1998

CHARACTER AND IDENTITY

PHILOSOPHICAL FOUNDATIONS OF POLITICAL AND SOCIOLOGICAL PERSPECTIVES

Edited by
Morton A. Kaplan

A PWPA Book
St. Paul, Minnesota

Published in the United States of America by

Professors World Peace Academy
2700 University Avenue West
St. Paul, Minnesota 55114

Trade distribution by Paragon House Publishers

A Professors World Peace Academy Book

The Professors World Peace Academy (PWPA) is an international association of professors and scholars from diverse backgrounds, devoted to issues concerning world peace. PWPA sustains a program of conferences and publications on topics in peace studies, area and cultural studies, national and international development, education, economics and international relations.

Library of Congress Cataloging-in-Publication Data

Character and Identity / edited by Morton A. Kaplan
        p. cm.onum bj1521
    "...Issuing from the Conference on Character and Identity which the Professors World Peace Academy held in November, 1997"—V. 1, pref.
    Includes bibliographical references and index.
    Contents: [1] Philosophical foundations of political and sociological perspectives.
    ISBN: 1-885118-08-2 (v. 1: hardcover) — ISBN 1-885118-09-0 (v. 1: pbk.)
    1. Character. 2. Identity (Psychology) I. Kaplan, Morton A. II. Professors World Peace Academy. III. Conference on Character and Identity (1997)
BJ1521.C48   1998
190—dc21   98-23786
                                                 CIP

CONTENTS

PREFACE

Character and Identity: Philosophical Foundations of Political and Sociological Perspectives is the first of two volumes issuing from the Conference on Character and Identity which the Professors World Peace Academy held in November, 1997. Volume Two is *Character and Identity: Sociological Foundations of Literary and Historical Perspectives.*

In a world in which "doing one's thing" has become so prominent, a conference on character and identity seemed a very useful counterpoint. Although the idea of doing things one's own way is very appealing, we want our mechanics to ply their trade with skill and seriousness. Who doubts that fewer do so than in years past? Even in my youth few had the work ethic of the street tradesman in Kyoto who sold some porcelain dishes and cups to my wife. When I suggested that he did not have to pack them so carefully, he replied that indeed he did.

Such standards do not occur as a result of abstract choice in which we consider a range of alternatives and then choose the best in the circumstances. They are based on concepts of right behavior and often take place spontaneously as a direct product of character. They persist if we are acculturated to social standards and take them seriously.

Although our current times are thought of as the age of autonomy, it is individuals such as the street merchant who are genuinely autonomous because their actions stem from character. The flotsam that drifts in the stream is not autonomous. The iron scraps that drift toward the attraction of the magnet are not autonomous. The concept of autonomy implicates inner direction—a direction that stems primarily from the character of the chooser and not primarily from the attraction or the repulsion of the external world.

Few of us would have had the courage of those German Christians who hid Jews from their Nazi persecutors. Or of some top officials of the Polish Communist Party, mostly Jewish by culture if not by religious affiliation, who surreptitiously saved some high ranking members of the anti-Communist Home Army despite the execution that awaited them if Stalin discovered their "treason." They knew who they were. Their freedom lay in their autonomous choice.

How many of us would want to live in a society that did not produce a significant number of individuals with such courage? Such individuals have characters that are strong enough to resist great social pressure, but they would not exist in the absence of institutional structures and frameworks of belief that helped to shape them, from infancy to adulthood, by setting standards that became integral parts of their character and sense of identity. Nature does not directly provide such standards. Only particular societies with particular sets of values can do so.

Cultural and social standards are far more complex and less determinate in kind than programs for computers, but they do share certain features. In the absence of standards based on acculturation— and *a fortiori*, these must be standards that provide firm, although not rigid, direction—individuals can no more make meaningful autonomous choices than a computer could grind out an answer in the absence of a program. If they have strong characters, individuals also have the integrity necessary to examine their societies critically, even though not entirely independently of the complex cultural interrelationships and sets of moral meanings that their history has bequeathed to them.

Consider our present nonjudgmental society in which the individual can choose from a farrago of conflicting standards, all of which are culturally accepted. How could that society expect individuals to run risks or make sacrifices when some other equally acceptable formulation will provide absolution? Why should not transient pleasure or advantage take precedence over more responsible behavior?

Character and identity are not goods in themselves. Hitler and Stalin also had strong characters and reasonable senses of identity. But those who lack a good sense of identity that informs their character will be easily seduced by transient advantage and pleasure. They will have weaker, less stable, and poorly defined selves. And societies filled with such weak characters easily will become the prey of those who wish to exploit or enslave others.

It was our purpose to examine the institutional foundations of character and identity. And then to illustrate this with examples from history and fiction of different types of characters from different cultures whose lives would make the subject of character and identity meaningful to our participants and the readers of the ensuing book. However, two papers—"Identity and Its Classical Greek Foundation" by Jude Dougherty and "Selves and Stories: From Descartes to the Global Self" by John Simpson—raised issues that were so important that we decided to put them into a separate volume, with other contributions that fleshed out the issues that these papers raised.

As Dougherty points out, Greek metaphysics provided a firm foundation for identity and character. This foundation rested on a metaphysical base that included natural kinds, a belief in the rationality of the world that mind could penetrate, and the reasoned belief that philosophical knowledge has a firm foundation. He is sharply critical of the contemporary "stories" approach.[1]

Simpson, who ignores the Greeks, correctly starts his account of the widely-accepted stories approach with Descartes, whose placement of certain knowledge in the lone thinking self is the core from which it descends, even if not without twists and turns. Descartes' failure, and the successive failures of post-Cartesian philosophers, to find a certain ground for knowledge, led to the post-modern stories approach. I will have something to say about this history in chapter 5.

Simpson legitimates the stories approach by reference to research on the brain that, he says, shows that the brain is tuned to narrative stories. If his article tells a story, it is one that has more in common with an assessment based on the fit between elements of an account and its surround—a subject that will be treated in chapter 5—than with narrative stories as they are more often understood. Moreover, if the brain did not also respond to theoretical treatments or assessments of them, it is difficult to see how analytical studies ever would have succeeded. His own story is based on hypothesis-driven and analytically rich work on the brain and how it processes thought. On the other hand, narrative stories, as they are ordinarily understood, are more congruent with the post-modernism represented in such writers as Heidegger, Foucault, and Derrida than with Simpson's own position, which he presents as true, even if not certainly true.

There is, of course, a version of "story" that can contribute to meaningful assessments. If by story, we mean a narrative account of how a character—or a nation—came to be shaped by history and experience in ways in which it can take pride, the internalization of this story in the understanding of individuals can provide a stable and meaningful framework for choice. This version of story, however, is incompatible with the wide-ranging freedom of choice that attends the concept of "just a story," which makes any individual story merely one among an infinity of personal choices.

The useful version of story, which few advocates of that position—certainly not Foucault or Derrida—take, constrains a person and a nation to behave as what they are rather than as merely personal choosers or as utilitarian optimizers who seek the greatest gain in individual situations. It provides a frame for moral evaluation and, with respect to the test in principle and the concept of transstability, for self-criticism. It does so from the standpoint of an assessment that reaches beyond the story to ground it in the human condition in a concrete set of circumstances. Embeddedment in a small circle of identification, for instance, family or nation, has an emotional connectedness that focuses concern and hence a willingness to accept responsibility, to sacrifice, and to seek to improve the group. The larger the unit, the more attenuated this relationship becomes. A truly global self would diffuse identification and responsibility, perhaps to the vanishing point.

Simpson's story of a developing global self is benign in its details. I share his disdain for the stories told by such as Nietzsche and Heidegger. However, his story is unconvincing. The fact that humans share virtually the same genetic foundation is not irrelevant to moral analysis. However, its weight is dwarfed by other considerations. And even its relevancy is dependent upon moral and scientific analysis and not the story he tells.

Because Simpson's story rests on "credo" as the foundation for "cogito," it cannot rise above the story level. It is true that experience, and thinking about experience, would be impossible in the absence of interpretation, as I show in detail in chapter 6. Perhaps how we come to believe theories or hypotheses is important to developing them. However, no story has a claim against contrary stories in the absence of philosophical and scientific analysis. Only if the story we share rests upon a mutually communicable account of the nature of the world—only if the story is replaced by a theory or an assessment—can we claim intellectual validity for it. Thus, only a contemporary version of the great Greek quest for rational knowledge can accomplish this task.

It would be excessive, even presumptuous, to attribute the turmoil—even a developing tribalism—in contemporary society to philosophical consensus on the stories approach. The flaws, if any, in alternative modern philosophies have been there for a long time. On the other hand, if the intellectual class develops a consensus with respect to the "stories" approach, intellectuals are the publicists and educators who will accelerate these trends by publicizing and justifying them. It would be even more presumptuous to suggest that this effort to counter those trends is likely to have much effect. But, while still alive, one attempts to do what one can.

Part One of Volume One includes the Dougherty and Simpson contributions. To these, I have added an article by Lloyd Eby from the July 1997 issue of THE WORLD & I, which sketches an alternative position that prepares the way for Part Two.

Part Two, The Philosophical Basis For A New Synthesis, serves two purposes. The first is to show why it has been difficult to carry out the great project that Greek philosophy bequeathed to civilization: finding a rational, common basis for knowledge. The defect in the classical Greek paradigm lay in the belief that language (logos) modeled necessary truth about the world, at least after intellection stripped away accidental elements from essence. Thus, the classical Greek approach reified language. Descartes broke with the Greek approach to language but not with the belief in a certain basis for knowledge. His approach to science, unlike that of Aristotle, was amenable to a rationalism that attempted to reduce the world to theory, while his *cogito ergo sum* made the individual mind, and not nature, the focus of necessity.

Descartes' failure, and that of his successors, to find a certain basis for knowledge ended with Hegel's even greater synthesis and failure. The Cartesian failure to discover a necessary foundation for knowledge stripped his paradigm down to what the individual mind constructs. The Hegelian failure left his inheritors with his account in *The Phenomenology* of how mind transacts with nature and society. The failure of both positions provides a basis for the stories approach to knowledge and appears to undercut the validity of the classical Greek project.

The second major purpose of Part Two is to find a synthesis that restores the Greek project. This synthesis builds on American pragmatism and the even earlier language studies of the nineteenth-century American anthropologist, Lewis Morgan. Morgan's studies of Indian languages and tribal practices showed how first-order accounts shape reality and its internalized legitimacies. For instance, in one tribe, "mother" referred not to biological parent but to a relationship between all females of a given age group and all children of an associated age group. However, unlike continental philosophy—and the superficially similar language studies of Foucault—this approach does not give up on the Greek project of rational knowledge common to different individuals, different cultures, and different times. I will show how pragmatism properly interpreted, with the aid of the test-in-principle and the concept of transstability, can build a synthesis that restores the classical Greek project.

There are valid insights in both the classical Greek and the stories approach, but each is one-sided. A successful synthesis rejects the idea of a certain foundation for knowledge, replaces the classical concept of univocal and universal sign systems with a better account of how signs function, and makes a distinction between first and second-order frameworks of reference.

These metatheoretic considerations permit the reconstruction of a common universe, but one more complex in its nature and moral implications than the classical framework. Such a synthesis retains the stories concept of placing first-order analysis of problems by individuals within the social and institutional settings of particular societies and cultures but shows how a second-order framework of analysis permits comparative judgment.

The selections in Parts Three and Four on political and sociological perspectives respectively are included to flesh out some of the implications of the philosophical synthesis of Part Two.

Volume Two will include papers on the human institutions that help to shape character and identity and papers on historical and literary figures from a variety of cultures and nations to show how they were socialized by their transactions with their cultures to develop a sense of identity and character that contributed for better or worse to their lives and their creative transactions with others and society. Some of the stories will show the terrible pressures that transitional periods create for conscientious individuals. Others will show how conscientious individuals helped to shift cultural understandings as they responded critically to some aspects of a complex culture by emphasizing other not entirely congruent aspects.

Note

[1]Dean Dougherty has told me that he disagrees with my discussion of Aristotle in an earlier, and less detailed, draft of chapter 4. He apparently believes I place too much weight on what he agrees Aristotle does say about the ability of mind to recognize the necessary truth of the axioms of (necessarily) true theories. He told me that he believes Aristotle's position is compatible with a contemporary philosophy of science and also with the position I take in my work in the philosophy of science. I respectfully disagree.

PART ONE

THE CONTRASTING
PHILOSOPHICAL POSITIONS

CHAPTER 1

IDENTITY AND ITS CLASSICAL GREEK FOUNDATION

Jude P. Dougherty

I

We still speak of Western civilization, and it remains a reality even though its spiritual foundation has been under siege within Western intellectual circles for more than two centuries. The skepticism with respect to the inherited, long present within the academy, has within the last half of this century reached the common man who is no longer in possession of the moral certainties that motivated his forebears.

The English Lord Patrick Devlin wrote in 1968[1] that if the morality of a people crumbles, the laws based on that morality will themselves crumble. Since 1968 we have witnessed, at least in this country, a rapid decline in both morality and the rule of law. In Devlin's judgment, "A recognized morality is as necessary to society as a recognized government."[2]

As more than one historian has suggested, if the twentieth century has taught us anything, it has forced us to recognize that ideas have consequences, that the barriers between civilization and the forces of destruction are easily broached. Barbarism is not a picturesque myth or a half forgotten memory of a long-past stage of history but an ugly underlying reality which may erupt with shattering force whenever the moral authority of a civilization loses its control.

The ancients took unity of outlook and respect of inheritance seriously. Plato regarded atheism as a serious offense against the state and in the *Laws* even prescribed the death penalty for the second offense, ignoring the first youthful offense. Even the noble emperor,

3

Marcus Aurelius, with good conscience could put to death Christians whose new God threatened to disrupt the unity of the empire.

In turbulent times a clear diagnostic voice is one to be cherished. This has long been recognized to be the case. The first-century Roman historian, Titus Livius (59 BC-17 AD), better known as Livy, recommended to a failing Rome:

> I invite the reader's attention to the much more serious consideration of the kind of lives our ancestors lived, of who were the men and what the means, both in politics and war, by which Rome's power was first acquired and subsequently expanded. I would have him trace the processes of our moral decline, to watch first the sinking of the foundations of morality as the old teaching was allowed to lapse, then the final collapse of the whole edifice, and the dark dawning of our modern day when we can neither endure our vices nor face the remedies needed to cure them.[3]

To know who one is, is to adopt a familial perspective. To acquire an understanding of ancestry, immediate and distant, is to achieve a sense of identity. One exists within an inherited culture, and to understand that culture, one needs both an historical and analytical sense. One does not have to be a scholar, but required is some knowledge of the spiritual ends, the material conditions, and the social processes which have created the culture, whether those ends are defined in religious or secular formulae. In the end to achieve identity is to adopt a set of principles.

History teaches that social consciousness can be the gateway to civic conflict. Marx's doctrine of dialectical materialism has been used to support totalitarian regimes the world over. The myth of Aryan superiority has led to genocide; the myth of women's suppression has led to alienation of the sexes; and the doctrine of social progress has been used to support social programs with disastrous consequences. Images and metaphors can eat into reality and force the world to take on false shapes and colors, encouraging the politically engaged to bypass common sense and reasonable doubt.

It must be acknowledged that history rests on the laborious accumulation of facts, but it is more than that. Specialized historical studies exist in overwhelming number, and even those which focus on a single century are beyond the mastery of any individual. Yet in spite of the intrinsic difficulty of mastering the relevant studies, perspective on the past cannot be circumvented. The way the past is viewed has a direct bearing on the present. Deep political commitment and open partisanship are often the result of historical understanding or misunderstanding. To vote in an election or upon a referendum may not be a simple political act; it is more likely to be an affirmation of faith in a particular social philosophy or a commitment to a particular theory of history. In some circumstances such decisions may even be judgments upon mutually exclusive forms of civilization. As Lord Devlin reminds us, sweeping and comprehensive changes in the framing and interpretation of law often rest on changing moral considerations.

Morton A. Kaplan reminds us of the importance of context, that is, the social milieu which consciously or unconsciously frames our choices. Echoing John Donne's, "No man is an island," Kaplan will say, as the title of a recent essay suggests, "The Right to Be Left Alone is the Right to Be No One."[4] In that essay, Kaplan shows the radically different character of programs grounded, for example, in principles supplied by John S. Mill and those grounded in an Aristotelian concept of human nature. There is ample evidence, Kaplan suggests, to hold that the conditions which Mill regards as essential for his form of liberalism actually foster the very control which liberals seek to avoid.

The right to be left alone with respect to social and moral matters may be a popular position,[5] but in Kaplan's view the doctrine of privacy is counterproductive because it fails to recognize how identifications and conceptions of the self arise within the social order. "External social constraints and internal inhibitions are complements to the enticements and opportunities that social structure, personality, and environment provide. They are required to diminish the likelihood of pathology and to preserve the integrity of the self that makes choices."[6] The freedom which any of us enjoys depends on cultural constraints. A social system which does not exclude some patterns of behavior even if they do not injure others is inconceivable. "If, for instance, every social rule—whether to bow to superiors, to dress for dinner, and so forth—was subject to personal calculation, society would be in danger of collapse."[7] The question to be confronted is: "Do we today have a recognizable social system?"

II

In a period of cultural decline, to speak of national identity is problematic enough; to speak of Western identity is even more hazardous. And yet the West, historically considered, is different from the East. We used to speak of Christendom and mean by it those lands touched by Western culture. In spite of the recent globalization of science, technology, and trade there remains a difference between European and Oriental cultures and among Latin, Islamic, and Confucian modes of thought. True, advances in telecommunication have united the world at a superficial level, particularly through access to global television, but as often as not those global reports display the vast differences which steadfastly remain. One has to acknowledge that in spite of the availability of worldwide channels of communication, in spite of the multinational corporation, and in spite of global trade, cultural differences prevail.

Although the world's major cultures are identified primarily with geographic regions, it is notable that at the same time they transcend continental boundaries. North and South America perpetuate Western culture in a way in which Indonesia does not. Similarly, the Islamic mind is not confined to North Africa and the Middle East, and Chinese and other cultural enclaves are to be found throughout the globe. While those differences are amenable to description by the sociologist, other modes of assessment are important.

When the sociologist talks about culture, he usually means a common way of life grounded in a community of thought and a community of work stemming from a particular adjustment of man to his natural surroundings and economic needs. Both sources, spiritual and material, need to be acknowledged. In the introduction to his *Critique of Political Economy,* Marx placed a heavy emphasis on material resources:

> The mode of production in material life determines the social, political, and spiritual processes of life. It is not the consciousness of men that determines their existence, but their existence that determines their consciousness.[8]

Christopher Dawson in his critique of Marx offers a different assessment:

The great cultural changes and the historic revolutions that decide the fate of nations or the character of an age are the cumulative result of a number of spiritual decisions--the faith and insight, or the refusal and blindness, of individuals. No one can put his finger on the ulti-mate spiritual act which tilts the balance and makes the external or-der of society assume a new form.[9]

No one can deny that important aspects of culture have a material basis in the economic life of the people, but the roots of any culture are certainly deeper. In China, we have the example of Confucian ethics serving as the moral foundation of Chinese culture for more than two thousand years, with the result that it is impossible to un-derstand any aspect of Chinese history without an understanding of Confucianism. In his many studies of Western and Asian cultures, Christopher Dawson often reminds the reader that the great civiliza-tions of the world have not created the great religions of the world but rather it is the great religions of the world that have created the great cultures.

Werner Jaeger in his monumental study, *Paideia: The Ideals of Greek Culture,* offers an entirely different but interesting notion of culture. Jaeger distinguishes between culture as "a simple anthropo-logical concept," as used by Marx and Dawson, and culture as a "concept of value, a consciously pursued ideal."[10] In its "...vague analogical sense, it is permissible to talk of Chinese, Indian, Babylo-nian, Jewish or Egyptian culture, although none of these nations has a word or an ideal which corresponds to real culture."[11] It was the Greeks who created the ideal of culture. "The culture of the present," writes Jaeger, "cannot impart any value to the original Greek form of culture, but rather needs illumination and transformation by that ideal, in order to establish its true meaning and direction."[12] "Hu-man nature," "objectivity," "universality," "timeless," "ideal," are terms inherited from antiquity. We cannot slip into the posture of regard-ing classical antiquity simply as a piece of history, "for education has from the very beginning been closely connected with the study of the ancient world. The ages which succeeded it always regarded clas-sical antiquity as an inexhaustible treasure of knowledge and cul-ture—first as a collection of valuable external facts and arts, and later as a world of ideals to be imitated."[13]

III

The intent of these reflections is not to belabor the distinction between East and West or to distinguish among Judaism, Christianity, and Islam. Nor is it to compare Oriental thought with that of the West. Its focus is on Western identity before the advent of modernity, allowing history to provide a standard for assessment.

Western culture is woven out of strands provided by Athens, Rome, and Jerusalem. Although the world was already very old when Greek science and philosophy began, the originality of Greek philosophy seems uncontested. In spite of a certain debt to the Egyptians and Babylonians in mathematics and astronomy, Greek philosophy emerged untutored by any other civilization.

Philosophy for the Greek was the pursuit of wisdom, both theoretical and practical. It rested on the assumptions that nature is intelligible and that the human mind is powerful enough to ferret out the secrets of nature. Science is to be pursued for its own sake, and yet it yields a technology as man cooperates with the powers of nature. Babylonia and Egypt possessed agricultural skills, knew how to work with metals, had invented writing and the calendar, possessed institutions such as kingship, priesthood, and an organized state. Greece owed much to these older civilizations and by incorporating inherited techniques was able to make advances in mining and metallurgy as well as in medicine and surgery.

The Greek philosopher looked upon the world through an atmosphere singularly free from the mist of allegory and myth in contrast to the thought patterns of the East, which were heavily dependent on religion. Popular Greek religion, crude and without speculative content, had little or no hold on the mind of the philosopher.

Greek philosophy in its origin and in its Hellenistic development was continuous with a common sense approach to reality. Common sense tells us that there are things apart from us and that they are what they are, independent of any human opinion or desire. It tells us that by painstaking observation and experiment we can acquire some knowledge about them. And furthermore, that such systematic knowledge is the safest and most reliable guide to human action.

These basic insights led the Greeks to differentiate between the study of nature and the study of being, later called metaphysics.

Metaphysics has as its object not only material being but the immaterial order as well. Metaphysics reasons to the existence of a *prime mover* (in the order of efficient causality) and to a *summum bonum* (in the order of final causality).[14]

Plato taught that nature is intelligible is the result of *nous* (intellect). There is a reality, he maintained, behind the appearance of things which is more real than that which outwardly appears to be real. Behind the constant flux of becoming there is permanence and universality. The existence of such universals as *goodness, truth,* and *beauty* is the key which unlocks the door to understanding and wisdom. Against the contention of the Sophists that morality is simply social convention and that might makes right, both Plato and Aristotle argued that there are certain universal principles of goodness and justice which man by virtue of his reason can discover. Man is by nature a moral and social being who cannot live apart from his fellows. To be moral is to be fully human. The primary purpose of the state is to enable humans to attain the good life.

For Aristotle, living beings come to be by a process that has a natural end or *telos*. Each organism comes to be not at random, but in an orderly manner, starting from some relatively undifferentiated but nevertheless specific seed produced by parents of the same species and developing, unfolding, and informing itself from within in successive stages that tend toward and ultimately reach a limit, itself the fully formed organism. There is a natural end to the process of development that defines the previous motions throughout the various stages to its proper end.

It is not without reason that Aristotle is frequently called the "Father of Western Science." The twin concepts of *nous* and cosmos produced the confidence that with effort the human intellect is able to discern patterns in nature with indications for control. The buoyant realism of Aristotle may in retrospect be contrasted with the second century skepticism of Sextus Empiricus which had a deadening effect on purposive aspiration, and by placing greater dependence on animal appetite, led eventually to purposeless drift and cultural decay.

The Academy of Plato and the Lyceum of Aristotle were to last nine hundred years and six hundred years, respectively. Although the Emperor Justinian dissolved the Platonic academy in 529 AD, Greek philosophy remained an important constituent of Western intellectual life and culture influencing Islam and in turn being enriched by that contact. From Greek philosophy, the whole of European philosophy has descended.

With the disintegration of the Greek city-states and the coming of the Alexandrian and later the Roman Empire, a number of schools arose, some in conflict with the inherited, some perpetuating its basic insights. Of the many schools that arose in this period, one in particular, Stoicism, exerted an influence that was to have profound consequences for Western civilization. It was through Stoicism that much of Greek philosophy was transmitted to Western Europe in the early centuries before Christ. Stoicism flourished for about five hundred years, from the time of its founder, Zeno (340-265 BC), to the death of the Roman emperor, Marcus Aurelius (121-180 AD).

For the Stoic the universe is governed by natural laws of reason which are immanent in nature. The wise man lives according to nature, allowing his reason to guide his conduct and restrain his emotions. By cooperating with natural necessity he achieves a harmonious relationship to the universe. The highest virtue and supreme good consists in obedience to the universal law of reason. Self-control through reason is the highest good. Man is free when he freely wills that which reason decrees. Man is linked to man by a common necessity to obey the universal law of reason. Recognized is the universal brotherhood of man.

True law, Cicero taught, is right reason consonant with nature, available to all, constant and eternal. It summons to duty by its commands and hinders fraud by its prohibitions (*De Re Publica* 111, 2).[15] Reason forbids enactments by the people or by the Senate contrary to the laws of nature. There is but one law, immutable and eternal, which shall embrace all peoples for all time. There cannot be one law in Rome and another in Athens. "There shall be as it were one common master and ruler, the god of all, the author and judge and proposer of this law. And he who obeys him not shall flee from himself, and in spurning the nature of humankind by that very act he shall suffer the greatest of torments, though he escape other which men consider pain" (*De Re Publica* III, 2).[16]

This conception of natural law was to dominate Western political thought until the period of Enlightenment. Not until then did men seriously challenge the idea of the existence of a law of reason which is eternal, absolute, universal, and immutable. In the Stoic conception, natural law is common to God and man. It antedates the state and all civil law, which is but the expression of this natural law of reason. The state is nothing more or less than a partnership in law, an assemblage of men associated in consent to law.

Roman political thought envisaged man as prior to the state. In Roman political philosophy we find the origins of the modern doctrine that government rests upon the consent of the people. This contrasts with Greek thought which had difficulty conceiving of man apart from the state.

It may be argued that these two ideas—the idea of a universal law and the idea of the state's being founded upon consent—taken together laid the foundation for the concept of "individual rights" so prized in recent decades. These ideas were passed through the Middle Ages by the great canonists of the period and are ultimately reflected in English common law and American constitutional law.

In the sixth century a commission appointed by the Emperor Justinian compiled and published a Digest of Roman Law.[17] Three other important works were published about the same time: the Institutes, a handbook of law; the Codex, a codification of the laws then in effect; and the Novellae, an appendix to the Codex containing the decrees of Justinian. Prepared by the Greeks to conceive of God as the embodiment of cosmic Reason and by the Jews to conceive of God as the embodiment of perfect Righteousness, Western man was prepared to recognize in Jesus the incarnation of perfect wisdom and perfect justice.

IV

Christianity taught that man is the creature of God, that he is essentially a spiritual being with a transcendent nature and destiny. Beyond the Kingdom of Man there is the Kingdom of God. The concept of natural law as developed by the Stoics was identified explicitly with divine law. The brotherhood of man became the brotherhood of man under the Fatherhood of God.

Christianity provided an uncompromising affirmation of a personal God, a provident God, directing the universe with loving, watchful care, a God who has revealed Himself to mankind through the

Hebrew prophets and in the person of Christ.

In its Judaic phase, Christianity may well have considered itself the particular religion of one people. But it soon understood itself as called to address every man and every class of man. Christianity inherited the traditions of the empire. Through its missionary efforts Mediterranean culture was brought to the barbarian north, which until the advent of Christianity had no written literature, no cities, no stone architecture. It was only through Christianity and the elements of a higher culture transmitted to them by the Church that Western Europe acquired unity and form.

Out of these elements—a Hebrew sense of justice, the love of the Gospels, Greek faith in the human intellect, and Hellenistic asceticism—the Fathers of the early Church molded an organic whole we know as Christianity. Historian John Randall, writing from a purely secular point of view, acknowledged:

> This body of beliefs the barbarians found ready-made for them, a thing of life and beauty which they were drawn to reverence, but which for centuries they were unable to understand. When the slow growth of social life brought them to the place where they could readily assimilate it, they found in it a vehicle admirably adapted to express their own aspirations and energies. By the thirteenth century this Christian scheme of things had really taken root in the soil of the Western mind.[18]

Randall adds, "and it is this great medieval synthesis that makes such an appeal to those weary of the cross currents and confusions of today."[19]

Christianity, Randall reminds us, had its origins in the semi-oriental world of the great Hellenistic cities where it offered new life and hope to classes and individuals spiritually estranged from the soulless materialistic culture of the Roman Empire. The mother tongue of the Church was Greek, and its theological development was mainly due to Asiatic Greek councils and Asiatic Greek theologians.

It was the acceptance of the teachings of Christ which gave Western peoples their spiritual values, their moral standards, and their conception of a divine law from which all human laws ultimately derive their validity and their sanction. Dawson remarks, "It is hardly too much to say that it is Christian culture that has created Western man and the Western way of life. But at the same time we must admit that Western man has not been faithful to the Christian tradition."[20] Europe, in spite of a common heritage, has been fraught with centuries of devastating conflict.

Trying to understand Anglo-German antagonism in the late nineteenth and early twentieth centuries, Paul Knaplund has written, "How these great nations became rivals and finally enemies has challenged and will perhaps for all time challenge the curiosity of students of history."[21]

Denis de Rougemont, in his book *The Meaning of Europe*, reminds us that it was Hippocrates who was the first author to describe Europe as an entity, contrasting it with Asia in the treatise attributed to him, *Air, Waters, Places*.[22] While de Rougemont is reluctant, in the manner of Belloc or Novales, to equate Christianity with Europe, he raises the important question, "Why was Europe the only, or the first, part of the world to adopt this religion which came from the Near East and not from Europe itself?"[23] The standard Christian answer is that Christ came in the fullness of time when the intellect of the West was prepared to receive the truths of divine revelation. De Rougemont makes the point that to identify Christianity with Europe is to do an injustice to the universal claims of Christianity, to its claims to be the vehicle of time-transcending truth of which Europe "is not a fitting embodiment and in which she has no copyright."[24]

V

Conclusion

These Chagall-like impressions of Western identity will have to do for the present or, should I say, in lieu of a 10-volume exhaustively documented study. They are impressions, but I trust they are faithful enough to the historical record. They leave room for the development of other impressions. As Martin Marty argues in his recent book,[25] we need our stories to achieve our identity. The above is but one story, a broken one. Clearly within what we are calling Western civilization there was a major break with antiquity during the period of the Enlightenment when the sacral and inherited political order, represented by mitre and crown, were repudiated in favor of what we today call modernity. The conflict was not resolved in the eighteenth century. The battle for the soul of the West continues. Is man a purely material organism with no end beyond the grave, or is he a material/ spiritual entity with a transcendent end? Is there an eternal order to which he is finally accountable?

Modernity's answer is but one answer. There are many lessons to be learned. It is the intent of this symposium to elicit accounts from all quarters of the globe as illustrated in the lives of prominent representatives of those traditions. We have representatives from Africa to India, from Western Europe to China, each with a perspective to share. A subtheme of the conference explores the locus of greatness; "prominence" may be the better word. Whence the impetus to achieve? How much is due to the culture, how much to the individual? In studying some of the major political figures of this century, our selection is not complete nor does it represent an endorsement of the figures chosen. Rather it is an attempt to understand the source of their self-understanding and achievement.

The ancients remind us that for centuries the West lived off a different set of principles from those fostered in the period of the Enlightenment. While modernity has its appeal, to understand the West, one needs a longer historical perspective. To understand the modern mind is to study its genesis, to study it within the larger intellectual and social milieu which gave it birth. Most of all, to understand modernity is to place it in relief against that which it repudiated and sought to supersede. John Herman Randall, Jr., in his valuable study, *The Making of the Modern Mind*, spends the first 250 pages laying the historical foundation for his discussion of the seventeenth and eighteenth centuries, the immediate context of the Enlightenment. Randall even uses as a subtitle to his work, "A Survey of the Intellectual Background of the Present Age." Christopher Dawson was convinced that the distinctive feature of the West has been its attempt to separate itself from the religious roots that had provided moral unity to European peoples. Whether one agrees with Dawson or not, the quest for Western identity is inseparable from a history that begins with the Greeks. One may interpret that history from various perspectives, but the historical map is accessible to all who choose to join the exploration. Livy's recommendation previously cited is to be taken seriously.

Notes

[1]Lord Patrick Devlin, *The Enforcement of Morals*, London: Oxford University Press, 1968, p. 11.

[2]*Ibid.*

[3]Titus Livius, Preface to his *History*, vol. I, Cambridge, MA: Loeb Classical Library, 1924.

[4]Morton A. Kaplan, "The Right to Be Left Alone Is the Right to Be No One," in *Morality and Religion in Liberal Democratic Societies*, Gordon L. Anderson and Morton A. Kaplan, eds., St. Paul, Mn: Paragon House, 1992, p. 290.

[5]*Ibid.*, p. 290.

[6]*Ibid.*, p. 292.

[7]*Ibid.*, p. 297.

[8]Karl Marx, *Das Kapital: A Critique of Political Economy*, Chicago: C. H. Kerr & Co., 1906-09.

[9]Christopher Dawson, *The Historic Reality of Christian Culture*, New York: Harper & Row, 1960, p. 18.

[10]Werner Jaeger, *Paideia: The Ideals of Greek Culture*, (trans. from 2nd German edition by Gilbert Highet) , New York: Oxford University Press, 1939, p. xvii.

[11]*Ibid.*

[12]*Ibid.*, p. xviii.

[13]*Ibid.*, p. xvii.

[14]Joseph Owens, *The Doctrine of Being in the Aristotelian Metaphysics*, 3rd ed. , rev., Toronto: Pontifical Institute of Mediaeval Studies, 1978.

[15]*On the Good Life; [selected writings of] Cicero*, trans. by Michael Grant, London: Penguin, 1971.

[16]*Ibid.*

[17]Justinian, *The Digest of Roman Law: Theft, Rapine, Damage and Insult*, trans. by C. F. Kolbert, New York, Penguin, 1979.

[18]John H. Randall, *The Making of the Modern Mind*, New York: Houghton Mifflin, 1940, p. 49.

[19]*Ibid.*

[20]Christopher Dawson, *op. cit.*, p. 17.

[21]P. Knaplund (ed.), *Letters from the Berlin Embassy*. Selections from the Private Correspondence of British Representatives at Berlin and Foreign Secretary Lord Granville, 1871-1874, 1880-1885. Annual Report of the American Historical Association for the year 1942. Washington, D.C., 1944, p. 5.

[22]Denis de Rougemont, *The Meaning of Europe*, trans. from the French by Alan Braley, New York: Stein and Day, 1965, p. 29.

[23]*Ibid.*, p. 16.

[24] *Ibid.*

[25] Martin Marty, *The One and the Man*, Cambridge, MA: Harvard University Press, 1997.

CHAPTER 2

SELVES AND STORIES: FROM DESCARTES TO THE GLOBAL SELF

John H. Simpson

A sign written in Latin hangs above the door of the small booth. It says, "Credo Ergo Cogito." Kathy and I are on the boardwalk in Scheveningen, Holland's popular coastal resort town four kilometers from The Hague on a blistering day in the summer of 1995. The long, inviting beach is jammed. Words painted on the booth indicate that it belongs to a Christian group. Apparently, the day is too hot for evangelism. The booth is closed, its keepers, perhaps, cooling themselves in the North Sea.

We have just come from Berlin, a city full of energy where a frontier-like spirit prevails, a city casting off the agonies that twentieth century modernity brought to it. Most North Americans have no palpable sense of the destruction wrought in Germany by Allied bombing during World War II. In Berlin in the summer of 1995—the fiftieth anniversary of the end of World War II—one could see the destruction in museum displays of photographs taken fifty years ago by American, Soviet, British and German news and military photographers. In some places—Cologne, Dresden, and elsewhere—incendiary carpet bombing created hellish firestorms that asphyxiated thousands. Most were civilians. Cities were reduced to piles of rubble, some still visible today.

In Berlin in the summer of 1995 one could also view and touch the "wrapped Reichstag," the old German parliament building draped with aluminum coated material and hidden from sight by the artists, Christo and Jeanne-Claude. *Der verhullte Reichstag: Christo und Jeanne-Claude in Berlin* was *the* artistic event of the European summer of 1995. From June 23rd to July 7th the building appeared as a shimmering, sculptured monument—a covering of the past and, then, an uncovering laden with hope as the future location of the German Bundestag.

Standing on the boardwalk in Sheveningen I chuckled at the wordplay in the sign over the door of the booth. But the sign was more than an amusing placard, for it seemed to hang there as a profound challenge to four hundred years of self-sufficient modern Western thought: "Cogito ergo sum." Descartes was a person of faith but the epistemological apple that he plucked from the tree of knowledge, once bitten, led away from a necessary connection between faith and knowledge. Thinking was Being and "I" did the thinking.

But what is "I" and how does "I" perceive and conceive (today, we would say "construct") a world where "I" can usefully deny that nature abhors a vacuum or that it is in the nature of an apple to fall from a tree, deny, in other words, deductions from a physics of essences and accidents? Kant's "I" underwrites that denial. It is provided with categories that allow it to construct the empirically predictable space-time world of 'real' physics. While the "I" can never know the inner truth of things, it knows their empirical surfaces and that is all it needs to know, according to Kant.

Sensing the Parmenidean stasis of Kant's categories, Hegel put the "I" into a dynamic world of categories-imposed-on-movement where new categories arise out of the work of the "I" fed by perceptions and the results of its own work. Hegel's "I" does its work in the context of ordinary life (a point successfully obscured by generations of Marxists). There in the ongoing moments of labor, desire, and the 'freedom' of being ruled by the 'common' good expressed by the state as lord, the "I" makes speculative, dialectical sense of everything, according to Hegel.

Where Cartesian thinking via Kant removed God from the abstracted world of physical causation, Hegel's thinking (extended) took God out of ordinary life. In a world lacking a necessary God, Schleiermacher argued that one ought to have a sense of ultimate dependence. When Nietzsche was done, all that remained was the "I" of unbounded will shaping the world and creating its own civilization and culture. Against this background one read "Credo Ergo Cogito" on the small sign hanging on an outpost of evangelical endeavor in the pleasure town of Scheveningen, on a hot summer's day in 1995.

Fresh from Berlin one also read the sign hanging on the booth against the background of destructive modernity memorialized on museum walls and in tension with a beautifully shrouded Reichstag whose unwrapping seemed to signal resurrection and hope. "Credo," "Cogito," dark images of ruined cities, and a powerful symbol of rebirth played with and against each another. Did the self-sufficiency of "Cogito" lead to the cities of rubble and the death camps? Did a wrapped, and then unwrapped, Reichstag somehow signify a new empowerment through "Credo"—now trust not dependence that leads to blind assertion as its negation; a realization that there is no absolute self-sufficiency and in that realization that there is hope, not masochistic subservience? These questions reverberated in one's brain that day in Sheveningen. They are not unrelated to the question of the nature and development of the self. I will return to them, having explored some aspects of a sociological understanding of the self in the global context.

The Self in the Global Context

It is difficult to imagine that any group, society, culture, or civilization in the time of homo sapiens has lacked an indication that members thought that they were engaged in at least minimal ways with others who were like themselves. Homo sapiens must have always recognized that others, too, walk, run, use their hands, vocalize, and make love, among other things. It is not only difficult to imagine that homo sapiens somewhere and at sometime lacked engagement with similar others. It is, in fact, impossible to construct an account or story that such could ever have been the case without assuming that it never has been the case. Such an account could, itself, only be constructed by an organism that was engaged with others and realized that that was the case. The capacity to construct a story of non-engagement, in other words, depends upon the fact of engagement because only engaged organisms who know that they are engaged can construct stories about humans who do not know that they are living with other humans. I assert, then, the absolute universality among homo sapiens of engagement with others and the knowledge that we are engaged with others, an assertion that entails the necessary existence of the "I" and the other.

The fact of the existence of the "I" and the other is indisputable.

What is at issue are understandings regarding the nature, scope, valuation, role in action, and *telos* of the "I" or self. The stakes in this regard are high. Charles Taylor, for example, argues that without an understanding of what might be called "the self project," there can be no understanding of the modern West where... "(largely unarticulated) understandings of what it is to be a human agent: the senses of inwardness, freedom, individuality, and being embedded in nature..." shape everything from ordinary, everyday life to the most arcane debates on epistemology and the philosophy of language (1989:ix).

By the same token one can argue that without understanding what might be called "the family project" there can be no understanding of a modern, resurgent East Asia where what it means to be a human agent is embedded (again, undoubtedly, in largely unarticulated ways) in the Confucian absolute of kin and group. There an orientation to outwardness, limits, and the integrity and agency of the group shape everyday life, intellectual work, and the exercise of power. The "family project," of course, does not do away with the self or the "I"/other dialectic, but its terms and processes are substantively, if not formally, different from the range of possibilities that underwrite the Western project of the self.

Beyond an understanding of East and West and with reference to the global level of analysis, one might, furthermore, assert that the putative coming clash of civilizations and the remaking of world order as proposed by Samuel Huntington (1996) is rooted in and can only be understood by examining the practices, stories, interactions, and daily flow—the 'stuff' of ordinary, everyday life—that create and underwrite the substantively different selves of the civilizations of the world. This is both a vastly complex and very intriguing proposal—complex for obvious reasons, intriguing for the sociologist because it anchors an understanding of the globe-as-world and its future in the analysis of ordinary lives as they are lived on an everyday basis everywhere. At a minimum, it qualifies the utility of the grand narratives of economics, politics, the state, and international relations (and the exoticism of anthropology as well) as self-sufficient and entirely adequate means for understanding how the global system is possible and really operates.

The analysis of the self, then, is arguably a point of entry into an analysis of the globe-as-world. But can the analysis of the self or the idea of the self which, after all, is deeply rooted in the culture and civilization of the West, serve a universal purpose: the construction of an analytic unit of action that has global methodological validity? By "global methodological validity" I mean the construction of a unit of analysis that is simultaneously adequate in terms of the problems of universality / particularity, globality / locality, nature / culture, and stability / change. "Simultaneous adequacy" means that the construction of the self as a unit in the global context does not undo the tensions posed by the problems of universality / particularity, and so forth. Viewed in light of these criteria the inadequacy of various 'received' selves can be seen straightaway.

Descartes' "I" lacks the quiddity of bodily presence. His "I" exists in the eternal realm of logical/mathematical truths. It has no rootedness in particularity, locality, nature and culture and social change.

Kant's "I" is grounded variously in the action of a theorizing scientist (the epistemological "I"), a moralizing, liberal Christian (the ethical "I"), and the standards of taste of the European bourgeoisie in the eighteenth century (the aesthetic "I"). Kant's "I," ironically, lacks universality even within a Western frame of reference where its most important mode—the fixed epistemological "I" founded on the *a priori* categories of Galilean-Cartesian-Newtonian space-time— was deconstructed by Einstein's relativistic physics.

Although time was quickly running out, it was still possible at the turn of the eighteenth century to master the sum of (Western) knowledge. Hegel was, perhaps, the last of the great encyclopedists. His "I"—that is Hegel's model or idea of the universal "I"—engaged all knowledge and its ever changing possibilities and directions and in so doing, rose dialectically into the realm of pure identity where it finally met and recognized itself as the *telos* of the cosmos. Hegel's "I" is the 'world's greatest expert'. It reasons within the circle of a single, all-inclusive language game that was broken down, eventually, by the rapidly advancing division of labor in the production of knowledge (specialization) in the nineteenth century, the social and material disunities of entrepreneurial capitalism, and the divisions created by the idea of exclusive nationally-based states. Hegel's "I" is dissipated where unity is a practical or theoretical impossibility. (It had a brief resurrected half-life in the end-of-history argument at the end of the Cold War.)

If Hegel's "I" disappears where there can be no synthetic unity, Nietzsche's "I" thrives. Here we have the unlimited, unbounded will of the organism-as-power—the militarized aristocrat of the spirit creating and embedding his values in the world. "Unity, yes! But unity on my terms only. I will create unity by destroying and replacing your values and your ideas with mine and, therefore, see myself everywhere."

Nietzsche's "I" is truly the modern "I," the fundamentalist—religious or secular—whose self-calling is to subdue the other and obliterate difference in order to see the (my) "I" everywhere and in all. Sometimes this "I" is transmuted into the "common good" (really "my good"), the "general will" (really "my will"), or, simply, "the people" (really "me"). Nietzsche's "I" undoes the tension of the universal / particular dialectic by effacing all other particulars and making the particularity of the "I" into a universal. The best of all possible worlds is that world where every "I" is "me," that is reflects the dominate "I."

Other "I's" can be added to this brief survey of 'received' selves, for example, Kierkegaard's existential "I" or Heidegger's *dasein* (see Tiryakian, 1962). All in one way or another do not satisfy the criteria for a methodologically valid global self. They are Western selves that are answers to epistemological questions that since Galileo (1564-1642) have focused on the type of organism that invents 'the universe of the day', so to speak, and is, itself, assumed and constructed in the universe that it invents. For example, Kant's "I" is the inventor of a Galilean-Cartesian-Newtonian universe and is, itself, assumed and constructed in that kind of universe. Nietzsche's "I" is the logical 'end product' of a Kantian universe, a universe where there are neither necessary nor even optional gods. Necessity is replaced by 'one-dimensional' human voluntarism.

Is the self always local or relative (particular) in some sense? Within Western civilization, as suggested above, the nature of the self (at least since Descartes) varies with epistemological changes bearing on the question of how the organism knows and constructs the universe/world. Changes in the construction of the self can be traced to epistemological shifts. Given *that* localization and, indeed, the universality of localization (different civilizations construct different selves), is it possible to satisfy the criteria of universality /particularity and globality /locality, that is, maintain the tension in these categorical pairs that must be kept if a global methodologically adequate self is to be mooted?

The universality of the self—the fact that every human being has some kind of self—resides in the universality of the brain/body as a form. Every human being has a brain/body, a brain/body that is immersed in the world. The universal sameness of homo sapiens is a natural sameness. To us, today, that observation may seem obvious, trite and commonplace, even perhaps banal. But we must remind ourselves that the great horror of twentieth century Western civilization—the Holocaust—was perpetrated precisely by those who contested the assumption of natural sameness and constructed an ideology based on the 'truth' of natural difference which was, in truth, an ideology of absolute evil leading directly to the ovens of Auschwitz (Simpson, 1997).

It is scientifically false and ethically corrupt to derive absolute otherness and sociocultural differences from natural differences. Otherness and sociocultural difference exist *within* the universal and global context of natural human sameness, established by the difference in the central tendency and insignificant overlap in the variability (to use a statistical model) between homo sapiens and any other natural form. Homo sapiens is a combination of chemical elements, a combination whose 'parameters' establish within group sameness and between group (i.e., other species) difference.

Brain/body variability *within* homo sapiens clearly exists. However, differences between civilizations, societies, and groups in culture and economic, social, and political organizations—those differences that are the major sources of variation in the self across the globe—are not differences that are attributable to brain/body variability *within* homo sapiens. I stress the qualifier "major" in the last sentence because genetic variability within homo sapiens can have effects on the self but these effects are subsidiary to the location of the individual in a sociocultural context. For example, being at risk for Tay-Sachs disease does not define Jewishness, although Ashkenazic Jews are at much higher risk for the disease than, say, persons of Chinese descent. By the same token, being a poor metabolizer of alcohol because one did not inherit the genetically-linked capacity to metabolize alcohol does not make one Chinese although those of Chinese descent are more likely than others to lack the enzyme that metabolizes alcohol. Because nearly all those of Scandinavian or Irish descent inherit the genetically-linked capacity to metabolize alcohol, the risk of alcoholism is higher in Scandinavian and Irish populations than in Chinese populations. However, being a drunk does not make one Scandinavian or Irish nor is abstention a defining feature of Chinese culture.

In the search for a methodologically valid global self, the tension between universality/particularity, globality/locality, and nature/culture is maintained where there is a recognition of (1) universal brain/body sameness (Only a very small number of human offspring are born with brains that are so damaged or incomplete that they lack the biological basis for mind/self acquisition); (2) variation in the properties of groups, families, organizations, societies, civilizations; and (3) the contextual, responsive embeddedness of brain/body variation.

Variation in the construction of the self is a function of variation in social units where the universality of brain/body sameness guarantees the production of a self and where brain/body variation (including sex/gender) interacts with the properties of social units where the organism is embedded to produce the self. Mental intelligence and physical strength, among other things, are variable across homo sapiens. That variation occurs within the universal sameness of homo sapiens or the biologically-based capacity to acquire a self. It interacts with the properties of the contexts where the organism is located to produce the self.

Universal within-species biological sameness and social variability, then, are the foundations of the global self. This assertion might appear to be somewhat obvious and taken-for-granted were it not for two things. First, the assertion denies the taken-for-granted residues of nineteenth century racial theories that still lurk about in some places. Social differences between people—the differences that count—have their sources in the variability of social contexts and not in brain/body variations. Blacks in the United States, for example, suffer from the socially reproduced long-term effects of the institution of slavery. They are not victims of their brains and their bodies as such except as those brains and bodies interact with the enduring effects of the institution of slavery to reproduce the central tendency of social misery and deprivation in the Black subpopulation.

Second, the assertion denies the radical independence of mind/ self and brain/body. Variations in mind/self can only occur because of the sameness and nature of the brain/body substrate which is the universal 'tool' for acquiring a mind/self. Mind/self and brain/body are not separable. One cannot be bracketed with finality where the other is being studied. They are codeterminative, a point that has been consistently overlooked in the sociological tradition where mind and the self tend to be cut free from the body and the anchoring of consciousness in the body.

In most sociological thought, the body is a taken-for-granted object that plays no analytic role as a source of the knowing subject. Thus, the sociological tradition has maintained and deepened the Western dualism of mind and body by failing to account for the body's presence as an agent in action. This is a major failure in light of accumulating evidence in cognitive science, neuroscience, developmental psychology, linguistics, and literary analysis that mind/self and brain/body are codeterminative.

What has been forgotten or repressed in contemporary sociological thought—a forgetting/repression that underwrites the sublation of the body—is "Mead's conjecture." The reference is to George Herbert Mead (1934) who, ironically, is generally considered to be the progenitor of the modern sociological analysis of the mind and self. Recalling Mead's conjecture provides additional insight into the nature of the global self.

Mead called himself a "social behaviorist," a designation that was intended to bridge behavioristic psychology as developed by John B. Watson and earlier psychologies such as the parallelism of Wundt who sought the sources of behavior in representations of the external world in the central nervous system. Behaviorism was, clearly, a major breakthrough in the study and explanation of the activities of living organisms. The stimulus-response paradigm externalized the problem of understanding behavior by constructing a set of observables that matched the behavioral outputs (responses) of organisms with the causal inputs (stimuli and reinforcements) of the environments in which organisms are located. Matching could be fixed as in the case of reflexes or probabilistic where the organism is engaged in learning.

Enthusiastic behaviorists such as B. F. Skinner would eventually claim that human observers could know enough about the environment in which human organisms are located—that is, could isolate and control all relevant stimuli—so that it would be possible to produce an optimally socialized individual. That belief, obviously, did away with the need to posit a mind or a thought process that somehow was engaged with the environment in the codetermination of behavior. Mind/brain for the behaviorists is a 'black box' that the scientist or philosopher does not have to enter in order to understand human activity.

But the necessity to open up the 'black box' of mind/brain within a naturalistic framework persisted despite the major advances of the behaviorists in understanding the activities of organisms. Chomsky's damning observation reveals the heart of the behaviorists' problem: humans produce sentences in speech that they have never heard, learned or could possibly produce by generalizing to something that has been learned. Thus, the production of speech must be tied to something in the 'black box' of the mind/brain that cannot be adequately understood or explained without going beyond the observables of behavior.

Mead, himself, held a similar view. He noted that some human behavior proceeds on the basis of choice. There can be an inhibition of response in the presence of multiple stimuli with subsequent stimulus selection by the organism. Response occurs after deliberation or the conscious processing of possibilities in the 'black box' of the mind/ brain and the response may be novel, that is not associated precisely with any stimuli present in the environment prior to deliberation and response.

Mead, however, did not hold the view that all human behavior involved choice or stimulus selection. In that regard he was a qualified behaviorist who insisted that the object of study was human behavior, that is, what is available in an environment to an observer. But he also insisted that mind/brain was part of the environment where behavior occurs and that some kinds of behavior can only be understood with reference to unobservables.

Mead's conjecture refers to his unwillingness to divorce mind from brain and body, on the one hand, and his unwillingness, on the other hand, to posit physical locations in the brain where the unobservables that are needed to explain higher order behaviors reside. He thought that the human brain was a processor embedded in natural and social contexts (the environment) and that the way that the brain processes and responds to environmental inputs and constructs its own environment, in effect, is what enables humans to have minds and selves. Minds and selves, according to Mead, are behavioral flows. They are not providential causal structures. Mead's conjecture, made more than 80 years ago, is remarkably consistent with contemporary understandings of the brain/mind.

Mead assigns universality to the operation of the brain/processor and variability to the self that is traceable to between group variations (in the statistical sense) in the social contexts and locations where the brain/processor operates. Mead's theory of the self guarantees its expression as a function of local embeddedness.

Mead would agree with Heidegger's contention that a human being (*dasein*) is "throwness into existence." We enter time at conception/birth and leave it at death. What counts, as far as the human organism is concerned, is the local, empirical world into which one is "thrown" and where one lives, moves, and has one's being over the life course. An implication of this view is that thematizing the origin of society and social order as a problem to be solved leads to just-so stories. Society and social order are givens into which homo sapiens are cast. Societies are not a coming-together-of-individuals who make a deal and thereby constitute a society. Human interactions occur within the prior given context of society, according to Mead.

The human organism, then, is "thrown" into a social context. Like all behaving organisms, humans respond to stimuli in their environment. When a stimulus is attributable to a behaving organism, Mead calls it a "gesture." Much of human behavior, according to Mead, is a response to gestures, and such behavior can be understood within the behaviorist paradigm of stimulus, response, and reinforcement. However, some human behavior occurs because the human organism has the capacity to be simultaneously a stimulus to itself and to an other by "calling out" in the other what it "calls out" in itself. Before the other responds, the organism has an 'idea' of what the response will be and, thus, is able to gauge its response accordingly. That kind of process cannot be fully explained by the behaviorist paradigm since there is an unobservable, reflexive, symmetric moment in the stimulus-response sequence. Mead argues that the reflexive, symmetric moment occurs only among humans. It defines the human act. The human act, then, consists of a stimulus (gesture) produced by an organism and based on the calling out by the organism of what the organism calls out in the other (the initial phase of the act) with the same pattern occurring in the response of the other (the completion of the act).

The "me," according to Mead, is the set of conventional stabilized responses that arise in the process of the act. The "I" is the unpredictable novelty that may occur in responses. The possible modification of responses by the "I" provides for evolution in the social process in the sense that the next response can be different from the previous response. Where the next response is a modification of the last response and the modified response is stable and repeated, social change has occurred.

Mead's self is an "I" (defined in his terms) and a "me" engaged in the ongoing social process. Mead's self, in fact, *is* the ongoing social process at the individual level. Where the process proceeds, in terms of the flow of reflexive symmetry described above, that is, the process is not simply the interplay of gestures in a pattern of stimulus and response, Mead refers to it as the operation of *significant* gestures or symbols. Significant gestures *encoded in language* are the most important components of the human act. It is, then, to language that Mead ultimately refers the operation of the self and its ability to proceed reflectively in the social process, an ability that is universal.

The 'localness' of the self is attributable to limitations and boundaries in the social process that 'dam' the flow of reflexive, symmetric action. These 'dams' are networks of communication that are relationally dense within a network and unlinked or lightly linked to other networks. Families, groups, communities and organizations are familiar 'dams'. As Mead noted, language is a vehicle that allows humans to construct responses to these 'dams' or relationally dense patterns of communication as *units* to which action can be oriented. Mead calls the symbolization or reduction in language of dense patterns of communication the "generalized other."

In the final analysis it is the 'dams' between dense networks of communication—the limited 'stretch' of generalized others—*and* substantive differences in the contents (cultures) of the dense networks into which the organism is "thrown" that produce the observable global variations in the self. A civilization is, perhaps, the ultimate boundary ('dam') for the self of everyday, ordinary lived life.

Mead's perspective provides a way for thinking about and constructing a globally adequate self, a self that is anchored in nature and culture and satisfies the criteria of universality / particularity, globality / locality, and stability / change. This self is not derived from a doctrine or ideology of individualism. Nor is it intended as a support for such a doctrine or ideology.

With the spread of notions of human rights and the worldwide constitutionalization of the individual as a unit with economic, political, and social rights there is a contextual global 'press' underwriting individualism. Where doctrines and ideologies of individualism hold sway, that is, where they enter into the conversation of gestures in everyday life as significant symbols, the self can be constructed as an individual in the sense of being treated as an autonomous unit in the social process, with rights to define action and rights as the object of action. However, not all selves in the world are individuals or will become individuals in that sense. Where some people live and move and have their being, the conversation of gestures does not include individualism as a significant symbol. Whether it should is another matter.

Selves and Stories

Having laid out a perspective on the self as a unit of analysis in the global system, the question of its application can be raised. Where does the claim that the properties of Mead's self are a necessary and sufficient set of descriptors for thinking about the self in the global context lead us? One answer is: not in the direction of cultural studies. Mead, I would argue, would not define himself as a "symbolic interactionist" in the Blumer-Denzin mode. Unlike Blumer and Denzin, he accepted the epistemological validity of the logic of the experiment as a way of understanding human behavior. He would not reject the notion of measured variables as legitimate, reliable, and valid means for exploring and understanding human behavior. He would see measurement as a moment in the social process and the results of measurement as an analog of differentiation in the mathematical sense, a more or less instantaneous cross-section of the social process with respect to a point in time. Where the unit of analysis is the individual, the point would be on the time-line of an individual's life course.

Mead would not see himself in most contemporary symbolic interactionist scholarship. He would find his thought consistent with developments in the contemporary sociological study of social sequences, the life course, biography, and, especially, the study of contextual effects over time. Mead was, above all, a contextualist. Society, in his view, is the source of minds and selves. Minds and selves are not the source of society. This view is remarkably consistent with recent developments in the analysis of language, literary forms, and cognitive processes.

Turner, for example, argues that the brain is not an "...agent who 'deals with' language..."... or a container that momentarily "...'holds' [a] language [construction] while examining it for storage or discard..." (1996:159). Rather, it is a processor whose neurobiological and cognitive activity "...based on all the sensory modalities and submodalities, on motor capacities, and on perceptual and conceptual categorization..." produces "...image schemas and dynamic integrative connections across different distributed activities in the brain" (1996:157). The integrated summarizing capacities of the brain underwrite human communication and they could have conferred reproductive advantage only where there was prior proto-linguistic communicative engagement that enabled organisms to take advantage of speech when it appeared.

The fundamental 'product' of brain/mind, according to Turner, is narrative imagining: *a story*. "Etti watered the garden" and "Zadok anointed Solomon" are stories. The brain is a storyteller according to Turner. Its integrative connections across distributed activities make small stories: "Kris rows the shell"; "Vicki tosses the rock." These stories are projected or mapped onto other stories. One story is a parable for another story. Parents can tell life-course stories: "Kris rowed her boat gently down a stream." "Vicki played hard ball."

Small space stories are mapped to form time stories: "The years with you, dear, have been a delightful journey, so far."

The mind is fundamentally literary. We proceed through time by abstracting 'brain stories.' The category structure of a 'brain story' can be projected to vocal sound which has grammatical structure. The structure, however, does not reside in the sequence of speech sounds. "Kris rows the shell" and "Vicki tosses the rock" share nothing in common as sound sequences in speech. They are precisely the same grammatically. They share a "generic space," in Turner's terms.

The conceptual 'brain story' or narrative projected onto sound is language. The parabolic mind operates in such a way that the structure of the conceptual 'brain story' is projected to create grammatical structure. The grammatical structure of the spoken sentence 'fits' with the structure of the conceptual 'brain story' or narrative although they are not the same thing: one is sound and the other is a complex integration of distributed activities that occurs in 'the flash of a eye'.

Once he specified the nature of the human act, Mead, as noted above, was cautious about claims regarding what was going on in the brain although he clearly never abandoned the notion that the act depended on the brain and that the act someday could be understood in terms of the brain. That was his conjecture. The notion of the brain/mind as a parabolic process appears to be an important breakthrough in the understanding of the nature of the brain/mind. *It is consistent with Mead's analysis of the act.* Symbolic gestures, or the taking of the role of the other, are in Turner's terms the projection or mapping of one story onto another story. Taking the role of the other is a parabolic process where the "I/me" story—the self's story—is projected as the other's story (the initiation of the act) and the other's story (now another self-story) is projected in turn as an "I/me" story (the completion of the act).

The idea of the brain/mind as literary—as, fundamentally, a spinner of narratives—is based on research in cognitive linguistics, developmental psychology, and neuroscience (Turner, 1996). A similar conclusion regarding the operation of the brain/mind has been reached by researchers in computer-related fields such as artificial intelligence. These researchers approach the problem of modeling the brain/mind in terms of comparisons between what humans can do and what computers can do. Computers don't tell stories. Humans do. You can't ask a computer why it did something and get an answer. Ask the school girl why she did the arithmetic to find the value of pi given the radius and circumference of a circle and she might say, "It was the homework assignment." A computer wouldn't even know that you asked the question even though it could digitalize the sound and store it on disk.

When Mead was thinking about the brain/mind problem 80 years ago or so, the comparison would have been with, say, a chimpanzee. With the development of computers, we tend to compare ourselves less with other species and more with computing machinery in order to find out who we are. When we compare ourselves with computers, we are comparing ourselves, obviously, with a product of our own minds. (If we ever evolve computers to the point where they can answer the question, "Why did you compute pi?" the Hegelian/Marxian 'dream' of seeing ourselves in the other and in that which we have made will have been realized.)

Humans, then, tell stories and the quality of the stories we hear others tell is, according to Schank (1990), the basic measure we use to judge the other's intelligence. Ages before someone invented formal tests of intelligence, humans were assessing others' 'smarts' in terms of how well they told stories in everyday life: "Why wasn't the hunt successful?" "Why did the crop fail?" "How come she got the man and I didn't?"

Schank (1990), like Turner (1996), recognizes the parabolic nature of brain/mind. A general story can be projected and used to create a helpful, plausible story in a specific situation. "Should I buy more Barrick Gold convertible debentures?" "Look before you leap." If attended to, the proverb-story is mapped into a search-story: "Where is the price of gold headed?" "What are Barrick's average production costs?" "How much production is sold forward and at what price?" etcetera.

There are many different kinds of stories, some more gripping than others. Well-known stories that are widely recognized in a society provide general models that may help people sort out action in specific situations. That notion has been applied by Greeley in his elaboration of "religion as poetry" (1995) and in other research as well.

Greeley hypothesizes that persons' images of God will have an impact in daily life. Following Tracy (1981), he argues that images of God in the Judeo-Christian tradition tend to be either dialectical—God as father, master, judge, king—or analogical—God as mother, spouse, lover, friend. These images are anchored in the Bible, theologies, teachings, rituals, and experience—all the 'stuff' of the countless *stories* that create, inform, and underwrite a religious "career" over the life course including the career of "no religion." ("No religion" has its stories too.)

Do images of God (propositional assertions or beliefs derived from stories) make a difference in behavior? Greeley shows that they do. Between 1968 and 1975, American Catholics reduced their weekly church attendance by one-third marking an unprecedented decline in Catholic religious observance. A popular interpretation of the decline linked it to changes in the Church as a result of the Second Vatican Council. Having analyzed a variety of data bases, Greeley and his colleagues concluded that is was not the actions of the Council that caused the decline. Rather, it was the 1968 papal encyclical on birth-control, *Humanae Vitae*. They noted that there was little change in Catholic observance between the end of the Council in 1964 and 1968. The decline in observance began in 1968 and leveled off in 1975.

Analysis of data gathered from representative samples of the US Catholic population showed that about half of American Catholics accepted the birth-control teaching in 1963. The figure declined to 15 percent by 1974. A similar change occurred in the acceptance of papal authority. The change in weekly observance was accounted for by declines in the acceptance of the birth-control teaching and the acceptance of papal authority. The change could not be explained by age-related lifestyle factors, changes in the demography of American Catholics, or secularization.

The decline in observance stabilized in the mid-seventies at about 50 percent. Among those who still attended church weekly there were, in fact, many who (like the infrequent attenders) did not accept the birth-control teaching and questioned papal authority. Why did *they* remain observant Catholics? Greeley shows that the key variable was how people imagine God. Those who reject the Church's sexual ethic and have an image of God as kind, gentle and loving are the ones who are most likely to go to weekly Mass and Communion. They justify the reception of the sacraments by appealing in their minds to an image of God who as kind, gentle and loving understands the importance of sex in marriage (Greeley, 1996:448-58).

Stories have impacts.

Conclusion

The study of selves in the global context is the study of the stories of civilizations, societies, schools, communities, families, etcetera, and their mappings in the brain/mind of the human organism. The self is local. The stories that make up the self have their boundaries in the networks of communication where local stories circulate.

Many local stories are parables of civilizational stories. If we are to understand and deal with the clash of civilizations in the global system, we need to know more about how civilizational stories are mapped into local contexts where they become selves.

The Western "self project" and the East Asian "family project," for example, are anchored in grand civilizational narratives projected onto local stories that are projected onto family stories that become the way that the agent of socialization of the infant responds to the infant. "The hand that rocks the cradle rules the world." The stories that the mother/father/sibling/aunt/uncle/ grandparent, etcetera, tell to the child become the self of the child. They are the stories that the child projects to make sense of the flux of life. They are the ways of the child's world. The stories that we tell our children and the stories that they learn in the expanse of their world are the stories on which the future depends (in some very complex sense, of course).

In the West, in the past five hundred years or so two very general civilizational storylines have developed: the secular and the religious. Each can be regarded as a censoring of the other. Telling a religious story ("Credo") means that you cannot tell a compatible secular story ("Cogito") and, by the same token, telling a secular story has become incompatible with telling a religious story. Secular stories and religious stories are not parables of one another in contemporary Western civilization. One cannot be projected or mapped onto the other.

My story that day on the beach in Scheveningen raised the question for me of whether there can be hope apart from a mapping of the humility of "Credo" onto the Promethean march of "Cogito." I am not certain of it, but I think that the answer is "No!" (cf. Barth, 1933).

References

Karl Barth. 1933. *The Epistle to the Romans.* London: Oxford University Press.

Andrew M. Greeley. 1995. *Religion as Poetry.* New Brunswick, New Jersey: Transaction Publishers.

_____. 1996. *White Smoke.* New York: Tom Doherty Associates, Inc.

Samuel P. Huntington. 1996. *The Clash of Civilizations and the Remaking of World Order.* New York: Simon and Schuster.

George Herbert Mead. 1934. *Mind, Self & Society.* Chicago: The University of Chicago Press.

Roger C. Schank. 1990. *Tell Me a Story.* New York: Charles Scribner's Sons.

John H. Simpson. 1997. "The Social Construction of Plagues." *Concilium,* forthcoming.

Charles Taylor. 1989. *Sources of the Self.* Cambridge, Massachusetts: Harvard University Press.

David Tracy. 1981. *The Analogical Imagination.* New York: Crossroad.

Edward A. Tiryakian. 1962. *Sociologism and Existentialism.* Englewood Cliffs, New Jersey: Prentice-Hall, Inc.

Mark Turner. 1996. *The Literary Mind.* New York: The Oxford University Press.

CHAPTER 3

BACK TO OBJECTIVITY: CAN WE UNDERSTAND EACH OTHER AFTER ALL?

Lloyd Eby

In the past several decades, many philosophers and others have asserted that people who come from or represent significantly different mindsets or language communities cannot really communicate with one another. Those who have held this view have expressed it through claiming that differing conceptual schemes—also known as frameworks or theories—are incompatible, incommensurable (meaning that they cannot be compared), and untranslatable (meaning that one cannot be translated into the other). (For brevity, I'll call this view the IIU thesis.) An especially blatant—and outrageous—example of this claim occurs in the oft-seen T-shirt slogan, "It's a Black thing. You wouldn't understand."

The IIU thesis has a long and seemingly persuasive philosophical pedigree. Noted ethicist Alasdair MacIntyre, for example, has written that "debate between fundamentally opposing standpoints does occur; but it is inevitably inconclusive."[1] The central and questionable term here is "inevitably," and, as we will presently see, the central ideas behind the IIU thesis have come primarily from philosophy of science. But others have also contributed to it. In particular, theologians and literary scholars have often spoken of what they have called a "hermeneutic circle." Hermeneutics has to do with the principles and practice of interpreting texts, and the claim that a hermeneutic circle exists means that whatever principles of interpretation are used by any interpreter are themselves part of the interpretation process, so that the process is circular—each differing interpretation group or policy having its own circle that is unique to itself, and closed to other, differing, circles.

The debate about this problem or question is not just an academic exercise; it has many implications for our lives and our behavior. The present-day concern with multiculturalism, diversity, and historical relativism has roots, among other places, in the view that different racial, ethnic, cultural, and historical groups cannot really understand or speak to or for each other—that only a black person can really understand or speak for black people, only an American Indian for American Indians, only a Jew for Jews, only a woman for women, and so on. The issues in this debate draw on many fields: they include, among others, linguistics, philosophy, theory of science, and ethics.

If the underlying thesis is correct—the claim that differing language or conceptual frameworks make it impossible for those holding them to really communicate with one another in such a way that genuine interaction and change is possible—then genuine understanding between persons or groups with major differences is in principle impossible. This would mean that Jews and Muslims, or Christians and Hindus, or agnostics and religious believers, for example, live in worlds that are so different that genuine understanding of one by the other is impossible; attempts by any side to explain itself to another, or efforts by any side to really understand another, would inevitably be doomed to failure. This would seem to mean that the hope or goal of making a universal human community could not succeed.

If, however, the IIU thesis is false, then things such as the T-shirt slogan mentioned above are not just factually wrong, but ethically repugnant, because they promote racial and other animosities and divisions where these are unnecessary.

Thomas Kuhn

Many of the arguments and contentions that lead to the IIU thesis are based on the seminal work of the late philosopher and historian of science Thomas S. Kuhn, as presented in his most influential book *The Structure of Scientific Revolutions* (first edition, 1962). There, Kuhn claimed that when a major shift in scientific theories occurs, the two theories—he called them the pre- and post-paradigm-shift theories—are incompatible and incommensurable with one another. Kuhn called the change a paradigm shift, and compared the change to one of religious conversion. He claimed that backers of the new paradigm could not be understood by proponents of the old one.

The late philosopher Sir Karl Popper, among others, attacked Kuhn's views, especially Kuhn's claim of incommensurability, pointing out that Kuhn's claim on this point is mistaken. If two things are really incommensurable, then they cannot be compared, thus they cannot be incompatible and they can coexist without any problem; for two things to be incompatible they must be compared, and comparison of two things requires that they be commensurable. So if they are incommensurable, then they are fully compatible. Kuhn was mistaken in tieing together incompatibility and incommensurability.

Popper also attacked Kuhn's view about the problem of translation. Kuhn seemed to hold that a new theory cannot be translated into the language of the old theory in such a way that it can be understood by those who hold the old view. The untranslatability thesis, if true, would mean that one theory cannot be translated into the other or compared with the other by means of any common language or shared (third) language.

But Popper refuted Kuhn's view by writing:

> I do admit that at any moment we are prisoners caught in the framework of our theories; our expectations; our past experiences; our language. But ... if we try, we can break out of our framework at any time. Admittedly, we shall find ourselves again in a framework, but it will be a better and roomier one; and we can at any moment break out of it again. The central point is that a critical discussion and a comparison of the various frameworks is always possible. ...My counter-thesis is that [Kuhn's view] simply exaggerates a difficulty into an impossibility.[2]

Popper did admit that it is frequently difficult for people who exist in different frameworks to discuss things with one another. But he pointed out that there is nothing more fruitful than such discussions, and that such a clash—a clash between people of different cultures or conceptual frameworks—has brought about some of our greatest intellectual revolutions.

As a matter of fact, translation and comparison of differing languages and views does occur—at least sometimes. These translations may be difficult and only partly successful, but the different sides (or different language speakers) often can and do make comparisons, cross-references, and so on. Thus, the untranslatability thesis must be mistaken.

Interpretation Circles

The view that interpretation theories or principles are themselves part of what is under consideration when we investigate anything is often called the circularity thesis. The circularity thesis says that theories—or paradigms or interpretative principles—are circular in character, because, whenever we debate about or explain or attempt to justify any theory, then we necessarily must use that theory or paradigm or interpretative principle itself in carrying out our investigation. Kuhn, and others who hold to this view, claim that the result is a circular argument whose only force or utility is persuasion.

In response to that, we must acknowledge that the premise of this argument is correct: It is true that paradigms—or theories or interpretative principles—are indeed used when we debate about the adoption or justification of those selfsame paradigms or theories or interpretative principles. This suggests that the process of criticism and justification must be circular. But, we must ask: Are these arguments really circular, as the circularity thesis asserts, or—if it is true that these arguments are indeed circular to some extent—then is it necessarily the case that the resulting (circular) arguments can have only persuasive force?

Kuhn and others have answered "Yes" to those questions. But, if we can present an account of language that demonstrates that the circularity is only partial, and show that there can be a place or position that permits us to have an independent evaluation of the theories or paradigms or interpretative principles in question—meaning an evaluation that is not fully dependent on those interpretative principles, but which brings in something from "outside," so to speak—then we can show that Kuhn's answers are incorrect and that the circularity thesis is not the translation-stopper that its proponents say it is.

In his book *Science, Language* Morton Kaplan explains this supposed circularity problem further. He says that the arguments for circularity claim that "... metaphysical worldviews establish an interpretative framework that cannot be criticized from competing frameworks."[3] Therefore "... differences in worldviews cannot be adjudicated, although a worldview may fail because its own criteria are not satisfied." The result—that is, the result that those who hold to the circularity theory defend—is that criticism exists or operates only within its own framework, and this framework cannot be criticized from competing frameworks. [Popper called this view—a view he himself completely rejected—the "myth of the framework."] According to such views, the root metaphors of metaphysical systems cannot be disproved because, as Kaplan says, "... the assumptions that characterize them as such, and that shape their [explanations] are present in their formulation."

But, as Kaplan points out, that view is incorrect because data can be used to critique theories in a noncircular way. One reason is that worldviews or hypotheses about the world can only be constructed in a partial or elliptical way, not in full detail. Such theses always have holes or gaps, and data can be used to show that the theory is defective where it has gaps or holes. Only some aspects of philosophy and experience are organized into theories, either philosophical theories or scientific theories. Thus, although data is influenced by the theory, it is not completely determined by it, and it can be used to critique the theory.

Another reason that the circularity thesis is incorrect is that there do exist ways to assess the relative merits of such differing or competing "rough sketches" because there is actually, as Kaplan says, "a great overlap between the methods and interpretations of theories. If this were not so, it would not be possible for opposed philosophical formulations or scientific theories to grow out of the same cultural base." They would be excluded because there would always exist an interpretative framework that would determine the kinds of observations that could be reported and the interpretations to which they could be subjected. But opposed—or at least differing—scientific theories and philosophical formulations do grow out of the same observational or cultural data. For example, two researchers may share the same data, but differ on the theory of polygraphic detection of lies—one holding that this is possible and another rejecting that theory.

One observation that has contributed to the circularity thesis was made by those philosophers and researchers—such as the late philosopher Norwood Russell Hanson in his book *Patterns of Discovery* (first edition, 1958)—who pointed to what they often call the theory-laden character of observations. They noticed that no one can observe or collect data unless there is some theory underlying this process of data-gathering or observation. Popper himself, for example, pointed out that if someone goes before a class of students and says, "Observe, and write down what you observe," the students will be perplexed and unable to comply with that order unless they are told what to observe, or unless there is already a tacit understanding about what they should observe.

The philosophers who pointed out the theory-laden character of observations often went on to suggest that this means that the observations are fully controlled or determined by the theory underlying the observations. But that is not so. The fact that observations are theory-laden does not mean that observation cannot be used to defeat a theory; theories are often defeated by observations. Theories are—at least sometimes or at some point—what we might call data-controlled or data-sensitive. The theory that Jones was killed by being fed poison, for example, is defeated by the coroner's observation that Jones died from strangulation. Moreover, as we have already mentioned, theories are at best sketchy affairs, with many points not filled in. This "sketchy" character of theories arises not just because no theory can be as rich or complex or thorough as whatever it is a theory about, but because a theory has a different character and purpose from the data it encompasses.

The dynamic nature of the relationship between theories and observations helps provide a foundation for relatively neutral assessments in which we are able to compare one theory or framework with another. Since neither theory-making nor the process of observation and data-gathering is wholly determined by the other, each can, in turn, provide a partial stance for criticism of the other, and each is at least partly neutral in relation to the other. Each can—and does—influence the other, so that what we might call a dynamic give-and-take relationship occurs between them.

Since a scientific or theoretical system may be inadequate on its own terms, or weak in comparison with a competing system (it may fail to explain something that the competing system explains, or the competitor may offer a more complete explanation), it is entirely possible to argue against theoretical systems, or to give reasons why one such system should be preferred to another. So, while it may be true that root metaphors of metaphysical systems cannot be disproved (in the strong or logically certain sense of 'disprove'), this does not mean that good reasons, arguments and discussions cannot be offered that show the superiority of one such system over another. Moreover, such arguments are not simply exercises in rhetoric or persuasion, as Kuhn claimed.

There is, we must acknowledge, some truth to the circularity arguments: All knowledge and reasoning is circular in the sense that, without having some initial system for coding or processing information, no perceiver can exist. A mind that was a complete tabula rasa, as the philosopher John Locke supposed and as empiricists have generally held, could not generate useful information. But all that does not imply that the conclusions drawn by supporters of the circularity thesis are true.

Historical Relativism

Understanding the open character of knowledge circles allows us to link the process of knowing to the facts of history and historical development without succumbing to historical relativism. (Historical relativism is the view that all our knowledge is determined by our history, that we cannot achieve any ahistorical stance.)

What we know at any time is linked closely to both contemporary historical conditions and the historical paths by which our knowledge has been reached. But, in reply to historical relativism, we can say that, although we never achieve absolute neutrality of perspective in any of our observations or in our knowing, we can gain relatively neutral perspectives and we do this with greater and greater power as knowledge increases. There are limits to communication, but there are no completely closed circles for any problem that we can clearly specify.

Our relatively neutral perspectives are gained through the process of assessment. We do not, in fact, prove all our conclusions, but we do assess some. In addition, the assessments that we make are usually not deductive proofs. Thus, in the process of assessment we do not need to succumb to any vicious circularity because the dependence of the whole theory on its elements, and of the elements on the whole, is limited. As a matter of fact, we make such assessments quite often, and we especially make them in science. Scientific knowledge is not completely circular; it is not completely historically determined, and decisions based on assessments can be made in a way that is at least partly non-equivocal.

Noncircular assessments—for instance, whether light bends when it passes a gravitational field, a crucial experiment in favor of Einstein's theory, and a refutation of Newtonianism—are common in science. Consider the possibility that the scientists Kepler, Newton, and Einstein could have met to study that question. If the IIU thesis were correct, they could not have communicated or agreed about what they meant by crucial terms. But, in fact, all three would have agreed, for the purpose of the relevant experiments, on what they meant by the terms 'planet', 'perihelion', 'curvature', and 'light', although they might have disagreed in other respects. Kepler and Newton would have been unfamiliar with some techniques of measurement used by those experimenters who checked Einstein's prediction, but their science itself would not have precluded such an understanding, only the state of their technology.

As Kaplan says, "The three would have disagreed on what they meant by 'mass', 'time' and 'space', but this disagreement would not have been relevant to tests that compared the competing theories in this respect. Such assessments are not circularly dependent upon the theory to be tested. Nor do they depend on the absence of interpretation." The conclusion is that arguments that claim to prove the IIU thesis—arguments that purport to show the existence of closed interpretation or hermeneutic circles—are mistaken both because they assert too much and because they do not fit what actually happens in science and scientific argument and assessment. If they do not fit scientific language, then there is no good reason to suppose that they fit moral or religious language either.

A Theory of Language

To deal more thoroughly with the IIU thesis, it is useful to examine a theory of language, a theory that does not give rise to the developments which seem to lead to the IIU thesis. Kaplan has proposed such a theory of language, and it will be worth our time to look at it here.

Kaplan begins with three considerations prior to his analysis of language; he calls them "metatheoretical considerations," meta because they are considerations about the theory, therefore existing above the theory itself. Nearly all other theories of the language of science have ignored one or more of these metatheoretical considerations, but they form the background of Kaplan's proposed theory of language, especially scientific language.

First, Kaplan distinguishes between what he calls a first-order reference and a second-order level of language or reference. A first-order reference depends on the location of the observer, actor or system; a second-order one is independent of the location of particular observers or actors or systems, and exists at a higher level of abstraction. For example, your location in the cosmos will determine whether you see a supernova happening at a particular time or at a much earlier or later one (because your distance from the supernova will determine how long the light takes to get to you). So two particular observers living on different galaxies will differ in their reports—their first-order reference—about the time of the occurrence of the supernova. But if they both hold to the same physical and cosmological theories, they will reach the same conclusions about the reasons the supernova occurred and its influence on the cosmos— that is, they will agree about their second-order assessments of the occurrence.

People may agree or disagree about either first-order or second-order considerations. It is quite common for observers to agree on first-order analysis—two observers may agree that an indicator pointer has made a squiggle on some graph paper at a particular place, for example—but disagree on what second-order analysis to give to this. In this particular case one observer may claim that a particular squiggle shows that the person being tested is lying, while another rejects this claim because he rejects the theory of polygraph (lie-detector machine) detection of lies.

This distinction between first-order and second-order analysis is important for an additional reason: It gives us a way to reject complete epistemological relativism—the view that knowledge is completely relative to the knower and/or his conceptual, perceptual, and historical circumstances—while still admitting that every knower's perceptions and knowledge have a primacy for him.

Admitting the existence of second-order assessment allows us to retain and make clear the idea that one theory is better than another for good reasons. In the real world, scientific theories are actually compared, using criteria such as adequacy and progress. Kuhn himself clearly wanted to be able to do this, without providing a sufficient basis on which to do so. Kuhn himself rejected the notion that one theory could be "nearer to the truth" than another because we do not, in fact, know the truth. But Kaplan's view permits us a way of showing how one theory can be better—in a strong sense of "better"—than an earlier one; it is better because it fits more adequately our second-order assessments.

Part System Analysis

For his second metatheoretical consideration, Kaplan introduces a notion that he calls part-system analysis. A part system is one that is independent of a larger system in such a way that changes in related subsystems have little, if any, effect on it. For example, the tires are a part system of your car, as is the electrical system and the exterior paint, and a change in either of these does not (usually anyway) have any effect on the other—a flat tire does not make the car's lights go out, nor does a dead battery or a paint scratch have any effect on the tires.

When we are analyzing an entire system—an entire car, for example—we tentatively hold information about some part systems to be constant, while information about others is revised. In the case of the car, for example, if it will not start, a knowledgeable mechanic will not consider that the problem may be scratched paint because we know that the condition of the paint is irrelevant to whether the engine will start.

We do not analyze or revise an entire system all at once, but only one or more of its parts. For example, if the system or theory utilizes numbers, we do not consider the possibility that the theory of elementary arithmetic should be revised. In other words, any theoretical system is a complex entity, composed of subparts. We do not analyze or criticize an entire system at once, but only relevant subparts, while assuming that other subparts are OK or uncontroversial.

Because scientific systems are made up of such subparts—parts which are at least partly independent—it is possible that one part can be revised while another part is untouched; you can repaint your car in a different color, for example, without this affecting any other aspect of the car. As we have seen, Kuhn and many others adopt the metaphor of a circle, and see argument as circular. But Kaplan argues that, in fact, we use one limited area of the entire realm of all our knowledge to assess other limited areas. This means that scientific knowledge grows, or changes, not in a linear fashion but in a spiral one. Rather than a closed circle, the evaluations and changes we make in our knowledge take the shape of a spiral, in which the circular action does not close back on itself, but moves to a higher level.

Strong And Weak Orders

In his third metatheoretical consideration, Kaplan distinguishes between what he calls strong and weak orders. This notion may be difficult to understand. Kaplan says that "most real orders are weak," but he admits that "the concept of a weak order is not intuitively clear."

A strong order can perhaps best be described by presenting examples. As Kaplan says, "In some early views, the world constituted a simple strong order such that God, if He knew the starting state of every atom, could predict all of history." Newtonian physics is an example of such a strongly ordered, deterministic system; a system that supposedly has no uncertainty. We must note, however, that even in Newtonian physics, any uncertainty in measurement—and both in practice and in theory every measurement has some uncertainty—implies a future that is not fully predictable. So even Newtonian physics has a residual uncertainty, an uncertainty that is obscured because the theory ignores the influence of instruments on measurements and predictions. This obscuring of uncertainty becomes philosophically misleading because it allows the theory to seem more strongly ordered—more deterministic—than it, in fact, can ever be. Other examples of a strong order might be axiomatized logical or mathematical systems.

From such strong orders, we move to weaker and weaker ones; we can say that there exists an unending stream of weak orders. In present-day subatomic physics, for example, position and speed are both meaningful concepts but we cannot know both simultaneously. Thus quantum phenomenon are not strongly ordered. In economic theory, price may be strongly ordered in a perfectly competitive system, but in imperfectly competitive markets price is weakly ordered. Still another example of a weak order is the biological notion of evolutionary advantage.

There is a hierarchy of strong and weak orders, with the physical sciences having the strongest orders. But even in the physical sciences a fully strong order hardly ever occurs. In such sciences as biology, sociology, and psychology the ordering relations are even less strong.

It is also possible to consider two theories, even about the same thing, that do not coincide. "There need be no conflict," Kaplan says by means of example, " between a theory that treats a Portuguese man-of-war as a single organism and one that treats it as a collectivity of organisms, for the definition may depend on the types of outcomes that lie at the focus of the investigation."

Kaplan now moves to presenting his (partial) theory of language. A theory employs signs such as words and symbols. The meaning and implications of a theory depend on the relationships among the systems of signs employed in the theory, the concepts used, and reality. "Concepts are correlative in character," Kaplan writes, and "they necessarily have nonexplicit and nonconscious penumbra." Or, as philosopher Michael Polanyi explained, in terms that are perhaps less opaque, our explicit concepts and knowledge always rely on a background of nonexplicit, tacit knowledge.

The Role of the Person

Kaplan points first to the person doing the knowing—the transceiver, to use his apt term. This knower is central to the process of knowing. Without this personal component in the knowing process, knowing could not occur. Knowing always requires the active participation of the perceiver and knower—the person doing the knowing, the transceiver.

The person—the transceiver—is central to language and message transfer. Meaning comes about through a transaction between the knower—the transceiver—and the world. Experience is not just having incoming signals. The transceiver—the knower—is an active agent in producing data; data does not just come about by itself, without a person to produce it.

The process of perception is complex; there is not a simple connection between an external datum and an internal perceptual state. Simple stimulus-response theories of perception and knowing, as held by empiricists and behaviorists, may fit a stable world or organism, or a simple aspect of a more complex organism. But as a general theory of the connection between language and the world, they are mistaken. Terms like 'red' depend on the transceiver or knower, the source of light, and the referent of the red sensation. From this it follows that simple correspondence theories are mistaken when proposed as a general theory of the language-world relation. The relationship between transceiver and experience is complex, and is revised by part-system analysis.

Correlative Concept Pairs

Kaplan proposes what he calls a correlative concept pair as the basic unit of language. Such a concept-pair functions by making contrasts, as, for example, between hot and cold. This correlative pair bridges the gap between perceiver and perceived. The corelated terms 'solid' and 'porous', for example, do not characterize anything by themselves, but only function for a knower—a transceiver—within a context. A table, for example, is solid to my fist, but porous to an electron. The contrast between light and dark, for another example, gives meaning to the perceiver who is concerned with it.

This notion of a correlative concept pair is a very different notion of language and the language-world link than what was held by classical empiricist philosophers. In the empiricist view, there was supposed to be a one-to-one link between a word (or concept) and the world. But the notion of correlative concept pair is different because use of a correlative concept requires that the user—the transceiver—make a judgment with respect to some aspect of his experience, and making such a judgment necessarily involves other aspects of the judger's knowledge.

Correlative concept pairs make the connection, not directly with the "external world," as empiricist theory presumed, but with one another and with the perceiver and the object being perceived. This allows the perceiver to make judgments and assessments, and especially judgments of degree. So, for example, the water into which you put your hand is not simply hot or cold, but is hotter than the surrounding air, but also colder than the fire. The world is not just simply grasped or apprehended by the knower or perceiver; instead, a complex relation is set up between world, perceiver or judge—the transceiver—and language or concepts.

Correlatives can and do function as basic building blocks of experience. A pair functions as a basic unit, not a single concept or word. Moreover, if a pair functions as a basic unit, then a dynamic relation is also basic, because there exists, at the basic level, each of the two elements of the pair, as well as the connection or relation between them. So meaning is not a function simply of a word or concept, or a simple word-to-world relation, but a much more complex and dynamic interaction between perceiver (knower), the concept-pair, the relation within the concept-pair, and the world. A series of dynamic relations between four entities or units is basic, then, to perceiving and knowing.

Metacorrelatives

From the notion of correlatives as the basic unit of language, Kaplan moves on to a higher level of analysis by introducing a similar notion at what philosophers frequently call the meta-analytic level, the level where we analyze our analysis. Kaplan calls these higher-level terms metacorrelatives, and says, "If correlatives are the basic units of language, metacorrelatives are employed in analyzing their use and significance." So, just as we use correlative concepts at the basic level of perception, we use metacorrelatives to perceive and understand our analysis of our language.

This distinction between correlatives, as a basic unit of language, and metacorrelatives as a higher-order tool of both analysis and meaning-production, allows Kaplan a basis on which to break out of the so-called "hermeneutic circle" or "interpretative circle" mentioned above. Metacorrelatives may be used to criticize, or, alternatively, to ground or explain correlatives. Since correlatives can be grounded or explained (partially anyway) in this way, the circle set up by first-order language can be broken up or broken into by the higher-level metacorrelatives.

Some theorists have held that words have a meaning only within the sentence in which they occur, but other theorists have held that terms or words have an independent meaning. Kaplan finds a way between those two extremes by pointing out that the meaning of an element or term is related to the set or sentence in which it occurs, and yet also noting that terms in a sentence have a meaning that is independent of the sentences in which they are used. There is an interaction between elements of language—terms or words—and the sentences in which they occur. Each affects and influences the other. Attempting to establish priority for either the word or for the sentence is even more foredoomed than the proverbial attempt to establish priority for the chicken or for the egg. By calling this a part-system problem, Kaplan means that words are a part system of the sentence in which they occur, but the sentence is itself a system depending on the words. So analysis can occur at either level, and change and modification can occur at either point. Change or modification of one level may modify the other, or it may not, depending on circumstances. Thus, neither level is completely bound to or completely independent of the other.

Similar considerations to the word-sentence problem apply to concepts and truths. Kaplan explains that concepts are validated both internally and externally. This account of concepts and truth allows what we might call an interactive interplay—a give-and-take relationship—to exist between concepts and the external world. Internally, concepts are validated by definitions or by relations to other concepts. Externally, they are validated by the transceiver in relation to the empirical world. Thus, a person may know concepts without knowing how to apply them, but he may also have a kind of pre-conceptual, or conceptually unrefined knowledge of the external world, because he may not yet have refined or developed concepts in which to express that knowledge of the external.

Theories

All those considerations, finally, allow us to give an account of theories. Kaplan presents his view this way:

> A theory is a system of concepts mediated by signs, and the elements of a theory have meanings that depend upon their inner, that is, their

within-the-theory relationships.

"Mass," for instance, has at least partly different meanings in Newtonian and Einsteinian physics. And "line," for instance, has at least partly different meanings in Euclidean and non-Euclidean geometries. The application of a theory to the concrete world involves both inner meanings, meanings that are constrained by the system of signs, and meanings that are external, that is, that are constrained by other signs or systems of signs and the concepts they mediate; and, thus, ultimately by empirical assessment.[4]

Theories, then, involve concepts and signs, and these concepts and signs have both inner meanings—that is, meanings within the theory itself—and external meanings, that is meanings that come about through contact with the world. A theory is thus a complex; it cannot be reduced to or understood by either its inner or its external meanings without the other.

This account of theories shows the mistake in circularity accounts of scientific and other theories. It is true that the meanings of the elements of a theory depend on the theory and their relationship to it. But this dependence is only partial. There are also external constraints and considerations on the meanings. This makes breaking into the interpretative circle possible. Thus, although "mass" does indeed mean something partly different to Newton and Einstein, the difference is only partial. As we saw above, if Newton and Einstein were to have a discussion, they might have some difficulty communicating because they mean partly different things by the same words. But 'difficulty' does not mean 'impossibility'. There are external things—a world that is external to each perceiver and which exerts its force into the interchange, as well as certain signs and signals which are theory-neutral to the particular theories under consideration—to which the two could refer both to explain their differences to one another and to referee a discussion about which theory is preferable and better fits the empirical world.

In practice, such discussions and adjudications are frequently extremely difficult and even inconclusive. But that they are difficult is not the problem; the problem is whether any external referents and adjudication do exist or can occur at all. The theory of language sketched here shows both that these occur, and how to account for and explain them. As Kaplan says in speaking of the so-called translation problem, "...second-order procedures make possible the translation of English into, say, Russian or Japanese." But any such translation is almost never simple or one-to-one.

This theory avoids a purely relativist account of language, while acknowledging that language is, in fact, highly relative. This view supports a theory or account in which criticism can operate at both the first and the second levels, and each level has the possibility of serving as a standpoint for criticism of the other. Like Kuhn's, Kaplan's account of language recognizes the role of culture in language learning and language use; language is partly a socially-constructed affair. But, unlike Kuhn's, Kaplan's theory rejects any strong or thoroughgoing circularity.

Theory Change

Kaplan's theory of language speaks to Kuhn's problem of theory change. Kuhn held that change from one theory to another constitutes a radical break between the former and the latter theories, a break that Kuhn depicted using language appropriate to describing a religious conversion; in religious conversions there does seem frequently to be a radical break between what went before and what came after. But, the theory sketched here shows that there can be a give-and-take relationship between what went before and what follows, so the break is not radical or insurmountable. The change from one theory to another can indeed be traumatic (either epistemologically or psychologically traumatic—what Kuhn calls a crisis), but this break is not incommensurable. Kaplan's view allows for scientific progress, and makes sense of both change and permanence in scientific knowledge. Those two may seem to be in conflict, but a higher-level analysis shows that they need not be.

All this does not mean that we will always—or even in any particular case—succeed in finding a way to compare differing theories, or, to use philosophers' jargon, make differing theories commensurable or to translate them into each other. But it does mean that there is no *a priori* reason why we must fail. It also means that, with additional effort, we are likely to find a way to succeed.

Practically speaking, all this means that the central philosophical underpinning for the notions of multiculturalism, diversity, and historical relativism has been taken away. Although the discussion here has been primarily concerned with science and the language of science, this also has important implications for ethics. Those views are mistaken that claim that different people cannot understand one another, or that different ethical views cannot be compared, or that every system or theory or view is as good as any other. Therefore, attempts to uphold those mistaken views or to base social policy on them are ethically offensive, promoting social division and rancor where it is unnecessary.

Notes

[1] Alasdair Macintyre, *Three Rival Versions of Moral Enquiry* (University of Notre Dame Press, 1990), 5.

[2] Karl Popper, "Normal Science and its Dangers," in *Criticism and the Growth of Knowledge*, Imre Lakatos and Alan Musgrave, eds. (Cambridge University Press, 1970), 56-57.

[3] Morton A. Kaplan, *Science, Language, and the Human Condition* (Paragon House, revised edition, 1989), 26.

[4] Kaplan, 55.

PART TWO

THE PHILOSOPHICAL BASIS
FOR A NEW SYNTHESIS

CHAPTER 4

THE CLASSICAL GREEK THESIS

Morton A. Kaplan

I shall turn in Chapter 5 to the elements in contemporary continental philosophy that undermine belief in the authority of the social norms that buttress character and identity and in the absence of which anomie and the pursuit of transitory goals take precedence. But my first task is to show why the paradigms of classical philosophy, which made character and identity intellectually determinative, cannot be resurrected—at least within the confines of the contemporary realm of knowledge. Therefore, if a philosophical basis for the obligatory demands of social norms on character is desired, it will have to be done on a revised basis.

The Classic Greek Paradigm

I shall present a general view of the classical Greek paradigm and then defend the position that the differences between Plato and Aristotle do not undermine the conclusion based on this general account that there is a fatal flaw in the paradigm. The classical Greek worldview, best represented by Plato and Aristotle, was that there are natural kinds based on univocal and universal essences underlying the diversity of appearances. Each type of being is a natural kind. The essence of humankind, which receives its fullest and best expression as a member of society, is the foundation of human character. Its accidental expression might differ from culture to culture. Failures in development, as in that of a tree dwarfed because of shortage of water, might impede its adequate expression or even corrupt it. But its inner core remains the same in all times and places.

The existence of natural kinds is a necessary truth in the classical

Greek view because such kinds represented essences. The importance of character in the Greek paradigms rested to a significant degree on the existence of natural kinds—on the potential for a person to be an appropriate expression of human essence.

The classical Greeks distinguished between knowledge, which had as its subject necessary truth, and opinion or belief, which did not rest on such a firm basis. Mind examined experience by means of philosophical reasoning or theory in the quest for knowledge. However, for reasons that will soon become clear, neither form of analysis could directly reveal necessary truth. Instead, mind, they claimed, had a natural capability to recognize necessary truth in the process of reasoning about experience.

However, the claim of the great Greek philosophers that mind has a natural capability to recognize necessary truth is not valid. This can be shown initially by examining their understanding of theory. It later will be made clear that the flaw is not restricted to theory. Finally the reasons for the flawed assumption will be presented.

The path-breaking Greek account of theory, including the role of necessarily true axioms, or first principles, is provided in *The Posterior Analytics* of Aristotle. The very title of Aristotle's book announces that its subject is the method of treating formally how one may deduce necessary truths in theories which depend upon prior knowledge.

The Posterior Analytics resembles a contemporary philosophy of science in some important respects and differs from it in others. It remarkably included an assessment of the extent to which the various sciences are theoretical that largely accords with contemporary understanding. The Aristotelian position also accords with contemporary philosophy of science in permitting hypothesized elements that cannot be reduced to, or deduced from, experiential elements as critical parts of a scientific theory: a position at odds with the mistaken formulations of modern positivism. The concept of an electron, for instance, is not derived from experience but hypothesized to account for experience.

Aristotle's position differs critically from contemporary understanding in that it specified that theories, if true, are necessarily true. As Aristotle explicitly stated, theories are true not because observations confirm their derivative theorems (in our modern terms, predictions), but because their premises, including definitions, are necessarily true and because the theorems necessarily follow from them.

He just as clearly stated that mind has a natural capacity to recognize true axioms and definitions as necessarily true, even if experience and philosophical analysis are required to provide the evidence that leads mind to recognition.

This position with respect to the necessary truth of theories was related to logic, for theories involve an analytic chain. The derivative theorems of a theory flow necessarily from the axioms and definitions but are necessarily true only if the axioms and definitions are necessarily true. Therefore, if true theories are necessarily true, it must be because the premises are necessarily true.[1] The thesis upon which the foundation of knowledge rested would fail if the capability of the human mind to recognize the necessary truth of the premises of true theories could be called into serious question.

Aristotle's claim concerning the ability of mind to recognize the necessary truth of the axioms and definitions of theory can be examined usefully in the case of geometry. If it can be shown to be false with respect to a purely analytical, that is, demonstrative, discipline, then it will be false with respect to subjects that are not as theoretical and, hence, not purely analytical. His position was not shown to be false by the invention of non-Euclidean geometries, even though he considered mathematics to be the most theoretical of the sciences. One could argue that Euclidean geometry represented realworld truth and that non-Euclidean geometries were only curious inventions of mind.

The claim concerning the capacity of mind to recognize necessary truth, however, was invalidated by the discovery that the physical universe is non-Euclidean. Neither intuitive understanding nor philosophical reasoning could have sustained such a counter-intuitive conclusion. Only evidence with respect to competing theories and analysis of that evidence within the framework of the contemporary realm of knowledge that left older beliefs in deep trouble could have convinced the scientific establishment. Before Einsteinian relativity, including its non-Euclidean axioms, was accepted by the general scientific community, great resistance had to be overcome, even though many related concepts that accorded with relativity theory had already been accepted. (See the discussion of assessment with respect to a new synthesis in chapter 5.)

Quantum physics reinforced the falsification of the Aristotelian argument in a way that left no reasonable doubt. We cannot understand intuitively or on the basis of philosophical reasoning that electrons possess a definite position or momentum only during tests and that no test can make both position and momentum determinate simultaneously.

Even more radically, the successively more compelling confirmations of Bell's theory conflict with intuitive experience of space/time so thoroughly that disbelief needs to be almost unbelievingly suspended in view of the weight of the evidence. The Einstein/Podolsky/Rosen thought experiment was designed to show that the implications of quantum theory were so ridiculous that it had to be wrong or at least incomplete. Yet these very implications that Einstein considered proof that quantum theory had debilitating flaws repeatedly have been confirmed by tests of Bell's theory. There is still no framework of intuitive understanding that permits us to understand these results in ways that can be related to the larger body of knowledge other than as derivatives of a set of equations.

Quantum physics, put simply, is incommensurable with common sense or ordinary logical or philosophical thinking. There is a more intimate, if far from simple, relationship between acceptance of a theory, including its axioms, and the results of tests or other evidence, including assessments of the general surround of knowledge, than Aristotle was prepared to concede. This relationship remains continually revisable on the basis of new evidence or better analysis. The truth, let alone the necessary truth of the premises of physics, is not guaranteed by a natural capability of mind to recognize it. And this difference from Aristotle's position is crucial for a contemporary philosophy of science.

The evidence presented above shows that Aristotle is wrong about the capability of mind to recognize necessary truth as such. It still has not been shown that the concept of necessary truth is incorrect. Later at several points in this chapter, and in chapter 6, an account of why this is the case will be offered that will be related both to the relations of signs to their referents and to the distinction between first and second-order frameworks of reference.

Dialectical Reasoning

Can the Aristotelian account be saved by relaxing the requirement that the definitions and first principles of theory must be known to be necessarily true? Suppose one started with hypothetically true premises and definitions and used dialectical or philosophical reasoning.

Dialectic reasoning rests on beliefs that are believed to be probably true. Although analogy is the primary method of reasoning in dialectics, deductions may be made from premises. These follow necessarily from the premises. However, if one starts with premises that are probably true, the deductions, like the premises from which they follow, are probably, but not necessarily true.

Aristotle, who distinguishes between demonstrable and indemonstrable knowledge, clearly states that theory permits demonstrable knowledge. However, the theorems of theory cannot be demonstrably true unless the premises are necessarily, even if indemonstrably, true. Thus, it is not possible to relax the constraints Aristotle offered and remain within his system.

If it is not possible to know necessary truth about the world, theoretical science, as Aristotle portrays it, is not possible. If Aristotle had believed that, it is difficult, nay virtually impossible, to understand why Aristotle would have written *The Posterior Analytics* with such care and detail. We will soon show why Aristotle believed there was such a thing as necessary truth and why he believed mind could recognize it.

Ironically, metaphysics in Aristotle rests on dialectical reasoning. Thus, the first principles that underlie both the theoretical and the practical sciences, as Aristotle himself recognized, cannot be demonstrated to be necessarily true. If that is the case, then the only way in which theoretical science can play a meaningful role in the Aristotelian paradigm is if mind can recognize first principles as necessarily true. That is the claim that Aristotle, the first and greatest analytical philosopher, did make.

The Role of Logos

How can Aristotle claim that necessary truth can be known if there is no way to demonstrate first principles as necessarily true? The concept of logos likely provides the needed clue. In early fifth century Greek philosophy language (including logic) is the underlying controlling principle of the universe. Some form of logos, involving the relationship between language and reality, remained part of the Greek worldview into, and past, the time of Aristotle. Therefore, how did the concept of logos in its Aristotelian incarnation support the concept of necessary, knowable truth?

I am not a close enough student of Aristotle to attempt to decide precisely how Aristotle reached his conclusion concerning necessary truth. However, the underlying reasoning, whether explicit or implicit, is amenable to detection. Aristotle was the author of a treatise on logic, *The Prior Analytics*. In his view, the principles of logic underlie all posterior analytical science, even though the latter are not deduced from the former. However, even the principles of logic rest on other first principles.

For instance, if we assert that a lion is yellow, that is either true or false. Aristotle distinguishes necessary elements from accidental ones; hence the example assumes that the qualities to which reference is made are universal to the kind, although predicated in this case of an individual member of the kind. Thus, if one objects that the lion's hair may turn gray, he is really contending that yellow is an accidental attribute, not that the principle is incorrect.

If the assertion that a lion is yellow is true, it (language, logos) corresponds with reality and, hence, according to Aristotle, is necessarily true, for a true statement cannot be other than what it is. Thus, even with respect to statements about individuals, truth is necessarily true, for it cannot be otherwise.

Aristotle is not saying that one sees a yellow lion and, therefore, it is true that the lion is yellow. Assertion of truth in the intended sense, whether demonstrable or indemonstrable, is always universal and unchanging, hence, necessary. Truth in this Aristotelian sense, therefore, always asserts either an indemonstrable or a demonstrable claim concerning the universal in the particular.

How is this related to logos? What is the underlying reasoning? The underlying assumption clearly is A=A, which the Greek philosophers did not doubt. This is what Aristotle calls indemonstrable knowledge. (We will see in chapter 6 that even the truth of A = A is subject to interpretation.) Since A can be neither more nor less than A, A = df. A.

With respect to A = A, clearly, as Aristotle must have understood it, one A is identical to the other, the mental concept is identical to the linguistic embodiment, and both are identical to an actual A, the referent. The embodiment of the particular A has no accidental elements, except perhaps its being carved in stone or printed on parchment. Thus, mind immediately recognizes A = A as a necessary truth. Thus, there is a universal, univocal relationship between concept and reality and mind can recognize it.

Suppose one considers substituting for A = df. A: for instance, human = df. human. However, categories such as human presumably cannot be directly recognized as such, for hair, for instance, does turn gray. As things stand, the relationship between the two equalities constitutes an analogy by proportion and, hence, is not necessarily true. Yet Aristotle did not doubt that an entity is identical to itself (logos). How could this problem be solved?

In the Aristotelian system one would recognize human = human or human = df. human as a necessary truth subsequently to dialectical reasoning based on experience. This would separate df. human, or essence, from accidental attributes of particular humans. When this winnowing has been accomplished, mind then recognizes necessary truth and acquires knowledge of the underlying identity, even though this truth is not demonstrable. This is the case with respect to all posterior sciences.

Thus, after necessary truth has been recognized by mind, df. human = whatever it properly is, for example, rational animal or political animal. Whatever that essence is, it necessarily is because it is equal to itself. Hence, it is this something irrespectively and independently of the functioning of mind. Thus, it is this something univocally, universally, and necessarily. And language captures exactly what it is in nature.

Thus, when I argue that Aristotle had a univocal correspondence account of language, this most likely misrepresents the case. It likely is more than correspondence and yet not a copy. "Identity" between name and unchanging core would better represent what we are talking about. In any event, definition, which determines kinds in Aristotle, and which is less well developed in Plato, is explicitly univocal and universal in Aristotle. The essence of an entity is in this sense of "identity" identical to its name and contains no accidental elements.

This mode of conceptualizing the problem virtually fuses name and the universal within reality because, if true, it is necessarily and exactly true. It leaves out nothing of the necessary and adds nothing that is not necessary. Thus, only if one knows necessary truth does one have knowledge as distinguished from opinion. And only then will deductions be as necessarily true as the premises from which they are derived.

Aristotle is correct in believing that the definitions employed in a theory must be univocal, because otherwise determinative deduction would not be possible. However, the concept of logos likely is what leads him to believe, as he does believe, that true definitions are both univocal and universal. If necessarily true, as would be universally applicable definitions, their truth is not restricted to the theory in which they function. Later we will show to the contrary, in chapter 6, and from the standpoint of physics in chapter 8, that all definitions are from frames of reference and that these frames do not necessarily coincide. Definitions need not be the same in different contexts. And something that is true is not necessarily true in the Aristotelian sense.

Is Plato's Account Significantly Different?

Perhaps the reader suspects that my account of the classical position ignores a crucial distinction between Aristotle and Plato—that Plato's metaphor of the cave shows that he did not rest his metaphysical analysis upon a capacity of mind to recognize necessary truth concerning the world of experience. Plato's position, according to most accounts, was that mind has a capacity through philosophical reasoning, perhaps based on a supersensory insight into a fundamental mathematical reality, to show that metaphysical truth, including the existence of natural kinds, is the bedrock of the real on which fallible opinion concerning the world rests.

Plato clearly distinguished between knowledge and opinion. Therefore, how can one obtain knowledge in Plato's paradigm? If philosophy could reach to the world of experience, two methods of application were available within classical Greek philosophy: intellection and deduction. Were these methods sufficient to justify a claim of necessary truth?

Consider intellection. The methodology of how reason can use experience to find necessary truth was left less than fully determinate by the dialectical method of the Platonic dialogues. Intellection or philosophical reasoning, which is not fully deductive, falls short of the determinate character of theory. It, thus, is insufficient to permit so momentous a determinate claim as necessary truth. But even determinate theory cannot support such a claim.

Consider deduction. No subjects are more theoretical or determinate than mathematics and logic. (Gödel has proved that mathematical systems are not as completely determinate as Aristotle considered them to be. See chapter 8.) Even in logic, as Aristotle himself argued, it cannot be shown by a determinate method that the axiom set is true, let alone necessarily true, unless it is deduced from some other axiom set, in which case the same problem would arise. Yet the assertion of necessary truth is as determinate a claim as can be made.

Intellection or philosophical reasoning, being less than demonstrative or determinate, cannot have as firm a claim to knowledge of necessary truth as demonstration. Even if, contrary to the case, it had an equally firm foundation, it would not possess a better claim. When intellection operates in areas that are not theoretical, the lack of determination in the process is even greater. Thus, only recognition of necessary truth by mind is left. And there is no significant difference between Plato and Aristotle about the character of the problem or the necessary, if not necessarily sufficient, mode of solving it.

Earlier, we speculated about the role of logos with respect to Aristotle's position on necessary truth. We can come to the same conclusions concerning necessary truth, and somewhat more directly, from a somewhat different path. Consider again the implications of Aristotle's *Posterior Analytics*. Aristotle's inclusion of mathematics within the realm of theoretical science tells us that the classical Greek paradigm did not make the distinction that most contemporary philosophers do between strictly analytical or purely formal constructions and interpreted theories. (These are correlatives in my metatheory, neither dichotomous nor fused.)[2] Aristotelian theories apply directly to the world of experience, without need for interpretation.

Both Plato and Aristotle, thus, fuse language and reality. Aristotle's paradigm, however, extends the fusion in ways that Plato's paradigm cannot. In Aristotle's system, the logic of theoretical constructions permits necessary deductions from axioms that have little, if any, descriptive content, but that mind can recognize as necessarily true, to derived theorems that may move closer to more particular elements of life that mind perhaps cannot or does not recognize as necessarily true. It is the move from indemonstrable knowledge to demonstrable knowledge that theory provides that accounts for Aristotle's discussion of it. Thus, even though Aristotle provides a more sophisticated methodology than does Plato, the concept of essence—or, more generally, what something is as such or definitionally—is central to the discussion of necessary truth in both Plato and Aristotle.

I think there has been an exaggeration in the literature—which I accepted until I tried to work the matter out in this chapter in terms of the subject I am addressing—of the differences between Plato and Aristotle, with respect to their concepts of essence and their empiricism. I say this with some trepidation because exegetical analysis never has been an interest of mine and I do not read Greek.

I accept that no exact translation or reading of a text is possible. One difficulty stems from the fact that we cannot reproduce the contextual meanings of words and the unspoken but common understandings of the then current realm of knowledge. Nonetheless, in my opinion, both Aristotle and Plato shared a general paradigm, within which certain differences were expressed.

Plato's concept of archetypes differed from Aristotle's concept of what something is in essence—or what its final cause will produce under favorable circumstances—in ways that were important within the terms of the classical realm of knowledge. The archetype appears to be an idealistic concept dealing entirely with form and to have no physical base. Or, did Plato instead imply that an actual universal was embodied in many particular entities?

Potentiality and final cause, as Aristotle considers them, appear to add material content, even if not directly present to sense organs, to form. The universals in particulars would be identical to each other and not part of some noumenal sphere if that is what Plato was saying.

However, the concepts of essence of both Plato and Aristotle determine what the existential entity is as an exemplar of its type. If that is a correct interpretation, the difference is real but not very important from the standpoint of the issues raised in this chapter. The core is the identity of the universal element with itself and with concept or name.

In fact, if not in the understanding of the authors, neither the Platonic nor the Aristotelian option can be detached from material content or ideational form. Platonic Ideas cannot, in fact, be characterized entirely by elements of form, even if Plato did mean to assert this.

The Idea "chair," for instance, cannot entirely be divorced from experiential elements, even if it can be divorced from elements of particular form or material content. It would have to include an object with sufficient solidity to be sat on by some being with legs, or comparable appendages, and a bendable torso. (How would its form or content differ from that of a one-step ladder in a metaphysic that claims each has an independent univocal and universal essence?) Although the Idea could be as limited in experiential content as "atom," for instance, this would not be true of "human" or "fish." Aristotle did not differ in significant ways from this position.

One could argue that Idea and final cause are categories within metaphysical positions designed to elucidate how the philosopher or scientist can winnow out what is essential from what is inessential in entities. Both concepts of essence then would refer to hypotheticals that are dependent upon experience for judgments of content. The differences between them primarily would lie in methodology and not necessarily in content.

Plato and Aristotle may have been looking for a philosophical framework that would account for a closer connection between permanence and variable realities than previous metaphysical speculations permitted. Previous philosophers had sought permanent building blocks in general substances such as earth or atoms to account for the unchanged somethings that underlay changing experience. As one necessary something came under challenge, the substitute faced similar challenges.

The ancients possessed no systematic, determinate way to link these elements to the actual world because the distance between such general categories and most actual things was too remote. It was one thing to attempt to relate water to river—although in the absence of theory they could not really do this either, at least in a determinate manner—and another to relate water or earth to tiger or spider. Plato and Aristotle likely used essences of (the great diversity of) things to account for permanence because they believed this would enable them to make the missing linkages between the necessary underlying logos and variant existence.

Thus, the move from air, etcetera, or atoms etcetera, to types of things allowed reason in the philosophy of Plato and reason, theory, and experiment in Aristotle to deal with real, recognizable entities more explicitly than earlier metaphysical systems could deal with more general substances. Aristotle, however, was not content with Plato's account because it remained too loose in determining what was essential and ineffective in accounting for change or variance.

Aristotle's Account and Contemporary Science

There are elements in Aristotle's account of science that create the appearance but not the reality of a contemporary account. Aristotle's discussion of the different types of cause—cause also was a category that could not be doubted because it linked antecedent to consequent and, hence, had its own necessity or logos—permitted a sophisticated experimental method that aided in separating essence (final cause or even formal cause) from variant actuality (produced by other types of cause). For example, a shortage of water stunts a tree. Successive experiments, thus, could portray a number of the interrelationships between essence, development according to essence, and deviations from essence that would assist in discovering the necessary core of essence. Recognition of this necessity, however, still depended upon a natural capability of mind. One must be able to comprehend that "musical" is an accidental attribute of man, and not part of the essence of the class, of the universal.

In the Aristotelian system, theory building and the methods of experiment with respect to his categories of cause go hand in hand. Definitions or essences (internal meaning)—the universal and unchanging core of language (logos) and of types of things—would provide a foundation of the necessary that would be affected by external conditions and, hence, accident, that in combination produce existential variability.

This is similar in some respects to the concept of fit that will be discussed in chapter 5. Aristotle would have been there if he had surrendered the concept of logos, the univocal and universal, as distinguished from the different sets of internal meanings of different theories or accounts, and retreated from the ability of the mind to recognize necessary truth.

Perhaps one could argue that the Aristotelian metaphysic is consistent with modern science because philosophical reasoning would have led Aristotle if he came back to life to drop the concept of logos and his belief in the ability of mind to recognize necessary truth. This is not necessarily wrong, but it is loose. It could lead to the conclusion that almost all philosophies are the same because the modes of correction in them would lead to changes that eliminated the differences, somewhat as the elements of a kaleidoscope can be shifted to produce endless pictures.

Consider that if Newton had come back to life in 1900, with access to the same scientific data base that Einstein had, he might have modified his theory which has a considerable theoretical overlap with Einstein's, to include Einsteinian postulates. Yet physicists correctly, I believe, deny that Newton and Einstein shared the same theoretical paradigm because there also are important differences.

The Aristotelian metatheoretical schema is similar to and different from current conceptions in important respects. Some important differences deserve note. Because a type of entity, represented by definition in Aristotle, is permanent and unchanging, one essence cannot evolve into another. Knowledge of it is knowledge of what it necessarily is. Such knowledge cannot be provisional. (Hence the problem of a contemporary with how the Ideas of chairs and ladders can be differentiated within a classical framework.) Thus, even if nature cannot be reduced to theory in the classical metaphysical systems, correct definition, or essence, exhausts concepts and the universal within the particular.

In some other respects, the Aristotelian system is more modern than the Cartesian system that replaced it. Despite the concept of necessary truth, the classical position does not lead to rationalism. This comes out most clearly in the Aristotelian differentiation between theories of different subject matters. Each discipline starts with first principles appropriate to its subject matter. Aristotle deals with theory in each area in terms of the elements of which it is composed and of the axioms that apply to it. In Aristotle's system, geometric truths, for instance, cannot be deduced from the axioms of arithmetic, although they may be developed in conjunction with the axioms and theorems of arithmetic. In the contemporary synthesis that will be presented later, different theories invoke different frames of reference, and this also guards against rationalism.

Thus, the initial discussion of the classical position is modified by the prior discussion but not changed in its most important respects. Knowledge in both the Aristotelian and Platonic systems depends upon the capability of mind to recognize necessary truth, in particular, although not exclusively, the necessary truth of essences. The positions of both Aristotle and Plato on essence establish an inseparable connection between names (correctly applied) and types of things.

The Kripke-Putnam Concept of Rigid Designation

The last important effort to make the classical concept of a necessary connection between names and things viable, at least metaphysically, although not epistemically, lay in the rigid designation thesis of the contemporary mathematical logicians Saul Kripke and Hilary Putnam. They sought to restore the Greek concept of natural kinds without resort to a capacity of mind to recognize necessary truths. If the concept of natural kinds could be given validity, even apart from the capacity of mind to recognize its necessary truth, or even its truth, the classical foundations could be reestablished in principle. This attempt on their part ultimately failed.[3]

The discussion in chapter 5 of different frames of reference will pave the way for chapter 6 on language and meaning in which the reasons for the failure will become evident. In that chapter, the reader will see Kripke and Putnam struggle to find examples of rigid designation, moving from concepts such as "yellow is yellow" to "water is H_2O" to "molecular motion is molecular motion." However, even though they drop the epistemic claim, the same ultimate problems that undercut the Aristotelian use of univocal and universal concepts, and the associated first-order framework of reference, confront theirs.

The Straussian Critique and the Problem of First-Order Analysis

Although it has been mentioned in passing, I have not yet examined the problem arising from the implication of logos that truth rests on a first-order account of the world. It may be useful to bring forward this crucial subject through a challenge to modernity that Leo Strauss posed.

Leo Strauss and his followers have long argued that the revolution in philosophy beginning in the seventeenth century is responsible for current misconceptions (including mine) and that we must return to the wisdom of classical Greek philosophy. Arguments such as those I have made are regarded as ignorant, because they are based on incorrect seventeenth-century assumptions concerning the relationship of theoretical science to reality. In particular, Strauss claimed, we fail to distinguish between theoretical and practical science.

Strauss is wrong on both counts. It will be thoroughly clear by the end of chapter 5 that contemporary philosophy of science, rather than being based on Cartesian assumptions, is incompatible with crucial Cartesian assumptions. Moreover, as will also become clear, the Aristotelian dichotomy between theoretical and practical science will not survive analysis in the dichotomous way in which he made it.

The more immediate consideration is that neither Strauss nor his followers ever examined closely how science is used in contemporary philosophy of science. Consider how I have used science so far in this chapter. Among other lessons, I did not use the (abstruse) subject matters of relativity and quantum theories to draw conclusions, at least directly, concerning human affairs but to provide clear examples of the intimate, fallible, infinitely revisable, and often counterintuitive, relationships between fundamental assumptions—in the case of science, definitions and the axioms of theory—and experience, experiment, and analysis when attributing truth to the former.

There are other important lessons from science that I will use later, for instance, one stemming from the distinction between systems employing mechanical and those employing homeostatic equilibria. This distinction is used to show that theory, or even more mundane methods of physics, cannot be used in accounting for the homeostatic behavior of such nonhuman systems as air-conditioning systems, let alone human systems. This is one of the key features of a contemporary philosophy of science that conflicts with the Cartesian paradigm.

However, the Straussian objection, although incorrect, points to an important reason the classical account accepted the assumptions that moved it off course. And this centers precisely on how humans acquire knowledge, not on a claim, which the Straussians imagine those of us who use contemporary philosophy of science must make, that theory of the type of physics applies generally to human affairs.

Let us examine one reason why the ancients were seduced into believing that truth necessarily abided in first-order accounts by considering how early interpretation of the world worked with respect to the geometry of space. Consider what our human senses tell us about space. No unaided human experience can tell us whether or not parallel lines meet at infinity. The Euclidean axioms appear necessarily true because of our inability to perceive spacial matters at celestial distances, where predictions of the two theories differ significantly. On earth, we are incapable of noticing the deviations because they are infinitesimal. Euclidean axioms, thus, were reified by the Greeks as a necessary truth, as clearly and recognizably true as A=A.

Although the concept of logos underlay the Greek concept of essence, the belief of the Greeks that the axioms of Euclid were necessarily true stemmed from bodily constitution, not from a natural capability of mind to intuit necessary truth, even if only after experience and intellection. The classical writers, great as they were, did not recognize that what is true of experience is a product (a characterization) of a transaction between human transceivers and an external world, not something with an entirely independent existence, which mind merely recognizes, even if it must winnow the accidental from the necessary. The characteristics of this product depend upon the medium in which the transactions take place as well as upon the characteristics of the transceivers and of the referents of the process. Thus, none of the three elements will be the same from every framework of reference. For instance, my desk is solid from the standpoint of my hand. From the standpoint of an elementary particle it is as empty as is the solar system from the standpoint of a projectile.

In addition to the physical character of the transceiver, there is also the mental apparatus (or the coding system) the transceiver uses in experiencing and thinking (or calculating) about the world. The classical Greek philosophers did not perceive, at least with sufficient clarity, that different languages characterize entities differently. That different theories and that different frameworks of reference can lead to different, even seemingly opposed, but equally correct character-izations, and so forth, is foreign to classical Greek philosophy. (See the discussion of rigid designation in chapter 6, the references to it in this chapter, and chapter 8.)

The Greek view of the world was a first-order view. Even though Aristotle detailed an extremely sophisticated and complex experi-mental process for winnowing out variation from underlying essence, his methodology required a resting point that was universally true on a first-order basis. This carried over to the Aristotelian account of definition, in which the "is" entails an essentialist character. And, hence, language in principle can exhaust the reality to which con-cepts apply, even if theory cannot exhaust the world. Even if Plato's account was less well worked out, it was not different in ways that are important to this discussion.

Einsteinian relativity, thus, would have been virtually incompre-hensible to the classical Greek philosophers. The distinction between the opposed but equally correct first-order judgments of an observer on each of two independent inertial systems that the other's system was moving more slowly through space than his was, and a second-order theory that reconciles these apparent contradictions, would have been so foreign to their metaphysic and its use of language that it would have taken an astounding act of intellect to comprehend it and to incorporate it into the current metaphysic.

Therefore, the great classical Greek philosophers—who thought and wrote in the beginnings of philosophy and before the great ex-plosion of scientific knowledge—were not in a position adequately to comprehend the fundamental role of interpretation, at least as that term is employed in contemporary philosophy, in understand-ing the world, including the world of ideas. (Chapters 6, 7, and 8 will include discussions of interpretation from different perspectives.) Their copy or univocal and universal correspondence accounts of language reified language.

Although the common sense of Plato and Aristotle was filtered through "theoretical" frameworks not available to earlier thinkers, it was informed by too little theory and empirical knowledge to permit the kind of critical examination that even merely competent and otherwise ordinary philosophical minds can employ today. Thus, my analysis applies, if anything, even more strongly to the humanistic realm, and its ordinary sense methods, than to the scientific, although I do not deny the leaven that common sense can bring to analysis.

The Classical Greek Legacy

The Greek philosophers of the fourth century left to their progeny a recurrent problem with which we are still struggling: how to use reason to justify the claim that we possess knowledge. It is this quest that distinguishes Greek philosophy from speculations that in other cultures are called philosophy. It is this glory of our civilization that is being called into question in our contemporary age. How we got to this impasse and how we can escape from it without abandoning the Greek project of rational knowledge is the problem of the next chapter and of those that follow in this part of the book.

Notes

¹Contemporary logicians do not use Aristotle's syllogistic logic, and for good reasons. Among them, Aristotle surely knew that the heads of horses are heads of animals. Among other methods, he could point to a horse, call it an animal, and infer that its head is a head of an animal. But there is no way to prove this in syllogistic logic. However, even in contemporary systems of logic, if something is necessarily true of an antecedent, it is necessarily true of the consequent, although not necessarily vice versa. This is one of the bases on which confirmation of theories by testing is rejected by some philosophers in favor of falsification. However, both confirmation and falsification are useful and neither is fully determinative. See Morton A. Kaplan, *Science, Language, and the Human Condition*, Paragon House Publishers, 1984, revised edition 1989, pp.103-114 for the range of issues involved in this conclusion.

²See below and also *Science, Language*, pp. 49-58.

³The reasons for the failure are too complex to be adumbrated here but will be presented in a later section of chapter 6, which includes most of chapter 4 of *Science, Language*. Heraclitus, who appears to reject the essentialist paradigm by regarding everything as changing, paradoxically assumes that change is unchanging. Otherwise, it could not be true that change is the permanent state of things. Moreover, he could not have delineated a specific changing something without reference to something that was unchanged. (See chapter 6 and the preliminary discussion of that chapter in chapter 5.) It should be noted that the brilliant mathematician and physicist Roger Penrose, who understands physics and mathematics impeccably, is a neo-Platonist who be-

lieves that the world is mathematical in nature and that mathematical truths, if not their necessity, are directly accessible to mind. His argument is based partly upon the success of mathematics in providing a framework for physical theory, partly upon how infinitesimally close theories come to predicting real world physical results, and partly on the argument that it is difficult to see how mathematicians come up with great mathematical advances unless they have direct mental access to that world of mathematics. My reasons for disagreeing with him are given in chapter 8. See also the discussion of theory or proof and assessment in chapter 5, which relates Einstein's discovery of relativity theory to this issue. If Penrose were correct, however, it is difficult to understand why it took thousands of years for mathematicians, including some of the greatest of all time, to think of the possibility of a world in which parallel lines meet at infinity or of a Moebius strip, which has only one side, not two. Even if he were correct, he has not advanced us one step in learning how to determine which mathematical axioms or theorems are true of the world of physics, let alone for believing that mathematics characterizes in major ways the world of human values or social choices. Nor would the correctness of his thesis make the argument for natural kinds any less dubious.

CHAPTER 5

FROM THE CARTESIAN ANTITHESIS TO A CONTEMPORARY SYNTHESIS

Morton A. Kaplan

Long before the decisive, and easily understandable, contempo-rary evidence for a fatal flaw in the Greek paradigm was avail-able, the major philosophers of the Western world believed there were sufficient problems with the classical paradigm to reject it. For instance, experiments in alchemy convinced Descartes that the ac-cepted technique, the manipulation of the names of things or enti-ties, could not account for the results of experiments.

Descartes took the position that a language adequate for science would make use of quantitative relationships among the qualities of things, not of their essences. If science did not proceed on the Aris-totelian basis, natural kinds became irrelevant in the search for truth. Regardless of whether either Descartes or the alchemists understood entirely correctly how Aristotle used theory, Descartes broke the nec-essary connection between names and things and, thus, dismissed the ability of mind to recognize necessary truth in nature.

Yet Descartes retained the classical thesis that proof required dem-onstration. If mind could not recognize necessary truth in first prin-ciples or essences, how could it achieve demonstration? This was the new problem that confronted philosophy. As we shall see, Descartes incorrectly believed he had solved this problem at the beginning of modern philosophy.

There were two strands to Descartes' position. His approach to language—the breaking of the determinate connection between names and types of things—is one we would accept today, although in a form (non-univocal correspondence) different from his. The other—making knowledge depend upon the isolated ego rather than on the character of nature—was the wrong solution to the wrong problem: the search for a new certain foundation to knowledge. It needed to be replaced by a distinction between first and second-order frameworks of reference.

Although the Cartesian program was incompletely stated and in fact incapable of complete statement, one strand of Descartes' philosophical program, the basing of theory on the quantitative qualities of things, was instrumental in accounting for the development of a reconstructed realm of knowledge. Even though contemporary critics of Descartes pointed to fundamental flaws in the Cartesian paradigm, it was difficult to restrain enthusiasm. Because Cartesian theory was not limited to types of things, or even types of subject matters, as in Aristotle, it could possibly achieve complete generality. The rapid development of theoretical science in the early modern period reinforced belief in the philosophical community that the Cartesian scientific program was valid, even if other aspects of his philosophy were faulty. (Although Galileo was a Platonist who sought truth in mathematics, his theory was consistent with Descartes' use of language.)

This early modern philosophy, resting on mathematics and theory, in time took the position that theory in principle could account for the world. In its most extreme form, an omniscient God could predict all future states of the world from its initial positions. Thus, unlike the Greeks who believed the world was subject to rational understanding but not reducible to theory, the Cartesian approach gave credence to rationalism.

In some respects, Descartes did move us closer to an adequate contemporary position. If instead of using the self as the guarantor of certainty, he had used the self as a first-order frame of reference and tied this to a second-order framework of theory and a non-univocal correspondence account of language, he would have partly traversed the route we needed to take. Instead, he set us off on a path that philosophically was a dead end, even if it appeared to account for the florescence of theoretical science.

Leo Strauss and his followers, thus, are correct in believing that seventeenth century philosophy represents a break with the great Greek classical philosophical tradition. However, they wrongly place emphasis on Hobbes rather than Descartes, misunderstand crucial elements of the character of this break, and are insufficiently familiar with contemporary science and philosophy of science to understand why their critique of contemporary philosophy of science is irrelevant.*

It was the Cartesian philosophical paradigm that produced a philosophical revolution by the mid-seventeenth century. This philosophical revolution placed the basis for knowledge in the isolated individual, since certainty beginning with individual thought could

---

*Leo Strauss asserted a dichotomy between the classic and modern approaches, with Hobbes as the archetypal modern example. Although Hobbes had taken the then current theoretical paradigm for physics as a model for politics—thus, breaking with Aristotle's thesis that politics is a practical and not a theoretical subject—he did so within the framework of an Aristotelian understanding of the epistemological status of the axioms of valid theories. Hobbes accepted the Aristotelian thesis that mind has a natural ability to recognize the necessary truth of the axiom set or first principles of a theory. Thus, Strauss misdirected attention from the most crucial aspects of the Cartesian revolution, the use of language and the method for founding certain knowledge, that led to the worldview that made the individual the measure of all things. Even so, as chapter 9 will make clear, Hobbes had to change his definition of freedom in midstream to support the obligation to submit to sovereign authority. However, even if counterfactually Hobbes' writings had represented the then modern position, a number of the most important of the Cartesian understandings no longer accord with science. For instance, the statistical mechanics of Gibbs and Boltzmann, Einsteinian relativity theory, and quantum theory are thoroughly inconsistent with Cartesian determinism and rationalism. Even in the most theoretical sectors of physics some problems are so complex that only computer simulations can work them out. Hence, even if the contrast between classicism and the modernity of the seventeenth century had been correctly understood, treating it, as Strauss did, as central to the critique of contemporary understanding would be not only irrelevant but, much more important, misleading. Strauss' interpretation directs attention from central issues with which contemporary philosophy must cope, including the use of signs and the differences between first- and second-order frameworks of reference. As we shall see, one could more accurately view the progression from classical Greek philosophy to the contemporary period as an example of a quasi-Hegelian dialectic, with Aristotle's system as thesis, Descartes' as antithesis, and the position outlined below as synthesis.

not move beyond its isolated putative individual source. (The radical implications of this thesis for knowledge of a world common to different individuals did not receive recognition until the nineteenth century.) Hence, morals, law, and authority had no source other than what isolated individuals would provide. Legitimacy of authority, therefore, rested in contract among individuals.

Contract theories, and the concept of individual natural rights which precede contract, easily can be shown to be fatally flawed. This will be explained specifically in "The Philosophical Preconditions of Democratic Theory," included here as chapter 9, other aspects of which are discussed briefly in this chapter. This is an aside, however, for the successive flaws in the attempts of modern philosophers to find a secure foundation for knowledge led to the seeming contemporary impasse in which the very idea of a solution is rejected by most continental philosophers. And it is this impasse which must be overcome if we are to establish a compelling philosophical basis for character and obligation.

Therefore, let us turn to the more basic question of the foundation of knowledge as it was successively understood—a story of successive failures that starts with Descartes. Chapter 2, John Simpson's insightful article on the modern philosophical grounding of the self, its identity, and character, correctly begins with Descartes' attempt to ground knowledge in what is certain, even if not necessary. This was soon shown to be flawed, although this did not seem to inhibit the search for certain knowledge.

Descartes' contemporary Gassendi pointed out that any bodily function would give evidence of existence and, hence, that the attempt to rest certainty on thought failed. Gassendi placed emphasis on experience and experiment but this did not provide a guaranteed foundation. Leibniz developed his concept of windowless monads but was forced to rely upon God's goodwill for the concordance of their experiences. (How close he came to, but missed, the need for a second-order frame of reference!) Kant denied human ability to penetrate to things-in-themselves but claimed that the human mind had the capacity to establish causality among experiences or representations. This led to the rejoinder that a concept of things-in-themselves had been made superfluous by Kant's account.*

Kant was led into the foregoing trap by his belief that a certain ground for knowledge was required to sustain claims about reality. If the concepts of mind corresponded with appearances, but not with the reality that lay behind appearances, then what things really were in their essence was beyond even partial knowledge. Even after giving up this claim, he could justify a claim to know truth about phenomenal appearances only if mind could guarantee this. However, he merely assumed this and offered no reasonable argument to justify it.

Hegel restored the connection between mind and reality by his conception of the dialectical interrelationships of what things were for themselves and for others, a process that unfolded in history. His *Logic* recognized that this process of obtaining knowledge explored reality but did not exhaust it, even in its essence, in historical time. His system went wrong in assuming that the unfolding of the Absolute was a determinate process in real time that underlay the accidents of actual history.

The determinism of the process required a strong coherence theory

---

*Kant proclaimed that he arrived at his solution after Hume awoke him "from his dogmatic slumber." Hume had tried to demonstrate that there was no way to experience cause and that the concept arose only from the succession of appearances. However, Hume had rested his denial of causation on a causal sequence: that the appearance of succession would lead the mind to the idea of cause. Furthermore, if one accepted his argument, there would have been no ground for distinguishing successions that were related from those that were not, although both ordinary individuals and scientists did this successfully. (Think of a case in which a man drinks a glass of milk and drops dead but in which an autopsy shows severe sclerotic damage to the blood vessels.) Kant's solution, apart from the problems already noted, suffers from a similar problem. If the mind is the guarantor of the application of the category of cause to representations, then it should impose the relationship without error, something Kant knew to be false. If the investigator must distinguish between true and false attributions, then Kant's solution is unnecessary, the ground for attribution resting elsewhere. And if the distinction cannot be made, the solution is not a solution. Of course, there was a problem with the then current concept of cause but it lay in the search for a certain foundation for attribution of determinism to relationships among realworld events or things.

of truth (in effect, Hegel's version of fit) in which the Absolute was identical to itself (necessity) while the necessary in the existent was a concrete embodiment of that historically transforming identity within a distinctive existential form. (Neither the German language nor Hegel's use of it is noted for precision, but the use some American Marxists such as Bertell Ollman made of Hegel's ambiguous concept of identity turned it into simple nonsense in which fish was identical to water.) However, even if Hegel's solution to the philosophical problem of knowledge was incorrect, he was the first philosopher to move beyond a univocal correspondence theory of the use of concepts.

Hegel needed to find a determinate method to account for the determinate unfolding of history, even if he had to reject Aristotelian logic to do so, a process that was eased for him by recognition that the Greeks reified names. The concrete universal was an integral part of Hegel's solution. The concept of the concrete universal produced a complex process in the Hegelian system that led to the confusion over whether Hegel believed that history would end. (I believe that Hegel's concept of "true infinity" and his language, if interpreted in the Fichtean ur-language terms that were common in this romantic period, lead to the conclusion that history has no end.)

Although it is clear that the concrete universal was a necessary part of the Hegelian system if necessity was to overcome accident, Hegel never provided an adequate account of how it actually did so. However, the linkage of Hegel's system to history and his break with univocal correspondence accounts of language moved us considerably forward on the path that had to be taken toward a contemporary synthesis.

Hegel's fusion of the universal and concrete was the counterpart to Aristotle's virtual fusion of the universal and the particular by not distinguishing, even in the correlative sense, between the formal analytical content of theorems and their uninterpreted application to the universal within particular existential contexts. It was not Aristotle's concept of essence that was guaranteed by logic but the fusion of universal concept and particular real world outcomes by theorems that directly applied to the world of experience, that is, to particulars in a necessary way.

Hegel's system was the last great attempt to account for knowledge systematically and upon a certain foundation. Recent developments in continental philosophy can best be understood in terms of

Hegel's failed attempt to use the dialectic of the Absolute, with its critical concrete universal, to repair the seemingly unbridgeable rupture between things-in-themselves and the phenomenal appearances available to mind that the Kantian critique of "pure" reason proclaimed. Although the Hegelian dialectic responded to the inability of any logical schema of the Aristotelian type (or indeed of any analytic system of logic) to exhaust the essence of reality,* his attempt to account for this by a dialectical self-movement of the Absolute through history could not be maintained because there was no common method for agreeing on the terms of the dialectic. Thus, the dialectic of the Absolute which provided the necessity that underlay the accidents of history in Hegel's system was rejected by all but a few neo-Hegelians. However, the account in Hegel's *Phenomenology* of how knowledge in historical time developed by means of transactions among people and with the world survived and fuelled most subsequent philosophical accounts, including the opposed continental and pragmatic philosophies.

Because Hegel's continental successors could not find a way to ground knowledge in the absence of the Absolute, we seemed, in their view, to be left only with stories. These stories included, among others, the irrationalism and relativism of existentialism, Heidegger's concept of being-in-the-world, and the post-modernism of Derrida and Foucault.

The Contemporary Predicament

Where, thus, does contemporary philosophy leave us? With the notable exception of the positivists, some American pragmatists, and some students of the philosophy of science, it was argued that knowl-

---

*It could be argued that Hegel's insights were precursors of Cantor's work on different types of mathematical infinity, in which some infinities were larger than others. Furthermore, there were insights he shared with Asian thinkers that hint at some of the strange aspects of quantum theory and complex problems of exploring reality. Whether or not this is correct, his account of non-Aristotelian logic placed so few boundaries on what can be claimed that it is not surprising that his system lost credibility. Still, his system was, and remains, the greatest attempt at a philosophical system since those of the classical Greeks.

edge depends upon, that is, is relative to, language or social convention: a story we tell to ourselves or others. These stories lack absolute status and are regarded by many philosophers as limiting. With Foucault, any set of social conventions, including language, is an imposition on human freedom. With Derrida it is language itself that constrains us. With Heidegger Being, which is not reducible to any reasoned argument, irrupts into being-in-the-world as brute, irrational fact. It is not inconsistent with his philosophy that he became a Nazi, for any mad thought can represent underlying Being. Or that Sartre could find freedom in accident or Communism, for his belief system is not subject to rational critique on a basis common to others.

Because the metatheoretic employed here does not allow either concepts or theories to exhaust the reality to which they refer, surprises are always possible, but they are in principle subject to retrospective rational analysis. It is no accident that when so many of the post-moderns talk of science or social science, they employ gibberish, speech uncontrolled by reference, that makes Medieval scholasticism seem highly rational by contrast. Even worse, their metatheoretic also eases the path toward obnoxious political doctrines. Heidegger's metaphoric and unexamined reference to Being's irruption into being-in-the-world, for instance, turns his commentary into a license to fabricate any sequence of words that makes him feel good. But it also absolves him from asking the critical questions that might have kept him from allowing his situation in the Germany of the 1930s to turn him into a Nazi.

How can we speak seriously of self and character if we take the accounts of contemporary continental philosophy seriously? These leave us only with what the individual mind can conclude in constructing its own story. Consonantly with such a perspective, freedom involves the escape from any confining social story. And also from rational control, for truth depends upon our mode of characterizing it and has no core common to different modes of characterization. Intellectuals who believe the contemporary account of truth—in effect, its absence—are as bereft as are theologians who succumb to atheism. In their despair they cling to their personal stories as tightly as a neurotic clings to his secondary gains in preference to a cure. Fortunately, absolute knowledge and stories are not the only alternatives.

Towards a New Synthesis

The prior account of modern philosophy has ignored those post-Hegelian philosophers who believed in the project of establishing a basis for objective, but not certain, knowledge. Some of these approaches had serious flaws. Positivists such as Hempel, by the late forties and early fifties, had used powerful analytical techniques to demolish their own positivist program of basing theory exclusively on what sense experience can convey—a result it took most political scientists a full generation to learn. Scientifically-oriented philosophers such as Popper had made bold efforts to find a route to objective knowledge. So had some American pragmatists who understood Peirce's attack on the concept of truth and his resort to meaning primarily as an attack on the classical conception of truth that was based on concepts that were a copy of or, alternatively, that corresponded univocally and universally with, external objects or events.

Chapter 3, Lloyd Eby's "Can We Understand Each Other After All?," has already presented the fundamentals of the argument for communication of objective truths across stories. An account of how one can build upon Eby's contribution to sketch a philosophically sustainable conception of objective truth—but one that does not rest on a foundation that can be known to be certainly true—is the task of the remainder of Part Two, while Parts Three and Four show how political and sociological considerations relate to such a synthesis.

Consider some of the more general features of this suggested metatheoretic. Distinctions are made between first-order and second-order frameworks of reference. The univocal and universal linkage between names and things is replaced by a tripartite one—signs (names) mediate between concepts and external referents (the signed)—that functions within a non-universal framework. Truth claims are invoked on a provisional basis and without assertion of copy or a univocal and universal correspondence between concepts, and the signs that represent them, and external world features. Instead, language characterizes the world (see chapters 6 and 8). Theory (internal criteria) and assessment (external criteria) in their correlative interchanges determine when truth claims, as that concept is employed in this metatheoretic, concerning these characterizations are warranted.

Assessment

Theory and assessment are not opposed methods but correlatives that are used in arriving at judgments. Although one may take predominance over the other in any particular investigation, understanding how they complement each other is central to understanding how scientific knowledge is acquired. Since assessment (fit, praxis) is less well recognized than theory as an appropriate scientific tool, let us start with it.

The realm of knowledge, in effect, can be divided into partly independent part systems, the characteristics of some of which are tentatively held constant while problems or controversies in others are examined. Assessment, thus, refers to a not fully determinate analysis that uses ostensibly related features of the realm of knowledge in evaluating the truth value of a theory or account for which there is confirming evidence.

There are usually experimental results that clash with accepted theories and that are ignored. The reason for doing so is that in the contemporary surround of knowledge the evidence that sustains the theory, and its concordance with other elements of knowledge in the same or related fields or part systems, is so dense that it seems reasonable to believe either that the seemingly disconfirming experimental results are mistaken or that they will be subject to reinterpretation when placed in a better context. Although some experimental results are more critical than others, there is, in principle, no such thing as a certainly critical experiment. And, thus, there is no substitute for assessment or judgment in these matters with respect to the fit between theory and surround.

If the fit is poor, assessment may give rise to a new theory or hypothesis. Sometimes the fit between elements of the realm need not be especially poor for a new hypothesis or theory to be offered. Changes in the surround of knowledge that most physicists ignored led to relativity theory. The development of non-Euclidean geometries, the mathematics of Lorentz contractions, and Maxwellian relativity—Einstein says he was unaware of the Michelson-Morley experiment and no other experiments called Newton's theory into question, at least directly—led Einstein to the belief that the speed of light was a constant and to Einsteinian relativity theory. It was this changed surround of knowledge that convinced some physicists, even if only a minority, that Einstein was right even before experiments confirmed his theory of relativity. (This perhaps constitutes a splendid answer to Penrose's position that was discussed in footnote 3 of chapter 4. Einstein's mind did not have access to some noumenal sphere, but his creative preconscious produced a theory that fit an existing surround—one that Newton did not have access to—even better than did that of Newton.)

Assessment, which influences judgment concerning the acceptance, rvrn if only provisionally, of theories because of a fit with the larger body of knowledge, thus, attends the evaluation of every theory. Assessment depends upon a recognition of fit, which makes use of a preconscious ability of the brain to compare patterns, that is then subject to judgmental analysis.[1] It was this preconscious and fallible capability of the brain to recognize fit that Aristotle possibly misconstrued as a capability of the conscious mind to recognize necessary truth.

Theory

Although I reject the concept of necessarily true premises, like Hempel I agree with Aristotle's concept of what a theory is. It is a deductive system that starts with definitions and axioms from which theorems are derived. Thus, it is demonstrative and invokes proof. I agree with Hempel that explanation, as contrasted with what I call assessment, requires theory. Like Hempel, I agree that counterfactuals can function in a theory. I also employ the term theory sketch for an account which is looser than a theory, although employing some deductive sequences. Unlike Hempel (who calls this an explanation sketch), I do not agree that a theory lies undiscovered behind every theory sketch. Some subjects are too complex. For instance, we still have no general formula for calculations in physics other than the two-body formula. More important, there are areas in which independent measures do not exist and, hence, in which there cannot be covering laws.* Aristotle was correct when he argued that some subjects are

---

*See *Science, Language*, pp.44-48 for a discussion of independent measures and covering laws. Homeostatic systems, and these include purely physical systems such as air-conditioning systems, are systems the behavior of which

less susceptible to theory than others. Assessment is the far end of this continuum.

Aristotle was correct in avoiding the reductionist approach to theory that later informed the Cartesian paradigm. Whatever Niels Bohr really meant philosophically by his principle of complementarity, it accurately accounts for one important type of relationship between knowledge and the world. Because incompatible test protocols are required to determine the position or momentum of particles, each reveals a contrasting but equally relevant truth about the world in which neither can be reduced to the other. The analyses of language accounts and of brain functioning are not reducible one to the other. Each requires its own first principles. Perhaps a general theory of the four forces one day may be discovered. Would a general theory of physics then exist? I do not know enough physics to speak with authority, but I suspect we would find the same relationships that Aristotle did between logic and mathematics on the one hand and mathematics and geometry on the other. That the principles of the logically prior discipline—the one embodying a theory unifying the four forces—can be used by the posterior disciplines, but that both macro and micro physics would require their own first principles.[2]

The Aristotelian dichotomy between theoretical science and practical science needs to be replaced by a correlative account. Some branches of mathematics and physics have been financed by the army in order to learn how to build better weapons. Some theoreticians of science may go into the field because of its prestige. On the other hand, some political scientists may study how politicians win elec-

---

cannot be accounted for by covering laws and independent measures, even though the laws of physics account for their physical aspects. (As they do also for humans.) For example, setting the thermostat at a given temperature keeps it within a given range but is not equal to anything. On the other hand, in terms of the physical system, one can calculate how much energy must be expended to raise or lower the temperature by any number of degrees. And one can diagram precisely how the parts of the homeostatic system accomplish this. Iterated application of the two-body formula is used to calculate multi-body problems. Some problems, involving the interactions of different categories of things, are so complex, even in highly theoretical areas, that only computer simulations using local measurements will work.

tions because they want to gain knowledge. The reason for studying how to inhibit the growth of cancer cells is to fight cancer, but the utility of the study depends on how well it explicates the functioning of cells. Aristotle was largely right in the ordering of his scheme of classification but for the wrong reasons. There are theoretical and practical aspects to all branches of science, but some may come close to one pole and some to the other in their internal accounts.

Hobbes was correct in one respect in disagreeing with Aristotle over whether politics is a theoretical science. If one could construct an axiomatic system, including covering laws, on the basis of principles, politics might become a theoretical science, even if the principles dealt with purposes of humans such as the avoidance of death. However, the absence of independent measures meant the absence of covering laws. And this severely limits the range and scope of theory.

Because Newton's theory incorporates covering laws and independent measures, one can calculate the effect of a resisting atmosphere or gravity on the path of a projectile. Thus, the counterfactual character of Newton's axioms with respect to motion in a vacuum can be compensated for in applications of the theory. There is no way within the Hobbesian theory to calculate the effect of a willingness to risk death on the generalizations that incorporate the counterfactual—the central flaw also in Nozick's theory—even had it otherwise been a properly demonstrable theory. Thus, although some economic theories of voting behavior do overcome this defect in cases in which large enough numbers of people do vote their interests in a narrow sense, politics in a broader sense is not a highly theoretical discipline.

Could one argue instead that Aristotle was right in depicting the difference between theoretical and practical sciences but wrong only in how he demarcated them? Possibly. Hobbes' theory and air-conditioning systems have an end in view: in the one case avoidance of death and in the other maintaining a stipulated temperature. But then how would we answer the objection that the end of a body in motion is to remain in motion? We are better off with the contemporary distinction between types of systems, for example, mechanical, homeostatic, multistable, and transstable that emerge from systems theory. And by regarding theory and assessment as correlative, but not dichotomous, methods.

Theory and Truth

Popper, along with American pragmatists, understood the logical fallacy in using experimental confirmation of a prediction of a theory as proof of its axioms. (Because Aristotle derived the necessary truth of the theorem from the necessary truth of the axiom set, this problem did not arise for him.) However, Popper erred in failing properly to appreciate that confirmed predictions provide confirming evidence of the provisional truth of the definitions, axioms, and associated theorems of a theory, that is, of their efficacy in accounting for phenomena. There is not, however, a necessary identity, or even a necessary eidetic relationship, between the sign system and the referent, even if not universal, particularly at the microphysical level. Popper also failed to recognize the equally provisional character of falsification. These are correlative methods for judgment of truth claims in the contemporary realm of knowledge, equally legitimate, and equally provisional.

The context or frame of reference within which the axiom set and definitions of a theory are regarded as provisionally true is central to judgment, for the *as such* concept of "true" already has been renounced. Alternative true theories of the world from somewhat different perspectives, thus, may enunciate seemingly conflicting truths that in some cases no more contradict each other than do the claims of observers on independent inertial systems that it is the other system that is moving more slowly. It is the task of a second-order account to reconcile what seems in terms of the use of words or signs to be a contradiction.

Well confirmed theories sometimes radicalize the worldviews that up to then were the basis for assessments. Consider experiments in two different periods of history, the theories that sought to explain them, and the worldviews to which they gave rise. The experiments that led to the development of chemistry, as distinguished from alchemy, changed the entire surround of knowledge. They helped to produce the Cartesian account of language, led to Galilean and Newtonian physics, produced methodological individualism and a natural rights philosophy, and fostered changes in other aspects of the previous surround.

The proofs of relativity theory turned time into a fourth dimension and made its measurement relative to placement on an independent inertial system, thus causing a major shock to common sense understandings of space and time that were consistent with Newton's theory. The confirmations of Bell's theory undermine local realism, and it is possible in time that much of the general framework governing how we interpret the world of space/time may have to be surrendered. These theories helped to spur the metatheoretical concepts advocated in this chapter.

Until quantum theory, we thought of the atom as a miniature solar system. Even apart from other radical changes quantum theory imposed on our understanding of the world, consider how it has influenced our understanding of elementary particles. For instance, an electron acts like a particle within one experimental framework and a wave within another. It can now be concluded that an electron in experiential terms is a dispositional concept that definitional concepts such as wave or particle misrepresent. Even where definitional or eidetic concepts work, however, they do so only within limited contexts and not universally. The concepts of dispositional and definitional are correlatives and, thus, it is not true that something either is or is not one or the other (the classical Greek position).

These radical transformations from seventeenth-century understanding show why it makes no sense for the Straussians to attempt to find the flaws of contemporary philosophy of science in seventeenth-century precursors unless detailed examination of current beliefs support this hypothesis.

The distinction between theory (proof) and assessment (praxis) was also the foundation of my argument against the Stephen Pepper and Thomas Kuhn theses that different metaphysical and scientific systems are incommensurable because the interpretive danda that characterize the relevant data are different. As Eby notes, I argued that no complete metaphysical or scientific system had ever been constructed.[3] It is the overlap of these supposedly incommensurable metatheories that permits their comparative evaluation or assessment. I have subsequently been able to use a variant of Gödel's *Entscheidungsproblem* to show that a conceptually complete metaphysical or scientific system is, in principle, not possible.[4]

Completeness and Language

Much of the turmoil in contemporary philosophy over language can be clarified by reference to the issue of completeness. Consider Willard van Orman Quine's "proof" of the impossibility of translation. Quine's brilliant demonstration works because he ignores how translations are made. Quine in effect insisted that translations be made by transforming one complete system—the original text—into the translated text.

If instead Quine had recognized overlap and used part-system analyses, his result would not have followed. We sometimes must use one English word for a French word and sometimes a different English word for the same French word and vice versa. We sometimes must explore similarities and differences to find the closest word. Sometimes we must substitute a phrase for a word. Sometimes we must use a foreign word and learn how it is used in the foreign language. And sometimes we must make up a new word and describe what we mean by it.

No global analytical exercise can capture this process. Only an assessment that deals with languages not as complete systems but as partly independent subsystems can critique alternative translations. Quine knew that we do translate with reasonable success in many cases. Therefore, one must assume that he was trying only to knock down the idea of precise and perfect translation.

Still, one must concede that translations are not merely imprecise. By virtue of the nature of the process they are weakly ordered, a subject to which I shall return when I discuss chapter 9. This means there may be legitimate disagreement on important elements of translations. This is a problem, but it should not be magnified to the exclusion of the fact that most translations are successful with respect to most important elements.

Let us put Quine's "error" in perspective and see why the real errors of Wittgenstein, Derrida, and Foucault[5] have a similar origin: the failure to see that their theses hold, even if in different ways, only if it is true that rational discourse requires that systems be treated as complete. Each fails properly to appreciate that there are three partly independent part systems in the use of language—concepts, signs, and referents—which can vary with partial independence and, hence, differently in different subsystems of the investigative process.

Elements of individual part systems are affected by other elements in the part system as well as by elements in the associated systems. For instance, the concept of line depends upon whether it is an element in a Euclidean or non-Euclidean concept system. The sign—but not the concept or the relationships of the sign to other signs—remains unchanged in the move between systems. Newtonian and Einsteinian theory do not use an identical system of signs and the relationships of the signs to each other are not identical. The referent of a non-Euclidean line, that is, the curvature of the physical space line, is partly independent of both the sign and concept systems of geometry. It is related to the concepts and sign systems of physics and the initial conditions of the actual physical system. Quantum theory introduced new signs into the sign part system of physics, with associated changes though all three part systems.

Partly independent changes continually occur in each part system. Thus, it is not possible for an individual exactly to recapture his beliefs from one time to another because changes have occurred in each of the part systems. That is why post-modernists would have to deny that an individual could communicate with him or herself if they were to maintain a consistent position. If this is what Derrida has misconstrued, it is no wonder that he relates language to madness. What he has failed to see is that such complete and rigorous relationships are not necessary for knowledge, even though they are necessary within closed (complete) analytical structures.

Wittgenstein's error in his concept of language games was simple. We can move outside of any language game to change it because each game is imbedded in a larger and incomplete language milieu within the terms of which we can critique any language game. Thus, we develop new systems of logic, new physical theories, and so forth. If we could reason only within a language game, we could not have developed new systems of logic and new systems of physics.

It must be emphasized that we are talking not about conversation but about the criteria and the realworld referents to which they apply that permit conversations to produce common understanding. That is why the posture of Jurgen Habermas is irrelevant both to philosophy and science. When scientists argued about Einsteinian relativity, they did not ask whether their conversations were uncoerced but whether the confirming evidence and the fit with other elements of the realm of knowledge produced a rational preference for one theory over the other.

The anthropologist Lewis Morgan implicitly understood that his comparative account of consanguinity systems did not undermine the project of common knowledge, although he did not place his discovery in a philosophical context. Morgan implicitly knew that he could use subsystems of both English and the relevant Indian language to relate the structure and norms of any tribal family system to history, initiating conditions, and other relevant cultural and sociological factors. This analysis then could have been communicated in the same way both to his community and that of the Indian tribe. None would have been confused because different first-order descriptive systems were employed and all would have been capable, at least in principle, of making a comparative evaluation.

Foucault incorrectly thought a similar discovery on his part did undermine the common basis of knowledge. If his study had not been truncated by his ideological blinders—if he had more systematically and comparatively explored the relationships of the different uses of language to different social structures and initiating conditions—he could have produced a second-order account or assessment. To the extent change was possible within the system, this assessment would have increased the range of freedom—that is, of conscious, rational control over decisions within the framework of the first-order system—of any individual who understood it. Rather than understanding how language, properly used, liberated by increasing the range of rational human understanding, he regarded language as a form of enslavement.

Like any tool, language provides control only by being subject to constraint. Tires could not help to move a car if they suddenly shifted into non-round shapes. Letters would not form into words if their shapes shifted radically. Words must retain their meaning, at least within first-order contexts, if they are to permit communication. If humans want the freedom to use tools, they must accept the associated constraints. If they understand how the constraints operate, then they have increased their power and freedom to modify or substitute for them when conditions or circumstances permit. This would not be possible in the absence of rational, structured employment of language. This is how engineers learn how to produce improved versions of tires that provide better traction in slippery conditions.

Only Derrida drew the appropriate counsel of despair concerning language from Foucault's signal mistake. The transstable personality, as I use that concept, is liberated from confinement to the belief systems of any first-order account, while recognizing the obligations that arise from existential placement in a first-order system. Thus, the transstable personality uses something like the test in principle, discussed in chapters 9 and 11, to critique first-order systems and to seek change, where feasible.

Thus, second-order accounts of science, language, morals, etcetera, are possible that reveal the conditions under which the first-order accounts function. These undermine the hypostasization of the first-order accounts, but accord with rational analysis of realworld matters that in principle can lead to a common account.

Back to Objectivity and A Common World

The metatheoretical framework just adumbrated includes consonant definitions of truth and objectivity, for instance, that are different from the contemporary standard ones as well as from those employed by Aristotle. It uses language in ways that fit this surround.

Unlike Eby I refer to my account of the correlative character of language as an assessment and not as a theory. The terms that are used in *Science, Language* are given specific definitions that accord with my metatheoretical account and are included here in an appendix.

The comparative evaluation of competing paradigms and the second-order mode of analysis invoked by Einsteinian relativity, and discussed with respect to the classical Greek paradigm, permit a framework of knowledge common to different individuals or different societies. We shall see later in this chapter during the discussion of chapter 9 how this permits comparative evaluation of different societies, although not necessarily the reconciliation of conflicting objectives or needs.

The latter may be a practical problem, but not an intellectual one. Someone who needs to carry packages in a waterlogged paper bag also has a problem. In a common universe, we understand that waterlogged bags cannot be used to carry heavy items and that a tribe that needs food to sustain its people will not lightly surrender the only growing area to another tribe, even though its need may be equally great.

Second-order analysis enables us to move beyond the Cartesian thesis, which restricts claims of knowledge and values to the isolated individual first-order source. It restores the classical Greek objective of relating the individual to nature and society, even if it does so only provisionally and absent a conception of unchanging and universal truths. It maintains the project of using reason, but not Cartesian rationalism, to understand the world. Thus, as suggested above, we are presented with a quasi-Hegelian dialectic in which the classical Greek paradigm is thesis, the Cartesian antithesis, and the instant one synthesis.

Meaning and Language

The remaining chapters of Part Two deal with language, logic, interpretation, and the nature of reality. Chapter 6, most of which is reprinted from chapter 4 of *Science, Language,* provides an account of language that differs from that of the Greeks and from many contemporary accounts. The correlative character of language, which inherently involves interpretation and characterization of the world by transceivers, is examined.

Language (sign system) mediates between concepts and the world of referents. Because these relationships depend upon the framework of reference, no univocal system of correspondences can hold. Observers on different inertial systems, for instance, make opposed first-order judgments with reference to such inertial systems and common second-order judgments on the basis of relativity theory. The optic systems of humans and dogs characterize colors differently. Colors do not exist for angstrom counters although given angstrom counts correspond with different colors for human optic systems, depending upon the quality of the light. Lying to protect a superior was honorable in the Samurai system but dishonorable in nineteenth-century America. It follows that no use of language can exhaust potential truth statements concerning the world because there is no way to limit possible systems of reference in a complex world.

Chapter 6 also analyzes why different systems of logic may be appropriate for different problems or subject matters. It, thus, denies that a single paradigmatic system of logic is sufficient for the analysis of reality. All systems of logic—indeed the signs they use—depend upon interpretation. Toward the end of the chapter, the prior analysis is used to show why the attempt by Saul Kripke and Hilary Putnam to preserve the classical conception of natural kinds, even if only on a non-epistemic basis, fails. This again shows why knowledge of the world cannot be exhaustive.

Chapter 6 also distinguishes correlatives such as structure and process and definitions and dispositions in terms of how language provides different foci for different modes of investigation. Things (structures) and processes are correlatives and no univocal permanent and unchanging reality underlies either concept. The concepts either of an unchanging reality that underlies experience or of a constantly changing reality use language in ways that reify experience. Something is unchanging only relative to some frame of reference in which other things are changing. And something is changing only with reference to something that is not changing. The ruler is unchanging (structural) relative to the atoms that compose it. But over time it does change (process), for it weathers and, of course, it is composed of particles that are constantly changing position. Definition and disposition also are correlatives. Electron is primarily a dispositional concept while billiard ball is a mostly definitional concept.

The categories within which things or structures are included depend on frame of reference. Humans can be included in the class of thinking creatures or in the class of featherless bipeds. Language can produce only pragmatic accounts that reveal boundary-related, limited truths, which in principle can be construed in common second-order objective ways. The placement of humans in the category of thinking beings may have greater importance from a variety of perspectives but it is not the only categorization by means of which nature may be explored. (Thus, the Aristotelian disjunction between theoretical and practical sciences is replaced by correlative theoretical and practical purposes in the use and development of a science.)

A cybernetic account of the psychological mechanism of projection is presented in chapter 7.[6] It shows that the acquisition of information involves a choice from among competing mechanisms for acquiring information and why the accepted noncybernetic psychological explanation of the mechanism of projection fails to account accurately for the phenomenon. The competing mechanisms are also treated in the same appendix of that earlier book.

Each mode of acquiring information increases the likelihood of receiving certain types of information and decreases the likelihood of receiving other types of information. There is no neutral or simply veridical mode of receiving information and the inputs must be coded (interpreted) for the inputs to become information. Nonetheless, because these mechanisms can be understood—and the use of any particular one compensated for—a second-order account that clarifies matters is possible. All transceivers, including the human, must be set in one of alternative ways in order to receive information.

Chapter 8 on the nature of reality reinforces Eby's argument that the world places constraints on what we can say about it such that we can indeed talk to each other. Among other things, it shows that second-order reconstructions place the time paradox of relativity theory and Schrödinger's quantum cat problem in a context that makes them less troubling to common sense than they ordinarily appear to be. The concept of truth employed in this chapter is pragmatic. Definitions of different types of truth may be found in the Glossary.

It is only fair to warn the reader that my discussion of the Schrödinger quantum cat problem is controversial. I know several excellent physicists, including one whose books on quantum theory have been translated into numerous foreign languages, who believe my critique of Schrödinger is exactly right. I know another distinguished physicist who flat out rejects it.

Political Legitimacy and The Realm of Values

"The Philosophical Preconditions of Democratic Theory," reprinted as chapter 9, provides some of the intermediary positions in the philosophical theses discussed above and establishes a basis for political legitimacy. It also relates integrity of the self to both positions. In addition, it briefly recapitulates the argument in *Science, Language* that moral evaluations are subject to objective treatment, even though these elements of knowledge are only weakly ordered and subject to assessment rather than proof, strictly understood—a condition that attends all sufficiently complex matters. Two elements are central to the analysis: the distinction between first- and second-order identifications or frames of reference and the weakness or looseness of the orders themselves in the valuational sphere.

The distinction between first-order and second-order identifications is as important in understanding the possibility of a common moral universe as it is with respect to other scientific or human affairs. Think of the clock paradox of relativity physics as a metaphor. Each of two observers on independent inertial systems will assert correctly that time is moving more slowly on the other. However, they share a second-order theory that accounts for this and that specifies that they will make seemingly contradictory first-order judgments.

Although in the ordering of values there is no theory to provide a common second-order explanation, it is possible in principle to provide a weak second-order praxical account (assessment) that establishes a common universe of understanding. This distinction, like the similar one in relativity physics, enables individuals who have strongly divergent first-order evaluations in principle at least to place them within a common second-order frame.

To clarify what I mean by the weakness or looseness of the realm of values, consider another metaphor. For any Pareto Optimal problem, it is possible to improve the situation from all relevant perspectives by moving from within the enclosed convex decision space to the Pareto Optimal boundary decision line. However, once on that line, any movement on it, although improving the outcome from one perspective, worsens it from another. For instance, think of an optimal air-raid warning system. Any attempt to reduce the rate of false alarms will increase the rate of unsignalled raids and vice versa. Although good reasons may be given for some of these choices, there is no objectively valid common second-order basis for singling out a particular choice as the best possible one.*

The situation with respect to the evaluation of social systems is even fuzzier than the air raid example. There will not even be a clear Pareto Optimal line or fungible units to use for purposes of comparison. Thus, although it may be possible to say on a common second-order basis that the Nazi and Communist systems were among

---

*This seems to resemble in certain limited respects what Aristotle says about precision. According to Aristotle, some subjects are subject to less precise analysis than others. What does this imply? From a contemporary standpoint, lack of precision invokes a measure that is more gross than desired. Precision always is relative to a standard of comparison and nothing is precise or imprecise in the absence of a standard. A quarter inch ruler is precise in

the worst of modern times, it is unlikely that a common second-order basis for asserting which is the very worst will be available. Different first-order evaluations in many cases will be objectively defensible. This will be true throughout the range of evaluation from best to worst, although a common second-order basis may exist for a rough order of good to bad.

Are the prior distinctions required? Although I would argue that one who understood the relevance of the air raid warning metaphor would be forced to agree, let us look to how some, who also reject the notion of mere stories, try to establish their position. Clyde Kluckhohn, for instance, argued that the fact that all societies have rules against murder, theft, etcetera, is proof of the universality of values. Other writers have argued that this proves that these values are embedded in human nature. In fact, all Kluckhohn's evidence shows is that a society is an organization and, commonly with other organizations, requires rules and regulations in important areas of activity.

The seeming evidence that all societies share the same values is based upon an improper equating of different things. Murder, for instance, means different things in different societies. There is no underlying essence for murder, in which its different manifestations are included. In some premodern societies victorious armies killed all defeated adult males. Some societies permitted slavery and did

---

measuring the mile run and imprecise in measuring the width of a bacterium. Both game and quantum theory are determinate at the level of theory but weakly-ordered. This is not a matter of precision. There is nothing imprecise about the air-raid warning example, even though no methodology or principle can single out a unique answer on a common basis. A unique answer on a common basis is not possible in such cases—for instance, in the zero sum game both minimax and minimax regret are defensible choices, depending on attitude toward risk—whereas, at least in principle, many calculations or measurements can be made more precise. Thus, in the metatheory presented in this book, it is the universe that is weakly ordered in many respects, that is, from many frames of reference, and strongly ordered in others. Because these issues do not arise in the same way in Aristotle's metatheory, I cannot say whether it is information about some less theoretical subjects that is imprecise while the universe is strongly ordered on a universal basis or whether the lack of theoretical character of a subject makes the implications of its first principles less precise.

not make killing the slave an offense. During World War II Romanian peasants led Nazi soldiers to hidden Jews so that they could be killed. In some Latin American countries husbands were permitted to kill their adulterous wives with legal impunity. In India, a husband could kill with legal impunity a wife who did not bring a big enough dowry.

To say that these societies shared the value of outlawing murder is to obliterate vital distinctions by raising the level of abstraction. If this mode of argument made sense, one might argue that men and women are both human, humans and primates both mammal, mammals and reptiles both animal, animals and plants both live, living beings and coal both organic, organic and inorganic both matter, matter and energy both existential, and everything the same as everything else. This progression is not entirely wrong—everything is the same in some respects, although different in others—but its erroneous use in context in the case of values should now be obvious. Kluckhohn has shown only that all restrictive norms can be made to fit into a common system of classification, although he has not shown that a different system cannot be made to work.

The fact is that some different societies have incompatible values as the Dutch burgher would have discovered in Samurai Japan. Not only was murder defined differently in the two societies, but the relationships of the individual values were different. Honesty was the mark of a good man in the Dutch system, but loyalty took weight over honesty in the Samurai, and became a signal element of honor.

If Kluckhohn's position that values are universal were correct, it would require the judgment that Nazi Germany and neighboring Denmark did not differ in important ways with respect to whether they shared better or worse values, for they shared the same values. Although some extreme relativists might argue that position, I doubt even they believe it.

In fact, it is obvious that values of some individuals and groups in contemporary society are sometimes incompatible. This is illustrated by the debates over abortion and same sex marriage. Although I believe a second-order examination would place these debates in a context that would tend to ameliorate the extreme positions on each side, it would not eliminate the fact of first-order difference.

Values and Human Nature

Values, even though they may be defined and implemented differently in different societies, are not divorced from our human nature. Society would not be possible unless individuals had an inbuilt capacity to be socialized, to become members of a group. Although we have properly advanced from earlier stages in which small membership groupings are the exclusive focus of moral obligation—a progress that the test in principle and transstable analysis (see below) can assist—detachment from the social context of moral analysis is destructive.

We are so seduced by utilitarian analysis and an abstract approach to moral rules that we forget how symbiotically related are humans and society. Our ability to function well depends both on effective social standards and symbolic behavior that reinforces our value as members of society. The failure to properly value identity in its group aspect, derived in part from the Cartesian revolution and the social understandings that feed upon it, constitutes a peril.

As Aristotle noted, individuals might be gods or beasts in the absence of society, but they would not be human. Becoming gods, as Nietzsche ordained, would not be a solution for reasons explored during examination of the dysfunction of "true" autonomy in chapter 11. Becoming a beast, on Aristotle's perhaps dubious judgment concerning the moral life of some animals, is not an option I believe any thoughtful person would choose—a judgment Diane Dreher makes concrete in her contribution to volume two: "Shakespeare's Cordelia and the Power of Character." In any event, it is highly likely that evolutionary mechanisms selected for some degree of altruism and social solidarity, and early evidence from some animal studies indicates this orientation may be located in so-called "social genes."

The potential for moral judgment and recognition of moral obligation, thus, almost surely is present in human nature. Children have an inborn potential to learn to walk, although not to walk in a particular style. Likely in a somewhat similar fashion, there is an inborn potential to distinguish between good and bad things which develops in specific, and perhaps incompatible, ways with successful socialization (that almost surely involves changes in the wiring of the brain) and later by means of independent comparative evaluation.

As the cases of Caspar Hauser and feral children have shown, this inborn capacity likely is based upon a potential, but defeatable, capacity for empathy and altruism that informs moral evaluations within existential and potential contexts but that does not concretize particular values. This does not exclude the possibility that some traits related to values may have some basis in genetic hard-wiring, but great caution is required in assessing these relationships. None of this diminishes the importance and objectivity of valuational judgments but it does remove them from *a priori* and overly generalized conclusions.

There is, I now regret, only the briefest discussion in chapter 9 of the "test in principle,"[7] which requires that the moral evaluator ask how he or she would react to society's values, depending upon placement within it, and then extend this to a comparative evaluation of different societies. Although this test cannot be carried out other than as a loose thought experiment, it forces the practitioner to a relatively neutral evaluational stance and, in this way, limits the kinds of arguments that can be made to others or indeed to oneself, for the process produces an internalized critique.

In principle, it is possible to build a common second-order framework of values, even if a very loose one, that can be used, in conjunction with the values of one's own society, to critique the current state of its value system or of any other society. Although there may be existential dilemmas that cannot be overcome, there are also critical periods in which individuals and societies can move beyond legitimate self or social interest to create a better world, although one in which new dilemmas arise. (With Socrates every philosopher is a subversive. Unfortunately, very few subversives are philosophers, including a great many who nominally carry that title.)

The philosophically-oriented reader will note that this position shares much with both the Aristotelian and Hegelian analyses, although the analysis is conducted within a metatheoretic position that, unlike theirs, is consistent with the contemporary realm of knowledge. Both great philosophers shared a synoptic empirically-oriented approach that placed great stress on what I have reformulated as assessment, rather than on theory, in these practical areas.

Most modern philosophers take an abstract or truncated view of moral issues that misses very important elements of moral analysis. The major positions of modern writers on morals including post-

Kantian formalistic writers such as Rawls, Nozick, and Gewirth, rules-oriented writers such as Donegan, language games proponents such as Toulmin, and consequentialist authors such as Glover and Smart fail to account adequately for moral understanding.[8] Unlike more systematic philosophers such as Aristotle and Hegel, they miss the complex connections between self, mind, and society that are integral to understanding the role of character in moral decisions and substitute a simplistic and abstract methodology.

If I understand some of the more sophisticated moral undertakings of the stories approach, as distinguished from some of the more abstract approaches referred to above, they do place the moral agent within the context of a particular society, although why their accounts should not break down further into unrelated group or individual accounts is never explained. (Or even to different accounts by the same individual, for he or she should have as much trouble communicating to self as to others.)

Stories, however, are not irrelevant. To the extent that character is embodied in a story, the story provides the first-order basis on which comparative testing against other alternatives, or stories, moves beyond direct individual or national development to a wider comparative frame that provides an objective basis for critique.

A parallel case, although not an isomorphic one, would be an account of how Einstein arrived at relativity theory. We cannot understand this without an understanding of Einstein's love of theory and of developments in mathematics and physics after the time of Newton. However, the assessment of the worth of relativity theory properly moves beyond these considerations. We cannot understand character, whether of a nation or an individual, except in the context of particular first-order development. But we cannot evaluate it more fully except by contrast with other types of personalities and other types of cultures.

The two cases differ in an important, but not necessarily decisive, respect. Einstein's theory is considered to be universally true, whereas social and moral truths cannot be considered apart from contextual features. Even so, some physicists are already speculating that there may be universes in which our laws of physics do not hold. Whether or not this is true, the laws of physics that apply to our universe depend upon certain constants that cannot themselves be explained by theory. If they were to change, the theory of physics would change as would our understanding of the physical world and of our relationship to it, provided that this new world were consistent with the existence of thinking beings. Thus, first-order moral groundings are to this extent a parallel case.

First-order relationships, thus, are surely essential to analysis. In their absence, it is not possible to understand agonizing dilemmas of choice. However, most of the writers who take a stories approach seem to undervalue analysis of the imperatives of maintaining a social system within which moral norms regulate conduct in a generally eufunctional manner. They fail adequately to ask what the agent owes society and seem to overemphasize how society must change to meet the needs of particular types of agents. They lack anything like the test in principle that permits second-order critical analysis of both standpoints, although proponents of this approach seldom seem to like any status quo. And most importantly, they fail to understand how embeddedment in a first-order social system or culture provides the constants within which character and actions stemming from character are meaningful. Thus, their libertarian philosophy strips the self of the character that is essential to authentic choice by reducing these constants to the playthings of disembodied will.

A universe that is ordered enough to sustain life would collapse if the constants of physical theory changed rapidly—and perhaps if any changes occurred, given the extraordinarily narrow range within which they do permit life. A meaningful social world and a meaningful individual life would collapse if the constants of first-order societies and characters were subject to complete free choice. The test in principle and the associated concept of transstability provide an orderly methodology for the consideration of change. The unadulterated stories approach and the libertarian thesis might not produce chaos while applied by those brought up in relatively stable cultures. However, as new generations are socialized—or, more accurately, not socialized—their belief systems would become incompatible with stable social life.

The Self and Its Integrity

Chapter 10 "The Right to be Left Alone is the Right to be No One" is the leitmotif for the conference. It is a refutation of the Millsian argument that individuals should be given the right to do anything that does not directly hurt others—the contemporary libertarian position. It shows that if a society produces a free-ranging multiplicity of stories, the integrity of the self breaks down. What Foucault regarded as an imposition on freedom is shown to be the very foundation of freedom and personal autonomy. What Mill regarded as the optimal account of choice is inconsistent with meaningful choice related to an autonomous personality.

Despite the fundamental flaw in the Millsian position, particular claims for changes in the norms of society or the rights of individuals are often warranted. Indeed, in their absence much of what most of us would regard as moral progress would not have occurred. The removal of the iniquitous segregation and antimiscegenation laws that were supported by so many Americans is an example of moral progress. On the other hand, some changes are retrogressive. The Nazi Nuremburg laws unleashed a horror on what had been a decent society.

Even when some of society's laws or customs are morally wrong, however, moral individuals who use comparative evidence to conclude that some values of their society should be changed may still reflect upon the possibility that a public refusal to act upon them in a context in which this judgment is not understood by others in some cases may be more damaging to society—and, in the end, to the integrated self—than is conforming behavior. In such cases, their obligations to others may preclude behavior that would be consistent with norms they have good reason to believe are preferable; for instance, a refusal to bow by a nineteenth-century Japanese who had experienced a more egalitarian Western society.

Much of Part II of *Alienation and Identification*,[9] which undertakes the philosophical/ sociological analysis of the categories of the self, is reproduced in chapter 11. It analyzes the relationships of identity, alienation, and authenticity. Authenticity in this account does not become the unexplainable thrust from Being to being-in-the-world that it does in Heidegger but can be understood through rational analysis within the framework of a contemporary realm of knowledge. In particular, it is shown that any mode of self-characterizing of one's being affects adversely any other mode of characterizing that being. Hence, some degree of alienation is an inevitable consequence of life. Nonetheless, it is possible to deal productively with alienation in developing an identity that helps to define character.

A discussion of the transstable personality is included in chapter 11. The transstable self is not rigidly committed to rules but distinguishes between those cases in which rules should be applied and those in which this would be inappropriate. The transstable personality perceives social concerns, if not always those of its own membership system, as obligatory considerations. These obligations extend past its own society and also past the standards of its own, or any other, society. This transstable character adjusts the applicable moral frame of particular decisions to the relevant social setting and refuses to reify the values of particular social settings.[10]

Integration and Synthesis

Thus, it is true that we learn in part at least by means of assessments or stories that fit things into a pattern of relationships. However, these stories do not copy some external reality or operate on the basis of univocal correspondences. A neo-Hegelian quasi-dialectic can be employed that permits a multifaceted exploration of the world. This permits the stories to be compared and judged from a variety of perspectives, even if not with the high probability of much of physical science. This approach, thus, shows why it makes sense to take values seriously; why self and character legitimately are matters of concern; and why the odd thoughts that may thrust into our consciousness lack moral legitimacy unless they fit the larger realm of knowledge.

That this is a matter of continual revision—that final truth is not available or perhaps not even meaningful—may be part of human fate, but the quest for intermediate understandings of truth is not merely worthwhile but essential to our humanity. The quest for character and identity, thus, cannot be divorced from our historical grounding. And their importance should not be underestimated because assessments of their possible content are only weakly ordered. The story we seek is neither fictional nor entirely subject to personal choice. Obligation and responsibility are inherent elements of the story.

For reasons that have been given, the classical Greek philosophical paradigms are no longer acceptable. But the greatness of their contribution to civilization—rational inquiry on the broadest of bases into the nature of the world and our place in it—remains a beacon that flares ever so brightly in the face of contemporary attacks upon it.

The belief that philosophy can be compartmentalized and its branches examined in the absence of accounts from other branches of philosophy and other subjects, which is held by some famous philosophers who hold chairs in great universities, or that we can reassert past philosophical paradigms without incorporating developments from the various fields of knowledge, is without merit. Either position, in its own way, is as serious a lapse from scholarship as the uncontrolled use of language of a Heidegger, a Sartre, or a Derrida.

The fact that concepts and theories do not exhaust the reality to which they refer does not legitimate a use of language that deals with what can be known in a mystifying way that impedes the limited communication that genuinely is possible. Such mystifying use of language, whatever success it may have in stimulating imaginative reformulations, responds to the defects in the classical Greek vision by surrendering the goal of rational knowledge. In principle, this produces solipsism and, if really believed, should end in silence, for communication is not possible.

It is amazing how Plato and, even more particularly, Aristotle built a great synoptic discipline out of a base that, in terms of our extant knowledge of it, does not seem sufficient to produce such a remarkable body of work. It is not surprising that much of what they said about metaphysics and science properly is subject to contraversion, at least in terms of their conclusions if not of their reasoning. What is astounding is how much of their accounts of science, ethics, and politics remains relevant, even valid, and often superior to contemporary accounts. It is upon the backs of those giants that the rest of us climb for our glimpses of the initial ascent of the sun into the heavens. Only a synoptic methodology that makes use of the vast developments in the various branches of knowledge—an advantage we have over the classical writers and of which we do not seem to make adequate use—will permit us even to climb upon their backs.

Notes

¹A more extensive and detailed argument for this position is given in *Science, Language*. For the initial discussion of assessment, see pp. 54-55. For a discussion of fit, see pp. 82-99.

²Many, but not all, physicists believe something is wrong with current theories of physics because relativity theory and quantum theory appear to predict puzzlingly inconsistent results at their margins. Whether or not a theory that incorporates the four forces can be found, or current theories replaced with better ones, this reason for searching for it, I believe, hypostasizes theories. If concepts do not exhaust their referents and if Bohr's position on complementarity is correct, then the expectation that theories resting on different axioms must make completely concordant predictions is at base mistaken. All that is required is that, properly related to their frameworks, theories do not contradict each other.

³See *Science, Language*, pp. 23-29, which also include a discussion of how one chooses from among conflicting paradigms on a common objective basis. Kepler, Newton, and Einstein, for instance, would have agreed on what they meant by planet, perihelion, curvature, and light sufficiently for the purposes of experiment, while they would have disagreed on what they meant by mass, time, and space. Pp. 136-141 illustrate how languages can be translated, thus helping to create a common framework.

⁴See chapter 7.

⁵For critiques of the approaches to language of Wittgenstein, Derrida, and Foucault, see *Science Language*, pp. 142-171, pp. 173-192, and pp. 129, 154, and 155 respectively. Lewis Morgan's classic work of the late nineteenth-century *Systems of Consanguinity* pioneered in the investigation of how language functions in interpreting the world and influencing, even constituting, social structure. This book either directly, or by influencing the climate of scholarly understanding, may have been one of the factors that influenced Peirce's development of his concept of meaning. I believe the insights that drive the approaches to language of Wittgenstein, Derrida, and Foucault have their origins in Morgan's pioneering work but that the former writers make one-sided, and to that extent mistaken, use of what is clearly correct in the analyses of Morgan and Peirce.

⁶Reprinted from *System and Process in International Politics*, John Wiley & Sons, New York, 1957, pp. 262-263.

⁷*Science, Language*, pp. 253-257. My first attempt at a discussion of what later was developed as the test in principle was in Appendix 2 of *System and Process in International Politics*. It is also discussed in Morton A. Kaplan, *Justice, Human Nature, and Political Obligation*, The Free Press, New York, 1976,

pp. 174-181. The objectivity of the moral realm is discussed in *Science, Language*, pp. 257-278.

[8]The central theoretical flaw in Nozick is pointed out in chapter 8. For a discussion of Rawls and Nozick, see Morton A. Kaplan, *Justice, Human Nature*, pp.107-156; for a discussion of Gewirth and Smart, *ibid.*, pp.156-162; for a discussion of Nozick, ibid pp.201-202; for a discussion of Toulmin, *ibid*, pp. 47-80; for a second discussion of Gewirth, see *Science, Language* pp. 225-228; for a discussion of Glover, see ibid, pp. 228-236; for a discussion of Donegan, see ibid, pp. 236-247.

[9]Morton A. Kaplan, *Alienation and Identification*, New York: The Free Press, 1976.

[10]See *Justice, Human Nature*, pp. 80-92 for a discussion of transstability and the objective status of values and their obligatory character.

CHAPTER 6

MEANING AND LOGIC

Morton A. Kaplan

John Dewey argued that our knowledge of "red" is not derived from a red sensation. The theory that perceptions are produced by sensations* itself stems from and depends on experience.[1] Yet physiology reveals the inadequacies of naive empiricism as surely as does epistemological theory. Because the pupil of the normal eye is in continual motion, no message, that is, signal or sets of signals, can present a stationary object as stationary to the brain. The message is first transformed by the nerves that transmit it and then further transformed by the brain. And this statement can be confirmed by experiment. Thus, experience always requires the active participation of the perceiving system, or transceiver.

Messages, thus, require transceivers. Meaning is a product of a transaction between a transceiver and a world; experience is not a simple or automatic display of incoming signals. The transceiver codes, or produces, data in transactions with referents within a milieu. In addition to interpreting sensory inputs, the transceiver also selects inputs that fit with the expectations, hopes, and fears of the system. Thus, for instance, it is less likely that the psychological mechanism of projection involves a biased interpretation of specific incoming data than that it involves a selection of data that accord with expectations and the censorship of incoming data that conflict with those expectations.

---

*It is not clear what empiricists mean by "sensation." The feel of a tingling or of warmth? The angstrom wave patterns that are transmitted to the eye? Or the content of the message that is carried by nerves from the optic receptor to the brain?

Thus, the processes involved in perception do not link a discrete coding element or sign to a discrete signal or signal pattern in any simple fashion. Stimulus-response theories, in which such discrete elements are assumed, may be good enough for a sufficiently stable world and a sufficiently stable organism, or even for simple aspects of a more complex organism. But such a discrete conception of physiological coding reifies concepts, by appearing to give a color like red, for instance, a meaning that is independent of the transceiver, the source of light, and the character of the referent.[2] The correlative terms "solid" and "porous" also do not characterize as such, but only with reference to a transceiver and a context. The table is solid when I hit it, but porous to an electron.

There is no simple correspondence between a transceiver's implicit or explicit codes and external things, events, and processes. Indeed, external things, events, and processes are experienced only as interpreted phenomena, and beliefs about their character are revised by implicit or explicit part-system analysis. The difference between perceptual coding and linguistic coding is that the former is continuous, nonserial, and analog whereas the latter is discrete, serial, and digital.

Correlatives

In my opinion, the correlative pair is the basic unit of language. It bridges the transaction between the perceiver and the object, process, and arena of action or perception. It functions by means of contrast. For example, the contrast between light and dark produces meaning for a perceiver. It does not merely match a sign to an external datum as the English empiricists and the positivists believed. Instead, a correlative concept is mediated by a sign with respect to an aspect of experience, an application that involves a judgment and, thus, one that invokes other elements of the realms of knowledge.

Correlative sign pairs depends upon each other for their meaning. Their use produces clear conceptual distinctions, for example, "light" or "dark." However, whether something is light or dark depends upon the context and a frame of reference that produces inner connectedness. It is not such *as such*, that is, things are not, in essence, either light or dark. Consider "determinism" and "indeterminism" in quantum theory. Quantum theory is indeterministic with respect to a particle's momentum or position, but deterministic with respect to the dynamic state transformations signified by the quantum equations.

It is not difficult to understand why language is correlative. The communication theorists have taught us that the bit, a binary element, is the smallest unit of information. The bit is a quantitative unit in computers and measures the distinction between one (positive) and zero (negative). However, the sentence in which I make that claim uses qualitative concepts: positive and negative. Their contrast alone permits qualitative knowledge, the qualitative bit. This is easy to see in pairs such as positive-negative, deterministic-indeterministic, and so forth.

Characterization, that is, description, requires contrasting concepts. They need not be binary in an analysis, but it is not surprising that they often are, for dichotomizing concepts are powerful. Locator terms, to be discussed shortly, permit finer distinctions in an analysis containing many (binary) dichotomies. They also function through contrast. Thus, for instance, when we learn to distinguish shades of a particular color, we do this by contrasting them to their neighbors. The discussion in this chapter of the relational character of knowledge makes characterization the key concept. We shall see that knowledge operates through correlative axes that are used to characterize the objects, processes, or events that are the referents in experience of signs and concepts.

The argument that language is correlative is an assessment, not a deductive proof. Many of the subsequent discussions in this book will provide corroborating evidence that treating language as correlative assists in the assessment of philosophical problems.

Willard van Orman Quine's well-known argument against an absolute distinction between the analytic and the synthetic[3] may hold only because it is an instance of the correlative character of language. The analytic can be distinguished from the synthetic. However, no proposition is either analytic or synthetic as such; an issue to which I shall return.

Thus, correlatives are fundamental building blocks of language: pairs, the meaning of each of which involves the other. And often, as in pairs such as "determinism" and "indeterminism" or "solid" and "porous," the same realworld entity or process can be characterized by either aspect of a pair, depending on the aspect of the world to which one is referring or the frame of reference.

Metacorrelatives

If correlatives are the basic units of language, *metacorrelatives* are employed in analyzing their use and significance. "Sign" and "signed," for instance, comprise a metacorrelative concept that is used in the production of meaning itself. For example, "solid" and "porous" are correlatives. They provide meaning. "Solid" has as its referent a solid entity. The former is the sign and the latter is the signed. "Sign" and "signed" are metacorrelatives, for they raise the level of abstraction.

Locators

Locators, that is, terms that help us to locate an object, process, or event, are limited to only one aspect of a correlative pair, and they permit distinctions within that aspect of the correlative pair. For instance, the correlative relation between "space" and "time" is irrelevant to geographic surveys. If a correlative concept (for example, "bright," "heavy," "finite," or "analytic") exhausted the object or event to which it referred, we would not need locators.

Moreover, for practical purposes, locators function in a multiple, rather than a binary, fashion. We know that our system of arithmetic is based on ten's but that a binary base is used in computers. The accident of ten fingers and toes almost surely played a role in determining our choice of an arithmetic base of ten. The connections within an electronic circuit, which can be turned only on or off, produce the zero-one base of electronic arithmetic.

At least implicitly, paired concepts are used in language to determine meaning. Almost surely some highly practical determinant of language—perhaps the fact that paired terms are particularly powerful in clarifying types of meaning while locators function primarily within a typology and with respect to circumstances in which the influence of the polar elements is vanishingly small—produced these differences. "Types" and "locators" are themselves metacorrelatives, and their meaning depends on their use.

Language and Meaning

Let me now encapsulate the view of language and of meaning that has been presented. Certain kinds of words, signs that mediate concepts, enable us to characterize and to locate aspects of the real. Sentences, expressions, and longer and more complex formulations are constructed according to rules that permit the particular meaning—as distinguished from the general meaning—of words to be understood within an exposition that employs a system of concepts.

Language has meaning because it uses signs to relate concepts to referents. Although some types of rules for its use, such as grammar, can be specified, many people can speak intelligibly without knowing all the rules of grammar. Meaning depends upon a host of cues to which people have become acculturated. The meaning of a word may be tacit or private, but it is usually fairly commonly recognized, more commonly in specific subcultures and less in the general culture.

Fiction and Reality

To write that a unicorn met a lady is to write fiction, although meaningfully so, because we can specify the unicorn's characteristics even though there is no evidence of its existence. Moreover, a unicorn may not be a fiction in a fictional realm; that is, it satisfies the criteria appropriate to that realm. An irrational number is not a fiction in the worlds of mathematics or physics.

Perhaps some readers have experienced bright spiralling lines under anesthesia. When we say that they were "tuning in" on a process that transforms sensory elements into perceptions, we do not mean that the formulas by means of which these processes can be characterized exist as "things" in the human organism. But neither are they fictions.

Was Newton's theory a fiction? Newton's theory was disproved. It was, however, a useful although incorrect account of the cosmos. Newton's laws have been shown to be not fictional, but marginally incorrect within solar distances. From the standpoint of relativity, Newton's theory is a good metaphor.

The foregoing statements require qualification. The appropriate application of theories treats their boundary conditions as if they are fully known. This assumption is a fiction, but a vanishingly small one in many cases.

Words and Sentences

I agree with Quine that the meaning of an element, or a term, bears a relationship to the set, or sentence, within which it is used.[4] I agree with Hilary Putnam that terms in a sentence have a meaning that is independent of the sentences in which they are used.[5] At least I agree in part. I know, for instance, what I mean by "eye," at least partly independently of a theory of vision or of particular sentences employing the term.

One need think only of "eye of the needle," "eye of the storm," "human eye," or "eye of the bee" to see that neither element nor sentence has absolute priority in the analysis of the meaning of eye. We do not know the precise meaning of eye except within the sentence. And yet we cannot know its meaning within the sentence unless we already have an initial set of meanings of the word to choose among, at least some of which depend for their meanings upon their contrasting characteristics. This is a part-system problem; and neither Quine's position nor Putnam's can be defended if pushed to an extreme.

Concepts and Truths

Concepts are validated both internally and externally. They are validated internally by definitions or by relations to other concepts either in a theory or in part-system codings of the mind. "Eye of the camera" and "eye of human" carry with them, among other concepts, those of inorganic and organic respectively. On the other hand, criteria such as "metal," "mechanical," "neurological tissue," and so forth, also have meanings that are independent of the particular concepts, "eye of camera" and "eye of human." Thus, they serve as external criteria for empirical truth: in this case, correct application of the concept. It is this interplay between "inner" and "outer" concepts and the use of part-system analysis that permits a theory of meaning and a theory of empirical truth to be reconciled. And it follows from this that one may know, at least partly, the meaning of something without knowing how to apply it, for the external criteria may not yet be understood. And vice versa, for its meaning may not yet have been refined.

A *theory* is a system of concepts mediated by signs, and the elements of a theory have meanings that depend upon their inner, that is, their within-the-theory relationships. "Mass," for instance, has at least partly different meanings in Newtonian and Einsteinian physics. And "line," for instance, has at least partly different meanings in Euclidean and non-Euclidean geometries. The application of a theory to the concrete world involves both inner meanings, meanings that are constrained by the system of signs, and meanings that are external, that is, that are constrained by other signs or systems of signs and the concepts they mediate; and, thus, ultimately by empirical assessment.

Signs and Referents

The previous discussion leads me now to a brief examination of Gottlob Frege's position on sign, sense (i.e., concept), and referent.[6] Frege was in error, as I shall attempt to show, in holding that the same referent may have more than one meaning.

Frege's distinctions among a sign, its sense, and its reference contain hidden ambiguities. He argued that "morning star" and "evening star" have different senses, but the same reference: Venus. However, this independence of sense and reference is artificial, for Venus is the referent of "Venus," and is a planet in the solar system, according to a first-order astronomical theory. The "morning star," "the evening star," and "Venus" have not yet been related. This matter can be clarified only by a second-order analysis, that is, one that is neutral with respect to the different frames of reference.

The argument that the terms "Venus," "the morning star," and "the evening star" have the same reference—the planet Venus—requires the use of second-order discourse to correlate the sign systems of astronomy and of ordinary common sense. There is an identity in meaning in the three signs in second-order discourse, but not in first-order discourse.

Einstein's theory of relativity accounts for differences in interpretation of first-order space-time phenomena by observers on different inertial systems. One of the remarkable achievements of his theory of relativity is to integrate seemingly contradictory first-order frameworks within a single set of second-order equations, a feat also accomplished in quantum theory. To use another example, second-order procedures make possible the translation of English into, say, Russian or Japanese. However, we cannot encompass the second-order reconciliation within a metalanguage that produces one-to-one relations between words or concepts. And this is the usual case.

Logic and Reality

Quine is often accused of having denied that there is a distinction between analytic and synthetic propositions or even of having failed to accept the existence of analytic propositions. Hilary Putnam, for instance, defended against Quine the utility of regarding "No bachelors are married" as analytic.[7] I do not read Quine as having denied the existence of analytic truths. There is, however, a question as to the conditions under which an analytic truth is an empirical truth. Consider a culture in which all males are married at birth but remain bachelors until the marriage is ceremonially consummated at the age of 13. The quoted proposition is not an analytic truth in that culture, for the analytic form, No $A = \bar{A}$ (no A equals not A), is not met. Even with respect to the form, however, Morris Cohen's argument— that $p \supset p$ (if p, then p) holds only if the p's are identical is valid. That this is not a mere quibble is illustrated by the difficulty of programming computers to read. How much variation in form can be permitted if the identity is to be recognized? That the human mind can solve most simple problems of this kind readily does not mean that no problem is present. "P's" do not exist *as such*.

There is both *intension*, that is, meaning, and *extension*, that is, examples, in these cases. P is only a sign. The problem becomes more complex when referents and concepts are involved, as in the "blue-colored" example below and even more complex in more sophisticated problems.

I don't doubt the existence of analytic truths. They are the correlatives of synthetic truths. Although the meaning of each depends upon the other, there is a clear distinction between the concepts. Whether "all blue objects are colored" is a logical truth depends on the inner relationship between "blue" and "colored." "All blue objects are colored is a logical truth" follows from the inner relationship between "blue" and "colored." That "all blue objects are colored" is true. But this last assertion of truth is not of logical truth. The judgment that the proposition is an analytic truth in this world—and possibly in all other worlds as well—depends upon external criteria that govern use and, hence, is its contingent correlative. Neither is such as such.

Logical truth invokes a world in which meanings are given and relationships are inner. A synthetic proposition invokes a world in which the relationships between referents and between concepts depend also on external criteria. For instance, the theorems of Euclidean and of non-Euclidean geometry are logical truths. But the meanings of analogous concepts, such as "line," differ in the two theories because of their relationships to other concepts. And differences in these analogous concepts are understood partly in terms of external criteria, including comparison.

For a long time it was believed that astronomical space was Euclidean. Now it is believed that space is non-Euclidean. Although Euclidean geometry provides fairly accurate approximations within solar distances, it is not believed to be true of any real space. On the other hand, "all bachelors are single men" may be a logical truth in some usages and not in others. (The arguments by Kripke and Putnam for *a posteriori* necessary truths will be considered subsequently.)

A more interesting argument—but also misleading and for the same reasons—is over which logical postulates are truly necessary. Take the principle of contradiction for instance.

Even a multivalued use of a concept translates into the principle of contradiction; for the argument that x is neither A nor not-A means that it is like A in some respects and not like A in others. On the other hand, every two-valued use can be translated into a multivalued one for an appropriate statement of a problem. These contrasting uses are correlatives. Which use should be employed in a particular case can be determined only by part-system analysis.

In logic, the rules of the notational system determine what statements are true. To determine whether a system is useful, its set of rules must be tested against experience. No set of general rules avoids problems. In Bertrand Russell's notational system, "Santa Claus lives at the North Pole" is a false statement.[8] But surely there is a sense in which this sentence is true. Contrast it with "Santa Claus lives at the

South Pole." Frege's notational system avoids this problem but permits statements with empty names, that is, names without denotation.[9] The problem created is obvious. Alexius Meinong avoids the problem of both Russell and Frege by recognizing that existence is not a quality.[10] However, his notational system permits statements such as "The circle is square" and "Bismarck has both a fat and a thin mother." Because Meinong does not assert that a round square exists or that both mothers exist, he avoids contradiction. Bismarck may, in fact, have had a fat and a thin mother; she may have gained weight or lost it. In this book we have seen that many apparently contradictory statements are not contradictory when properly interpreted in second-order discourse. Thus a table may be both solid *and* porous, depending upon whether we are referring to a human being or a gamma ray. A sweater may be both yellow *and* green, depending upon the light. And Sirius may be moving with respect to the sun *and* the sun may be moving with respect to Sirius, depending upon the inertial system from which the reference is made. What notational system works for a domain, or how it needs to be adapted to make it work, is determined by assessment at a literal level of analysis.

Systems of logic determine only analytical truth. According to formal logic, an antecedent, if false, entails the truth of any consequent. "Franklin Roosevelt was queen of England" entails "Harry Truman was the archbishop of Canterbury." This particular type of entailment, which logicians call material entailment, is not what we mean when we assert that one aspect of the world produces another, such as "When the sun rises, it will become day on earth." We have no difficulty in distinguishing such logical entailment from realworld connections. And, thus, we have no difficulty in knowing when *not* to use such logical entailment. Logic is merely a tool to be used. The failure of formal logic to deal with realworld relations says more about the nature of some systems of logic than it does about the world.[11]

Once we move past the basic postulates of logic—and, to some extent, even within them—we can vary our use of language. But we do this legitimately only to elucidate aspects of experience. Language and reality always condition each other, although not always in the seemingly simple and limited ways of the basic postulates of logic.

In effect, I reject formalism and all attempts to base logic on a single, correct axiomatic system. Although it might appear that my position then must be intuitionist, this is not the case, either. Systems of signs are merely tools for dealing with the signed world. I deny the existence in real time of infinite sets. I accept them as mathematical entities and also as potentialities in the real world.

Dialectics

Recently there have been attempts to formalize dialectical logic in both the Greek and Marxian senses. The classical Greek usage, in which dialectics involves the use of arguments generally believed to be true, is not inconsistent with the positions taken in this book. But Marxian dialectics is.

Some of those who have attempted to formalize dialectical logic have also attempted to justify the use of negations of negations and the appropriate nonuse of the principle of the excluded middle. Although the following is not an instance of what a Marxist means by a "negation of a negation," it is easy to see that two-valued usage has its limitations. "He is not unintelligent" is not the same as "He is intelligent." It would be easy to show that the Marxian concept of a negation of a negation is as metaphoric as arguing that "He is not unintelligent" is a negation of "He is not intelligent." In such sentences, the negation of a negation is a metaphor: the meaning of negation in two-valued use is being employed when one of the negations is not two-valued. The problem is that most Marxists have turned metaphors into verbal magic and employed them in the absence of that literal analysis that alone makes concepts applicable to a particular case. There undoubtedly are genuine phenomena to which the metaphor "negation of a negation" may be partly applicable. Conceivably the concept may have some heuristic value in orienting one to the possibility of reversals in the real world. However, scientific knowledge is transmitted only by literal language.

I suspect, although he wrote in too packed a way for one to be sure, that it is this error that underlies Jurgen Habermas's concept of dialogic* as well as many hermeneutical analyses.[12] These metaphors are more dangerous than those that give rise to the paradoxes of class

---

*To the extent that Habermas's concept of linguistic competence draws upon Anglo-Saxon language philosophy, the discussion in chapter 9 of *Science, Language* answers it.

or language discussed by Bertrand Russell and Alfred Tarski,[13] to which I now turn; for the Marxian metaphors pile uncontrolled use on top of uncontrolled use. Formalization of a concept is not a sufficient, or often a necessary, condition for controlled use. It is the *literal* understanding of a problem that provides the justification for both formalization and application.

Levels of Language and Types of Proposition

The previous discussion complements Tarski's concept of "levels of language." A sign always has a referent, even if the referent does not exist as an experienced event, object, or process. In principle, a sign is non-self-referring in its function as a sign, although by successive use in a *metalanguage,* that is, a language in which the prior language is discussed, it may refer to itself in its signed aspect; but, even then, only formally by the assertion of identity.

When a sign is used successively, it becomes the referent of a formally identical sign but not of itself. Thus, the metastatement may be a metaphor, an analogy by proportion—'x' as a sign is to x as signed as "x as a sign as signed" as a sign is to "x as a sign" as signed— if x as signed is not identical to, for example, " x as a sign" as signed. There is often a significant shift in meaning as signs are used successively in an argument. Whether this is the case is a factual matter in which external criteria are employed.

An equation involving proportions is not necessarily a metaphor: for instance, in mechanics, an area in which independent measures and covering laws exist, a proportional equation is literal. However, the problems addressed by Tarski's concept of levels of language and Russell's theory of types are in fact metaphors when their use of signs is correctly analyzed.

Thus, if the only sentence on a blackboard is "The first sentence on the blackboard is false," it might appear to create a paradox. If it is true, it is false. And if it is false, it is true. However, if the sentence is treated as a sign system, no paradox ensues. The sentence is neither true nor false, for there is not a properly constructed referent. "The first sentence on the blackboard" is a nounal clause; "is false" completes the sentence, and, therefore, can refer neither to the nounal clause nor to the complete sentence. However, a second sentence,

"The first sentence on the blackboard is true," is neither true nor false. For it to be true or false, the first sentence on the blackboard would have to make a claim that is true or false, and it does not do so. Only if the first sentence on the blackboard referred to itself without a distinction between its sign and its signed aspects would a problem arise.

Consider an envelope paradox: "The next sentence I am going to write is true," followed by "The previous sentence is false." This is a variant of Tarski's level-of-language problem. It has implications that bear on my earlier discussion of logic and reality. In the standard case, the second sentence or sign system would have a signed referent that is the indirect referent of the first set of signs. The paradox arises because mutual implications of the envelope type are not restricted in this system of logic. I am not arguing that this is necessarily true of every Gödelian-type problem.[14] Kurt Gödel's conclusion—that for any mathematical system, there are true propositions that cannot be proved within it—is uncontroverted. By incorporating information from part systems not included in the system of logic that produces the paradox, we can see that a restriction on mutual implications is required in the envelope type of argument. The logical system must be adapted to the realm of knowledge, not vice versa. Would it be a problem if the second sentence on the board read, "The previous sentence is not the first sentence"?

Consider Russell's problem: the class of all classes that are not members of themselves.[15] Is it a member of itself? If it is, it isn't. But if it isn't, it is. This, however, holds only if "sign" and "signed" are identical. It is a member of the class in its signed aspect, but not as a sign. If the use of the sign and the signed are not identical, and if they are correlative aspects of language, the paradox does not arise.[16]

Many statements at different levels of language that appear to be true turn out to be metaphors when the distinction between sign and signed is assessed. Even in mechanics, the meaning of measurements that appear to be entirely literal and concrete can become metaphoric. As Max Born noted, over a sufficiently long period of time predictions become impossible because of measurement "error."[17] There is no such thing as an absolutely precise measure or a fully determinate world.

Kripke, Putnam, and "Necessarily True" Definitions

More than fifty years ago, Morris Cohen argued that definitions are not arbitrary, that elements of definitions are factually connected: refined sugar, for instance, is "both white and sweet," because nature connects things in this way.[18] Saul Kripke and Hilary Putnam, however, argued that true definitions are necessary and true in all possible worlds.[19] This position is ultimately related to Kripke's rejection of connotational meaning for common and personal names.[20] Personal and proper names, according to Kripke, are rigid designators *de re* in all possible worlds, that is, they refer to things as they are in themselves and not as they are *de dicta*, that is, from a particular point of view. Thus, Aristotle would be Aristotle even if Plato had not been his teacher and gold would be gold even if it were not yellow. We may be mistaken that gold is yellow, according to Kripke, but scientific analysis will clarify that problem.

Kripke, thus, believed that there are no ambiguities of scope in modal logic. Leonard Linsky has shown at length why this position fails to hold.[21] For instance, in modal logic, if it is true that "Sir John wants to know whether Hesperus and Phosphorus are identical," and if it is true that Hesperus and Phosphorus are identical, then "Sir John wants to know whether Phosphorus is identical to Phosphorus" is also true. But this is clearly false. All we know of Ste. Anne is that she was the grandmother of Jesus. Thus, there could be no world in which Ste. Anne could be Ste. Anne unless she were the grandmother of Jesus. Hence, as Linsky noted, sense is essential to identification.

The concept of rigid designation in all possible worlds is too restrictive. Should Socrates have suffered brain damage as a child, would he still have been Socrates? Is the man the boy? The tree the tender shoot? What does it mean to say that two electrons are different electrons or that one electron at one time is the same as, or different from, that electron at a different time? When an amoeba splits, are both the new and the old amoeba the former amoeba? One? Neither? Is a second personality of a schizophrenic the same person as the first personality, or a different person? In what sense would Aristotle remain Aristotle in all possible worlds if no *de dicta* elements are specified? Suppose his parents had been different? His language? If he had not been a philosopher? What does it mean to say

Aristotle is Aristotle in all possible worlds *de re?* How do we determine what is *de dicta* and what *de re?*

Denotation *always* implies some connotative elements, if only to clarify that we are pointing to the same thing. The concept of denotation in logic is egregiously underdetermined and covertly borrows the concept of sense. Understanding sense and pointing, re-understanding sense and re-pointing, and so on are correlative techniques. Neither can be eliminated. And neither has priority.

The difficulties in the position of Kripke and Putnam are even more profound than Linsky asserted when he noted that their position requires logical and metaphysical omniscience. In an earlier section of this chapter, I pointed out that a statement may be a logical truth but that the assertion that it is a logical truth is not a logical truth. I shall use this mode of analysis now to show why the claim that a definition, if true, is necessarily true misstates in principle the ways in which we can know and speak about the world.

A logical truth is necessarily true as a consequence of internal criteria, but the assertion that it is empirically true, that is, that it applies correctly to a real world domain, depends also upon external criteria, that is, upon criteria from other part systems or domains.

But the crux of the sleight-of-hand by means of which Kripke and Putnam seemed to satisfy their claim lies in their illicit use of the "if true" stipulation in a context in which its meaning has varied. We have seen how variance of meaning affects Russell's type problem and Tarski's level-of-language problems. Does the stipulation "if true" overcome those difficulties? Or is this characterization of "true" different from the logical "true"? The problem is whether logical truths, if true, become truths as such, and hence metaphysically necessary, or whether they function as correlatives in characterizing aspects of the world.

Consider tautologies in which a substitution occurs in one of the elements of the tautology. For instance, for mammal $\supset$ mammal (if mammal, then mammal) substitute dolphin $\supset$ mammal. Or take a definition: water = H_2O. Here, Kripke's and Putnam's position requires rigid correspondence between the elements of the proposition or definition, a correspondence that is neutral and independent of all contexts and frames of reference. Putnam's argument to sustain this position rests, in addition, on the use of extensional logic, which gives absolute priority to the independent use of signs.

The preliminary answer to Kripke's and Putnam's claim, however, is that "sentence" and "words" are true correlatives and that neither can take absolute priority over the other. The importance of the sentence as the context of the signs has been confirmed repeatedly by experiments that show that an isolated word that cannot be understood, when it is heard alone, can often be understood when the other words of the sentence in which it occurs are heard. The earlier example of "the human eye" and "the eye of a storm" are evidence of the role of context in interpreting signs. Thus, the meaning of "truth" in "truth table" and in "truth of theory" are not necessarily the same. Perhaps, though, Kripke and Putnam would answer that the types of eye need to be distinguished *a posteriori* and that the correct use of signs would permit their rigid designation. Let us, therefore, carry on the analysis.

If, as Kripke argues, a table is not the same if it has been replaced by an identical duplicate (and how could this be known unless the substitution were observed?), what does it mean to deny that they are the same? Heraclitus argued that a river is never the same river, for different water is flowing. Most of the cells in the human body are replaced in seven years. Is it then the same body? What does "same" and "not same" mean in these examples?

"Same" and "not same" are correlatives, not truths as such. Something may be the same in one frame of reference and not the same in another. Second-order discourse eliminates the apparent contradiction. The river may be both the same and not the same, depending on the frame of reference. The body may be the same with reference to form and genetic characteristics, and different from the standpoint of cellular material.

Just as the "as such" concepts of "changing" and "unchanging" or "same" and "not same" are reifications, so is the idea of rigid designation or correspondence as such. Consider "yellow." How did Kripke handle this problem? Kripke argued that yellow is a manifest, and not a dispositional, property because if we had different neural structures, all this would mean is that yellow objects would not produce yellow sensations in us.[22] (By the way, no one ever had a yellow sensation. We see yellow objects.) However, yellow is a product and what becomes manifest as yellow depends on the lighting and the transceiver as well as upon its source. Furthermore, there are shades of yellow.

Can we resolve this problem by resorting to physics, as Kripke attempted to do with the problem of molecular motion? Suppose we define yellow by an angstrom number. But there is no yellow in physics. And, if we change the optic system, the angstrom pattern will no longer produce yellow. Is this difficulty perhaps why Kripke conceded that molecular motion may not be heat *de re:* because molecular motion might not produce heat in the physiological system? Nevertheless, he thought that this rigid relationship exists and said that "molecular motion is molecular motion" in all possible worlds.[23] However, molecules and motions are also products, and we are no better off than with yellow; for what counts as a molecule and what counts as motion is not entirely independent of transceivers, context, and frame of reference, and thus upon meaning in some respects. In any event, what varies with what is the rate of movement of atomic particles with temperature on a Kelvin scale.

I must admit that I do not know why Kripke regarded yellow as manifest *de re*, whereas he said that it is possible that heat is *de dicta*. The transactions that produce angstrom wave counts and temperature readings involve transactions with laboratory transceivers, whereas the experience of warm and yellow involves transactions with physiological transceivers. Angstrom waves are inferred entities, and degrees of temperature, or heat, are inferred quantities. Their meanings are not entirely independent of the range of transactions and of the theories that permit their existence or character to be asserted. However, angstrom wave production and color are not rigidly related, nor are heat production and hot. The same temperature is sometimes perceived as warm and sometimes as cool. "Hot" and "heat" are different concepts.

Would we not immediately spot something wrong if it were argued that human motion is human motion? However, what counts as human motion? A corpse's motion? A reflex? An intended motion? These questions have no answer as such; they can be answered only when the schemata of investigation and the problems to be solved are given.

Consider a well-known theoretical identity: water = H_2O. This definition is permissible (1) because by experiment we can show that two atoms of hydrogen and one of oxygen will result when water is vaporized and (2) because we will refuse to call anything water of which (1) is untrue even if it looks and behaves like water.

Hilary Putnam used the same example, H_2O, to attempt to make Kripke's point. If in another world, he wrote, people drink a substance that is not H_2O, it is not water.

> Once we have discovered that water (in the actual world) is H_2O, nothing counts as a possible world in which water isn't H_2O.[24]

This, he said, is a logical and metaphysical, even if not an epistemic, necessity. Whereas Kripke retreated to physics, Putnam refused to count as a possible world one in which water is not H_2O. Neither position withstands analysis. If we ask on what ground can one restrict the definition of water to H_2O, the somewhat different stances of Kripke and Putnam will be seen to have a common defect.

If liquid H_2O in a given world will not satisfy thirst, is it water? Below freezing, is H_2O ice or water? Consider, "He froze to death in a block of water." Solid H_2O and methane are both ice, but solid gold is not. Gold is a metal, but two atoms of gold do not constitute a metal. The relevant distinctions depend not merely upon physics or chemistry, but also upon meaning, and the frame of reference. There is no single frame of reference that serves as a foundation for necessary meaning.*

Necessity, in Kripke's and Putnam's thesis, is imbedded (1) in the structure of the logic of a theory, (2) in a decision to give priority to a particular theory, usually physics, and (3) in a decision to let (2) determine the use of names. However, either we can call both U235 and U238 uranium or we can designate them differently, depending on their atomic structure and on the purpose of the distinction. There is no necessity here, even though Kripke and Putnam draw their best examples from strongly ordered aspects of the world. The truth of a theory as a frame of reference and of the identifications within it is always dependent on assessment. A theory is never true as such. Neither are identifications.

The problem inheres in the important differences of meaning between the concept of truth in logic and the concept of truth in science. To call a theory true is not merely to make an epistemically

---

*Although Putman seems to take a similar position on frames of reference, the position developed here excludes his thesis on necessary truth.

fallible claim. It cannot be a fully determinate claim. It will always be based to some extent on external criteria that justify it in a specific domain, but that do not necessitate it. And the necessity of its internal logic is always bounded by this correlative nonnecessity. Kripke and Putnam offer no arguments for their inference from the identity of the two signs "truth"—the analytical and the empirical—the identity of the concepts and referents the signs mediate. This begs the questions of how language works and how the world is ordered.

The foregoing objections to the thesis of Kripke and Putnam are formidable. Thus, it is not necessary to show whether that thesis implies, as I think it does, that a theory of the world is possible in principle. Such an implication would be inconsistent with Kurt Gödel's famous proof of the incompleteness of mathematical systems, Isaac Newton's critical discovery that the initial conditions are contingent from the standpoint of the theory being applied, and Niels Bohr's complementarity principle. We may someday discover that one or all are wrong, but there is no reasonable ground for believing that to be the case. And each has metaphysical and ontological implications that are inconsistent with the thesis of Kripke and Putnam and consistent with my position.

Furthermore, the concepts "weight of evidence, "confirmation," or "falsification" have no algorithmic determination. There is no necessary order to definitions, theorems, and undefined terms in theories. Thus, what is defined within "true" theories—hence, rigidly designated, according to Kripke and Putnam—can vary with conventional differences in the construction of a theory.

My analysis also is not necessary, for it rests on part-system analysis and assessment. That does not mean that it must be doubted, although any position this complex merits some doubt. However, to clarify this distinction, take two sentences: "It has rained somewhere sometime on earth" and "At least one sentence in this paragraph contains more than three words." No sane person will doubt the first sentence, even though it is theoretically possible that our earthly life is only a dream. And discourse is not even possible unless we accept the truth of the second sentence. Yet we know that people who speak gibberish seem to think that they are communicating, and so perhaps our communication is merely gibberish. Actually, although we cannot doubt either of the two sentences, they are neither necessary nor logical truths.

There are *natural kinds*, that is, there is some sense in which the character of the world determines the classifications that are applied. But I do not mean[25] by the term what Kripke and Putnam do. They believe that only one hierarchical univocal order of classification can be true. In my opinion, an inquiry into what a natural kind is can be answered only by assessments, including theory, but not simply by theory. The classifying and ordering principles will be related to the frame of reference and subject to second-order analysis. The answers are not sharply delineated, at least at their peripheries, and they are not metaphysically necessary.

Thus, where the line is drawn between classifications of beings, for instance, depends upon frame of reference. If the hypothesis of punctuated equilibrium of biological evolution—according to which biological structure is highly resistant to change except when stressed beyond its capacity—is correct, species, as defined biologically, would not change gradually and competitive selection would be between species. The evidence seems to suggest that gradual evolution applies to changes in single-celled organisms and punctuated equilibrium applies to changes in more complex organisms. But, the biological framework of reference is not the only framework for classifications. Distinctions can be made according to types of responses to the environment, and beings can be grouped according to whether they are capable of rational behavior, moral understanding, and certain levels of intellectual accomplishment. These groupings might not be compatible with different frameworks, but they would be just as objective as biological designation. Similarly, "carnivorous" and "herbivorous" are classifications that overlap species.

No single ordering principle can be imposed on the concept of natural kinds. Furthermore, the fate of species, as distinguished from that of unions or factories, for instance, depends primarily on external conditions and, apart from procreation, only incidentally on organized relationships among their elements, that is, upon internal characteristics of their systems.

The type of simple but inadequate natural kinds in which Kripke and Putnam believe can be avoided by second-order analysis without giving up the concept of objectivity, or even of natural kinds, provided that one recognizes the limited contexts in which such designations can be used.

In a subsequent section, I shall explore the problem Kripke gets wrong in his discussion of yellow: the correlative character of the *definitional* and the *dispositional*. Whether one or the other governs is not an *as such* matter but one of frame of reference.

Structure and Process

The concepts, "structure" and "process," are correlatives. Thus, the decision to use either of the concepts depends on the context and the purpose of analysis. Structure consists of the static elements of a system. Process consists of the regular changes that functions produce in a system.

The sun, for instance, can be defined in more than one way. It can be defined as a luminous heavenly body. It can be defined as the element in the solar system that heats the planets that circle it. It can be defined as a body the heat of which is produced by the process of internal fusion and contraction. We can specify a number of experiments that will permit us to identify the orb in our particular solar system as a sun according to these definitions. Thus, we can employ multiple definitions in identifying structures or entities. A sun is a luminous body that provides heat to the planets that encircle it, and so forth. An ox is a quadruped, horned, cloven-footed, ruminant, and so forth, animal.

However, we can also study the sun or an ox in terms of their internal relations as these relations change. The human body may be subjected to a physiological analysis that is similar. We can study the body either as a structure of parts related to each other in a static fashion or as a process involving growth and decay. The body is both structure and process; and the two modes of analysis are complementary. Statements about the body as structure do not contradict statements about the body as process; they have different referents. Either structure or process may be dominant, depending upon the questions that are asked. And the two modes of analysis differ, even though both employ definitions. Thus the heart of an ox is an organ, and so forth that, in relation to the lungs, etcetera, has the following functions in producing, and so forth.

Definition and Disposition

Some concepts cannot be treated strictly definitionally, but only contextually and in complex conditional form. For instance, the term "electric charge" means, among other things, that if one body is placed near another body and is attracted by that second body, then it possesses an electric charge. The ensuing electric current can be inferred from the heat produced in a conductor, the deviation of a magnetic needle, the quantity of a substance separated from an electrolyte, and so forth. Thus, the concept of an electric current cannot be reduced to any one set of terms nor can it be measured simply by measuring a temperature. This is what I mean by a dispositional concept.

Dispositional concepts are necessarily employed when the interdependence of the element under consideration and its environment is great. However, this is merely the polar end of a series rather than a dichotomous usage. All manifest properties are products from one point of view as, for instance, the disposition of a type of optic system to produce a perception of yellow when a referent and light source produce given angstrom patterns. That is, they are dispositional in some respects. And all dispositional properties require reference to manifest properties if only to register their production: for electric current, heat, and deviation of the needle, for instance. Concepts such as "definition" and "disposition" are correlatives. Neither can be reduced to the other, and part-system analysis enables us to deal with them.

Although "electric current" is a dispositional concept in the area of mechanics, it is indicated on instruments that are considered virtually independent of context. The manifestation of yellow, on the other hand, depends on the conventional standard of sunlight, the chemical composition of referents, the angstrom pattern, and the normal optical transceivers of the human body. Variance in any of these, including the use of filters, would result dispositionally in a different manifest color. Rational and moral behavior are produced dispositionally and there is much greater variance, depending on context, than in color. There is no standard sunlight, chemical composition, or angstrom patterning to narrow the range of contextual variance in the area of moral or rational behavior. Given sufficient specification of transceiver and environment, however, good or rational behavior can be identified.

One of the striking results of von Neumann's development of game theory was the recognition that what was rational depended upon the context in which it was analyzed. Rationality is an extremely strong concept—that is, the criteria that define it are strong—in a situation such as the prisoners' dilemma, in which strictly rational independent behavior produces the worst joint outcome. It is a weaker and more restricted concept in the zero-sum game. The criteria for rationality are weaker still in some other types of games. When one turns to asymmetric bargaining games—that is, games in which the maximal outcomes for the players are different and in which they must agree on p, which stands for the proportion of his maximum that one player gets, if the other player gets $1 - p$ of his maximum—it is questionable whether a strategy pair can be picked out as rational, that is, whether there are adequate criteria for defining rationality in this context.[26]

Thus, when we try to analyze what we mean by a human being, our concept of it will depend upon how we structure the analysis and the context that we take into account. A mere examination of what individuals do in specific circumstances provides one framework of analysis. And examination of what they do under a variety of social and environmental circumstances provides another mode of analysis. An analysis of how they attempt to transform their environment in order to transform their alternatives and of how these attempts to change the environment differ in different societies requires still another framework. If we ask what capacities and dispositions they must possess to respond in these ways, we are at a still different level of analysis.

The comparative analysis of different but similar types of systems also can be helpful. We can learn more about human thinking and intelligence by contrasting computer models of computation and problem solving with human thinking and problem solving. We can learn more about human emotions by contrasting different theories of emotion with each other, for instance, Aristotle's, the James-Lange theory, and cybernetic or information-control theories. Such inquiries can also inform us, to some extent, about the interaction between different "housings" —biological in humans, electronic and metal in computers—and their related processes of thinking and problem solving as well as the subjects to which they are directed. In all these ways, we penetrate more and more deeply into the whatness and the meaning of humanity by means of the scientific methods of theory and praxis.

Pragmatistic Tests

The structure and differentiation of concepts depend not upon abstract conceptual analysis but upon the need to make distinctions that are important in the investigation of problems.

Thus, if we wish to investigate what we mean by "courage," we can do this best not by conceptual analysis but by contrasting varieties of behavior under different conditions. We may contrast the courage required to protect a family from assault by a bandit, the courage to fight for one's country in war, and the courage to think differently, to choose three arbitrary examples. Yet may it not sometimes be more courageous to surrender to the attacker and to limit the damage to one's family? And may it not be foolhardy, on going into battle, to begin a debate about the appropriate technique of attack?

With the aid of examples of this kind, we distinguish courage from foolhardiness or rashness. We may learn that what appears to be courageous is really cowardice: the preference for avoiding the appearance of cowardice regardless of the cost to others. We refine our concepts not only by analyzing them conceptually but by weighing them against the richness of the real world. We learn that different virtues are of different orders of importance in different societies. We learn that certain forms of moral behavior produce better people and better social conditions under existing historical conditions, but not necessarily under all.

The virtues that produce an integrated personality in a medieval society and those that produce an integrated personality in a modern society may be quite different. The values these virtues embody cannot be placed in any simple hierarchy, for their relationships with each other and with historical conditions are highly interdependent. Even the complex balance of values that are judged to be best because they produce the best people under the best possible conditions of one society will not be best in all sectors of the society or in all situations that arise within each particular sector.

To say that some values are more important than others does not mean that the less important values can be derived from the more important values—no system of logic will permit this in a way that accounts for actual experience—but that they will play a more important role in a class of situations or even in particular situations. Thus, one may lie to save one's brother from the secret police if he is merely a dissident, but not lie to save the brother if he will convey important information to an evil enemy nation. On the other hand, one may send secret information to the enemy to save one's mother if the information is unimportant or one's own society is not worth preserving. There is always a rich interdependence with other elements of the factual order in these judgments. If we believe that people are by nature selfish—that is, that except under restrictive conditions they will tend to act in their own interest against the public interest or the social good—then we would regard hypocrisy as a virtue, for the wise would be hypocritical and only fools would be taken in by claims to the contrary. Even so, truth-telling may be a virtue, in some situations, even for such selfish and hypocritical persons.

Whatness is revealed by the widest variety of testing possible: a variety that distinguishes between first-order and second-order types of statements and that reveals the dispositional shifts in both the meaning of terms and their relationships. This is similar to the reason the von Neumann utility axioms are insufficiently general, except for limited forms of economic analysis. A value is more important not because it ranks higher in an abstract hierarchy but because it will play a greater role in a decision that is itself more important than others.

This mode of analysis also illuminates the concept of "freedom," for freedom is not abstract, either. For freedom to have meaning, it must refer to the freedom of human beings to act according to their best understanding of what a human is. A drugged person is not free to analyze a problem, for an individual whose information has been severely restricted has lost the freedom to make significant moral decisions. At its deepest level, the understanding of human freedom requires a dispositional analysis. And this understanding will depend upon the facts of particular circumstances, particular societies, particular environmental conditions, particular available alternatives, and particular prospects for transforming those alternatives. Thus, our ability to understand the concept of freedom must be related to a praxical analysis.

Notes

[1]John Dewey, *Experience and Nature* (Chicago: Open Court Publishing Co., 1925).

[2]Morton A. Kaplan, *Justice, Human Nature and Political Obligation* (New York: Free Press, 1976), pp. 49 ff.

[3]Willard Van Orman Quine, *From a Logical Point of View* (Cambridge: Harvard University Press, 1953), pp. 20 ff.

[4]*Ibid.*, pp. 102 ff.

[5]Hilary Putnam, *Mind, Language and Reality,* Philosophical Papers, vol. 2, (Cambridge: Cambridge University Press, 1975), p. 52.

[6]Gottlob Frege, "On Sense and Reference," in *Translations from the Philosophical Writings of Gottlob Frege,* edited by P. Geach and M. Black (Oxford: Basil Blackwell, Publisher, 1952).

[7]Hilary Putnam, *Mind, Language and Reality,* vol. 2, p. 52.

[8]Bertrand Russell, "On Denoting," *Mind,* n.s., (1905).

[9]Gottlob Frege, "On Sense and Reference."

[10]Alexius Meinong, "The Theory of Objects," in *Realism and the Background of Phenomenology,* edited by R. Chisholm (Glencoe, Ill.: Free Press, 1960).

[11]For a powerful discussion of this topic see Brand Blanshard, *Research and Analysis* (La Salle, Ill.: Open Court Publishing Co., 1962), pp. 127 ff.

[12]Jurgen Habermas, *Theory and Practice* (Boston: Beacon Press, 1973). For a discussion of the neo-Kantian aspects of Habermas's philosophy, see Morton A. Kaplan, *Alienation and Identification* (New York: Free Press, 1976), pp. 29 ff.

[13]Bertrand Russell, *Principia Mathematica,* Introduction and chap. 2; Alfred Tarski, *Logic, Semantics, Metamathematics* (Oxford: Oxford University Press, 1956).

[14]Kurt Gödel, *On Undecidable Propositions of Formal Mathematical Systems; Notes on Lectures* (Princeton: Institute for Advanced Study, 1934).

[15]Bertrand Russell, *Principia Mathematica,* Introduction, chap. 2.

[16]A similar conclusion is argued powerfully from a different perspective in Edmond L. Wright, "Logic as an Intention-Matching System: A Solution to the Paradoxes," *Journal of the British Society for Phenomenology, 10* (1979).

[17]Max Born, *Physics and Politics* (Edinburgh: Oliver & Boyd, 1962), pp. 49 ff.

[18]Morris Cohen, *Reason and Nature* (New York: Harcourt, Brace, 1931).

[19]Saul Kripke, " Semantical Considerations in Modal Logic," *Acta Philosophica Fennica,* 16 (1963); Hilary Putnam, *Mind, Language, and Reality.*

[20]Saul Kripke, "Semantical Considerations."

[21]See Leonard Linsky, *Names and Descriptions* (Chicago: University of Chicago Press, 1977), pp. 66 ff., for a rigorous refutation of Kripke's view that proper names lack sense, a position that is necessary to Kripke's conclusion.

[22]Saul Kripke, "Naming and Necessity," in *Semantics of Natural Language*, edited by Donald Davidson and Gilbert Harman (Dordrecht, Holland: D. Reidel Publishing Co., 1972), p. 326.

[23]Saul Kripke, "Semantical Considerations," p. 274, fn. 71.

[24]Hilary Putnam, *Mind, Language and Reality*, p. 233.

[25]Saul Kripke, "Semantical Considerations"; Hilary Putnam, *Mind, Language and Reality*, p. 233.

[26]The reader who is interested further may turn to my discussion, "A Note on Game Theory, " in *New Approaches to International Relations*, edited by Morton A. Kaplan (New York: St. Martin's Press, 1968).

CHAPTER 7

THE MECHANISMS OF REGULATION: PROJECTION

Morton A. Kaplan

Projection occurs when the personality system has information which leads it to believe that a lethal danger threatens it. The system then devotes its regulatory capacity and its attention to the area of danger. However, it scans for a limited class of information, namely, information concerning that danger or concerning possible aid.

Projection does not involve a simple outward projection of internal motivations. The system readies itself for an appropriate response to a significant disturbance. To prepare an appropriate response in the area of sensitivity is an important mode of regulation. If danger is expected, a hostile response is in readiness; if aid, a friendly response. The situation may even be tested by an initial signaling response of the appropriate kind which stops short of final action. This signaling response has the function of informing others that, if they take certain actions, a particular kind of response will be forthcoming.

There is still another element to projection. Since the system uses scanning capacity for the information which threatens it or which it needs, it tends to be inattentive to information which does not come within this category. Therefore it tends to acquire a partial and misrepresentative picture of the external world. This is functional when the initial expectation was accurate but dysfunctional when it was false. Moreover, this selective scanning tends to inhibit the receipt of information that signals changes in the environment.

The preparatory responses may produce in the environment the very response which was anticipated. In the area of personal relations, it is a commonplace observation that some people create the very hostility they fear and that others arouse friendly responses where previously a friendly disposition may not have been present.

Projection may occur also when a system has hostile intentions against another actor in the environment. In this case, it may anticipate the appropriate response from that actor. If this information concerning the response of alter signals danger, the system may repress either information concerning the response or information concerning its own intentions. In this latter case, sensitivity in the dangerous task area may still be so great that the system continues to scan for and to anticipate a hostile response. This latter case, therefore, also constitutes projection.

When the information of a system indicates the presence of potentially lethal environmental disturbances or great internal stress, projection may be anticipated. Personality systems using projection as a characteristic mechanism may display great flexibility in interpreting information in conformity with anticipations. They may construct vast delusional systems designed to explain items of behavior which do not readily fit into the anticipated pattern.

Since, however, virtually all the regulatory capacity of such systems is devoted to task regulation in response to the great strain and danger confronting these systems, there is little capacity to scan for information which would permit a rebuilding of their information states. In short, projection is a sign that—at least in the area where projection occurs—the metatask regulatory capacity of the system is minimal. These systems are always "shoring up the levee" one bag at a time. Their hypotheses concerning the world are "one-bag" ad hoc hypotheses which add additional postulates for each new item of information because these systems lack the metatask regulatory capacity to construct economical hypotheses.

CHAPTER 8

THE NATURE OF REALITY AS ILLUMINATED BY QUANTUM PHYSICS AND MATHEMATICAL LOGIC*

Morton A. Kaplan

Although the world cannot be definitively described or understood, there are things that can be said that illuminate it or improve our understanding of its objective characteristics. However, some of those things, such as the character of space-time or particles, are less accessible to ordinary common sense than is commonly believed. In the course of the analysis, I shall analyze the conceptual error that led Erwin Schrödinger to his mistaken analysis of the black cat problem and show that it is his treatment of theoretical notations and theoretical formalisms that produced his mistaken analysis. It is this error that requires his brute-force solution of an absolute distinction between the macroworld and the world of quantum physics. I shall show also how the implications of Kurt Gödel's proof in the *Entscheidungsproblem*—which involves not merely the incompleteness of formal mathematical systems but the incompleteness with which they represent conceptions—refutes the concept of a world in which notations directly represent reality.

It is the triadic relationship among concept, sign, and referent that will play a key role in this analysis. Although differences in frameworks of reference lead to apparently contradictory but true statements, these statements, properly understood, are compatible with

* I am grateful to Marcelo Alonso and Saunders Mac Lane for helpful and clarifying comments.

each other. This framework employs terms such as first-order in a way that is different from the usages of physicists.

Both relativity and quantum theory raise significant questions about the character of reality. According to relativity theory, the first-order determinations—that is, the determinations made from their contextual placement on a particular inertial system—of observers on two independent inertial systems will establish correctly, but with apparent paradox, that time intervals are longer at the other frame of reference. Measurements of motion always are made with respect to the system or frame of reference. That relativity theory is correct in this regard is supported by the fact that the decay times of particles that enter the earth's atmosphere from outer space or that are accelerated in particle accelerators are slower than the decay times of the same type of particles when they are at rest with respect to the earth.

Observers on independent inertial systems nonetheless will agree on their second-order determinations—that is, the determinations that follow from their applications of relativity theory, which constitutes a relatively neutral second-order frame of reference for them. Both will use relativity theory to decide that their first-order determinations are mirror images. These frames of reference are only relatively neutral because they are not ultimate regardless of other considerations. Furthermore, there is no absolute space-time continuum from which determinations can be made.

There is no paradox in this claim, for time and space are not independent realities but only aspects of real things: entities the space-time evolution of which are represented by world lines (the path of a particle in space-time). Note, however, that an observer on the decaying particle noted above would agree that time passes more slowly on the particle. It has ceased to move on an independent inertial path, and its acceleration now can be noted independently. If one balks at an observer on a particle, we can return to the fabled twins, one of whom flies into outer space and then returns to Earth. Both now inhabit a relatively neutral frame of reference, in which their first-order and not merely their second-order accounts of reality coincide. Each agrees that the twin who flew into space is younger than the twin who remained at home.

There is a well-known thought experiment in which an attacking force is launched against an enemy in an independent inertial frame of reference. There is a third frame of reference, according to which the attacking force leaves before the decision to launch the attack force is made. This seems to be not merely paradoxical but impossible. However, if a common first-order frame of reference is found for the observers from all three inertial systems—if, for instance, the observers from the third system accelerate to the locus of attack—all three sets of observers will possess a similar first-order understanding of events.

It is worth repeating that this signifies only that there is no absolute first-order space-time within which placement and dating are uniquely given regardless of frame of reference. However, at the same time, there is a relatively neutral frame of reference at the second-order level and also first-order agreement—at least at the level of physics—when this has pragmatic significance.

The quantum puzzles collapse in a somewhat similar manner. The puzzles ensue from the interpretation given to the deterministic wave equations, which then supposedly collapse when the experiment is carried out. This is often identified with the presence of an observer rather than, as it should be, with the frame of reference, even though knowledge of events from a frame of reference always involves an observer.

Consider the two major puzzles: the position or momentum of the photon, and its particle or wave character. The wave equation specifies only probabilities with respect to position or momentum, whereas in an appropriate experiment there is always a definite position or momentum. Alternatively, in one type of experiment, quanta behave like particles and in another type like waves or fields.

The observer but not the frame of reference can be eliminated. For instance, each experiment can be ordered so that observers are absent but clocks and cameras are present. Furthermore, the experimental measures in which the positions of the photons are determined are incompatible with the experimental conditions in which the momenta are determined. This is also the case for the wave and particle experiments. The pictures will provide the results, in the absence of an observer. (I shall deal with the significance of the observer in each case shortly.)

The former examples are fundamentally different from the case of Schrödinger's black cat. Schrödinger suggested that if quantum laws applied to macroobjects, the quantum/macrophysical interchange would produce a bizarre result. This claim hinges on the fact that according to Schrödinger's interpretation of quantum theory, a radioactive particle exists in both a decayed and an undecayed state until observed. Consider a hermetically sealed physical apparatus with a cat, an inside observer, a quantum device involving radioactive material that would or would not release a poison that could kill the cat, and an outside observer. According to the common understanding of quantum phenomena, if the poison were released, the cat would be dead for the inside observer but neither dead nor alive for the outside observer until the experimental unit was opened.

Schrödinger knew intuitively that this interpretation is wrong. So he misleadingly made an absolute distinction between the world of macrophysics and that of microphysics. To reconstruct what is wrong with this quantum theoretical interpretation of the black cat experiment, substitute a camera and clock for the inside observer. If the poison is not released, the cat will be alive when the experimental container is opened. The camera recording will show that the cat always was alive, and it would be unreasonable to believe anything else. If the cat is dead, the camera will show the demise, the clock will record the time, and an autopsy will verify the time; and it will do so, at least approximately, even in the absence of the internal monitoring devices.

Note that Schrödinger's formulation of the problem requires that the outside observer know that there is a cat in the capsule and a quantum device that either will or will not emit poison. Otherwise, there would be no ground for Schrödinger's statement that until the capsule was opened, the cat would be neither dead nor alive in terms of quantum theoretical analysis for the external observer. These elements constitute a common or relatively neutral frame of reference for the internal and external observers, although their information may differ in other respects.

The external observer knows that cats do not exist in a state that is "neither dead nor alive." Thus, although the external observer cannot know whether the cat is alive or, if dead, when it died until the apparatus is opened, he does know that it is not "neither dead nor alive." This would remain true if the internal quantum device was absent as a condition of the experiment and whether or not the internal observer decides to release the poison. Although we cannot know whether it is raining in a foreign city until someone communicates the information, we would not say that it is neither raining nor not raining until we receive the information.

Note that the differences in the information possessed by the two observers about events inside the capsule are not the source of the problem, although most physicists insist that observation is the key to the distinctions. The photonic experiments are fundamentally different from the black cat experiment. There is no representational equivalent for a photon. Moreover, it does not have either a definite momentum or position, nor does it behave as a particle or field except in specific experimental or realworld contexts. However, the cat is somewhat like an independent measure. It is representational regardless of context (I ignore possible contexts involving different kinds of beings) and either is dead or alive.

The cat can exist only in either state (from our frame of reference), but we have insufficient grounds for asserting that the photon can exist only in the states revealed by the experiments we have performed. Therefore, it is licit in the current state of information to say that the photon is neither wavelike nor particle-like (but not both wavelike and particle-like) in the absence of the experiment, and it is true (at least in the present state of knowledge) to say that the photon has neither definite position nor momentum in the absence of an experiment or comparable realworld conditions. Although there may be legitimate disagreement about a definition of life or a transient moment in which it cannot be determined if the cat is alive or dead, neither of these considerations affects the assessment of Schrödinger's black cat experiment.

Thus, despite the hermetic sealing of the experimental chamber, the outside observer knows that the cat is either dead or alive, whereas the photon has a definite position, momentum, polarization, or dominant or field aspects only in the context of a relevant experiment or realworld situation. Furthermore, if the observer knows the probabilities with which the device will emit the poison, he also knows the probabilities that the cat is dead or alive. Thus, this problem does not differ from any ordinary macrophysical problem.

Note that even if an experiment in the hermetically sealed chamber is restricted to photonic behavior, for instance, Schrödinger's formulation also would misrepresent the experimental situation. The outside observer would know that if an experiment occurred within the chamber, the "neither/nor" aspect would be restricted to the period before the experiment, not to the period before the opening of the chamber. Whether the outside observer could know when the experiment occurred would depend upon the equipment inside the chamber.

Whether quantum effects may have consequences at the macrophysical level is a question to which we do not have an answer. They do not in the black cat experiment, but this does not exclude other contexts in which they may.

Before discussing the second error in the treatment of the collapse of the wave function, it is important to understand *meaning.* All meaning involves a triadic relationship among a concept, a sign, or word, and a referent, or signed. The signed, that is, the referent, is not given exhaustively by the sign or by the sign set (the set of terms and words) in the case of a theory. The sign or sign set merely points to a potentiality inherent in the referent.

What do we mean, more concretely, by the collapse of the wave function? In the first place, the wave function is the sign set and merely mediates between the potentiality in the referent and the concepts that the wave function (sign set) expresses publicly. Quantum physicists mistakenly have identified the notational form of quantum theory and its referents, or quanta. They have reified the theory. They have no basis for asserting that quanta are simultaneously in a state of decay and nondecay until observed upon the basis only of the notational elements of their theory.

In the second place, the frames of reference of the alternative outcomes are different. The experimental frames of reference do not conflict with the wave equations but merely produce specific outcomes that are consistent with them.

In the absence of the experiments, there is only a potentiality for these outcomes. The wave equations merely state the probability structure that will determine the results of a measurement or experiment. They do not describe reality. The claims made by quantum physicists are based on a failed metaphysic that asserts an identity between language and reality, whereas language is a pragmatic tool. It permits the investigation of reality and is consistent with claims of correspondence under carefully controlled conditions, and then only within the framework of nonprivileged frames of reference.

When quantum physicists refer to the collapse of the wave function, they fail to note that all empirical knowledge is transactional. Red, for instance, does not exist as an independent reality. If our optic and neurological structures or the characteristics of the sun or the environmental context were different, red would not appear to be red. It would have the same wavelength. But wavelength itself, in turn, conceivably could be something else if we possessed different theories, apparatuses, and sensory organs. Thus, there is no absolutely privileged frame of reference and no identity between the language used and the reality observed or described.

We designate particular sets of relationships between transactors and referents—humans perceive red and green and dogs do not—because we know from everyday life how transactional context affects phenomenal knowledge. But red and green do not exist as such for us, even at the human level in ordinary daylight. We can be trained to make finer distinctions as our conceptions of color are expanded by training.

Furthermore, the literal quality of notation varies with subject matter at the human observational level. A straight line literally represents both the concept and the referent for all practical purposes. The concept of motive, however, although representational, is much less literally representational. Any particular motive will vary with realworld factors as well as with the complex preconscious and conscious aspects of mental life. The notion that "motive" exists in the same way as "dead cat" or "live cat" is a philosophical error. Even the latter concepts are not absolutely dichotomous. Thus, Schrödinger's solution to the cat puzzle is misleading even though it makes a distinction between events at the macrolevel and microlevel that, on the whole, is correct.

The collapse of the wave function appears mysterious because we fail to understand that we have taken boundary conditions, context, or frame of reference for granted. Thus, we are mystified when they become relevant at the quantum level, where theory leaves them out of account.

In what sense is a theory or concept real? Their referents are the reals. The signs or sets of signs—that is, the public theories—that mediate between the concepts and the real referents contain notations that are not uniquely required. There is more than one way to compose them. Think of the rules of the road. It does not make much difference which side of the road we can travel on as long as rules of the road exist and are followed.

It is important to detach the concept of realism from that of verisimilitude. For instance, we can construct a physical model of a solar system or an analog computer model that employs the laws of physics and that is programmed for initial conditions that correspond to the inferred locations of the planets in the physical model. We can then compare changes in both with astronomical measurements. There is, however, no direct comparison between the models and the solar system. The correspondences have meaning only within a specific second-order frame of reference.

Perhaps the issue can be made clearer by moving to examples that are not as simple, as determinate, or as strongly ordered as in macromechanics, examples that also show how the correlative character of language fits the account that is being offered. The position and momentum of particles cannot be measured in the same experimental situations, for measurements of position require rigid instruments and measurements of momentum require instruments with moving parts. Note that "moving" and "rigid" are correlatives. Neither is such as such.

None of the foregoing alternatives is right or wrong as such. Each expresses a reality. However, some notational aspects of each may be purely conventional. To take one of the simplest examples, we may measure in meters rather than in yards. Yet no one would argue that if we cannot determine whether reality consists of meters or yards, then our account is subjective. If we were to reach the latter conclusion, it would rest on a failure to distinguish between the sign system (and its conceptual understanding) and its referent.

Meters and yards and clocks are merely alternative conventions for dealing with spacial and temporal concepts. Space-time is how we deal with certain aspects of physical reality. There may be other valid ways, particularly for beings radically different from ourselves. These alternative formulations deal with realities that need not contradict each other but that in Bohr's terms represent complementary aspects of reality.

We can now understand the error involved in the anthropic principle and also in the usual understanding of the collapse of the wave function. It is tautologically correct that the phenomenal world we know could not exist in the absence of observers somewhat like us. However, a substantially different phenomenal world may exist for beings radically different from ourselves.

The physical potentialities that make both sets of phenomenal worlds possible do not require observers, although knowledge of them does. For instance, knowledge of the existence of planets requires some type of observer, but the statement that planets existed before observers existed is an empirical truth. Only the ways in which planets are characterized depend upon transceivers (that is, observers) of particular types.

The concept of *in this context* or *from this frame of reference* is extremely important in interpreting quantum phenomena. Some of the experimental results with photons occur regardless of the width of separation between the slits in the experimental apparatus. Other results with polarization of photons in paired experiments have led to suggestions that one photon in a pair "knows" what has happened to its paired photon and responds accordingly regardless of the distance between them. This has led to the strange hypothesis of communication faster than light, although it more strongly calls into question space-time phenomena at the photonic level as they are integrated into the local space-time of human observers. Still other hypotheses have been offered for these strange phenomena.

This type of analysis also suggests that the space-time matrix involved in quantum physics and the matrix relevant to events involving entropy differ in meaning. Most quantum events are time reversible. But it does not follow that time has the same meaning for these events that it has for macrophysical events, particularly those involving entropy.

Quanta are considered to be identical by contemporary physical theory if they are of the same type. Thus, reversibility means only that the sign of direction is opposite. Thus, if quanta could observe, reversal in time would no more entail a disorientation than would our changing direction from left to right. If, however, we ever experienced an experiment in which the first phase of $-t$ (reversed time) occurred prior to the last phase in phenomenal time, I suggest that we would become disoriented.

Numerous examples have been designed to show the improbability of time reversal at the macrophysical level. Consider a glass that shatters. The shattering can follow more than one pattern. Yet, whatever pattern occurs in a particular case, the general form of that pattern will appear at worst to be not improbable. However, if one reverses events so that the glass is recomposed, this will seem to be so improbable as to be impossible.

However, there is an even stronger argument against time reversibility at the human macrolevel. If time reversed itself in a meaningful sense, we would grow younger. We would have to be born again. Thus if our mother were dead and cremated, she would have to be resurrected from the elements of which she had been composed.

Furthermore, our sentences and words would be uttered in reverse and we would become unconscious in the process, for consciousness entails meaning. Meaning would be lost in this form of reversal. Even if one wanted to argue that consciousness and meaning are epiphenomenal, this would imply a reversibility different from quantum reversibility, for the states would not be identical except for direction.

I cannot prove in the strong sense of "prove" that consciousness and meaning are integral aspects of behavior. But it would be a major and unjustified step, as well as an unproven one, to argue that they are not integral. Furthermore, for reasons soon to be made clear, every proof occurs within the framework of an assessment.

Let me back up a bit to make the relevant argument. Gödel's *Entscheidungsproblem* is well-known and undisputed. Gödel proved that for any mathematical system strong enough to contain some system of natural numbers and weak enough so that the rules of inference are recursive, it can be proved that there are relevant true propositions that cannot be derived from the axioms of the system.

Gödel's proof of the *Entscheidungsproblem*—and his undermining of formalism, in mathematics—is undisputed, but its commonsense implications for the layman depend on an implicit formalist position that its analytic truth value is independent of meaning, a position I reject.[1] For instance, a formalist would argue that the contradiction to which the class of all classes paradox gives rise is a true contradiction (I agree that the application of Bertrand Russell's axioms does produce a contradiction) and would avoid it by placing restrictions on Russell's axioms.

However, there is a different way to analyze such propositions. In *Science, Language, and the Human Condition,* I showed that when particular signs become the signed referents of themselves in the types of propositions that give rise to logical paradoxes, they are analogies by proportion—and hence metaphors—unless it can be shown independently that they are indeed identical.[2]

Note with reference to Gödel's thesis that some distinguished mathematicians have claimed that true propositions of arithmetic have been discovered that cannot be derived from its axioms and definitions. However, if we are dealing with pure formalism, then the axioms and definitions establish what arithmetic is, and one cannot overcome this by referring to a meaning for arithmetic outside of those axioms and definitions. Thus, on a strictly formalist account, if Gödel's proof is correct, it is incorrect; but if it is incorrect, of course, it is correct. Even a proof of incompleteness, thus, would be insufficient to determine that a true mathematical proposition is a truth of arithmetic unless the axioms and definitions represent a concept (arithmetic) not entirely embodied in them. Thus, there is an incompleteness not merely in the axiomatic structure of arithmetic but in its representation in formal signs. This is true for all formalisms.

If the thesis of incompleteness in this extended form is true of a system as precise or logically complete as mathematics—and it surely is—it is true of physical systems as well. Note, however, that I have not proved this; I have merely provided an exceptionally strong reason to believe that it is true. I call this assessment: a fit between the realm of knowledge and a particular assertion within it.

Assessment of the validity of logics or physical theories always involves outside elements. Logicians moved beyond Aristotelian logic because they knew that the heads of horses were the heads of animals and that this cannot be proved by Aristotelian logic, a fact that rules out Wittgenstein's approach to language games. Experimental results support the conclusion that space is non-Euclidean. The experimental matrices within which theories are judged are not themselves included in the theories, and even the concepts employed depend upon worldviews that cannot be encompassed by any theory.

The assertion that conscious meaning is not epiphenomenal fits the realm of knowledge. It accords with our understanding of our behavior. Our knowledge of evolution suggests that consciousness is an element of fitness. The acceptance of scientific theories also depends upon fit with the surround of knowledge, for there is always evidence going against a theory and problems of interpretation of data.

The acceptance of consciousness and meaning as integral to behavior does not involve us in Cartesian dualism. Niels Bohr's principle of complementarity applies here. Each mode of analysis provides knowledge about the world from its own frame of reference. Thus, accounts of conscious knowledge cannot be derived from physiological accounts and vice versa. Both are conceptual and sign systems that apply to a referent, not themselves different referents. Hence, no single frame of reference, or indeed any set of frames of reference, can exhaust the reality to which they refer.

Roger Penrose, in his brilliant *The Emperor's New Mind,* speculates that there is a Platonic world of numbers to which the mind has direct access.[3] Although I cannot prove this to be false, it does not fit the realm of knowledge as I understand it. In the first place, if that is how mathematical discoveries are made, then only a relatively small number of people have possessed such access. If the world of numbers existed in this sense, I think the number of minds with access to it would be far larger.

The mind is an evolutionary product. Furthermore, we know that it develops pathways after birth through its experiences with the world and that this is essential to various types of intelligence. We also know that the preconscious has an extraordinary capacity to come up with solutions to problems, even problems that are not mathematical.

Perhaps, as John von Neumann speculated, the preconscious mind uses a language different from that of the conscious mind. Or perhaps, it is the home of complex "fitting operations." We know that children can recognize individuals in ways that we cannot yet program computers to do. Is it not likely that the preconscious mind can recognize a fit between a solution and a problem? Once that fit is recognized by the preconscious mind, the puzzle unfolds to the conscious mind as if present at once.

In at least some cases, true conclusions are apparent to mathematicians but not the intermediate steps. Howard Raiffa gave me a manuscript copy of *Games and Decisions*—the book he did with Duncan Luce—in 1955.[4] Even with my vanishingly small ability in mathematics, I found several dozen errors in derivations but none in the authors' conclusions.

In fact, there is no such thing as a demonstration except to a mind that is "tuned" to perceive it. Some minds are not "tuned" to perceive that 2 + 2 = 4. Others, such as that of Professor Penrose, can perceive solutions with respect to enormously complicated problems. Some can perceive analogical similarities better than others. We misperceive at least part of this problem, because most people are aware that they cannot understand mathematical demonstrations but unaware that they cannot understand assessments of complicated situations when these use words in sentences that they believe they can understand.

Notes

[1]Morton A. Kaplan, *Science, Language, and the Human Condition*, rev. ed. (New York: Paragon House, 1988), 22-31.

[2]Chapter 6, pp. 117-118.

[3]Roger Penrose, *The Emperor's New Mind* (Oxford: Oxford University Press, 1989).

[4]Duncan Luce and Howard Raiffa, *Games and Decisions* (New York: John Wiley, 1957).

PART THREE

A POLITICAL PERSPECTIVE

CHAPTER 9

THE PHILOSOPHICAL AND MORAL PRECONDITIONS OF DEMOCRATIC THEORY

Morton A. Kaplan

The modern conception of democracy is supported by both practical and moral considerations. However, most attempts to provide this support fail significantly to distinguish between the seventeenth-century worldview that gave birth to liberal democracy and a worldview that is consistent with contemporary science. This failure merely replicates the more general failure of contemporary philosophy to provide an integrating worldview.

Although standard philosophical approaches have much to teach us, they tend to suffer from a significant defect. They more often than not attempt to investigate ethical and moral problems in isolation from those developments in the realm of knowledge that provide an appropriate interpretive context. This tends to be the case whether we are dealing with more traditional philosophers who come from the natural law school—although these do pay attention to prudential considerations concerning society—or with those who adhere to formalistic neo-Kantian or utilitarian approaches.

The great classic philosophers who wrote on ethics and justice were systematic philosophers. Their moral positions were consistent with, although not determined by, their worldviews. Those who carry on their tradition, perhaps through some variation of natural law, often fail to ask, however, whether that tradition needs to be modified by the contemporary understanding of the world. Are unmodified views of natural law epistemologically viable? Do they accord with a reasonable understanding of how signs mediate between concepts and referents? Is there anything in the contemporary understanding of the nature of the physical universe that works against them?

Many contemporary philosophers deliberately avoid discussion of the nature of the good. They seem unaware, or even to doubt, that moral and ethical concerns are related to the dispositional nature of humankind and the nature of the world. Until recently, John Rawls believed that one could choose the rules for governing society behind a veil of ignorance without knowing whether one would emerge as Attila among the Huns or as a bourgeois clerk in contemporary society.

Rawls argued that someone who believed in a true religion—including, for example, the Ayatollah Khomeini? —should accept tolerance in his actual world. He would opt for tolerance from behind a veil of ignorance, Rawls said, because, behind that veil, he could not know whether he could protect his religion in its absence. Thus, even though he knows he can impose his religion in the actual world, he is bound ethically, Rawls said, by the decision he would have made behind the veil. This shows only that Rawls does not know what a believer means by "true religion."

Allan Gewirth, for instance, believed that one's character as an agent and desire for freedom to accomplish one's desires logically entailed the recognition of the freedom of others for the same purposes. Thus, Gewirth argued that one could not claim a right in principle without recognizing that other agents could claim similar rights. This, he argued, would give rise to a regime of liberty. However, the "agent" about whom Gewirth reasoned is a completely abstract agent who lacks real contextually bound existence. He failed to perceive that if one were a deceitful agent who wished to enslave others, this would entail only the formal (and not necessarily public) requirement to understand that other agents have a similar formal claim to deceive or constrain us.

Moreover, even this purely formal constraint would depend upon the absence of relevant differentiation between us, for, if we are different in respects that can be related to potential rights or obligations, symmetry is not logically entailed. For instance, if 90 percent of adults were of what would be subnormal intelligence according to current standards, it is unlikely that we would desire formal voting equality.

The meaning imputed to the sign "agent" cannot be determined in the absence of contextual analysis. "Agent" as a universal is abstract. Actual agents, that is, the referents of the concept and sign, will be either more or less than what Gewirth calls agents. The concept "agent," on the other hand, has a meaning that is affected by the other concepts that provide its context, a philosophical conclusion that is supported by the latest developments in brain research. These types of mistakes can be avoided by reference to an adequate contemporary worldview.

All Knowledge Involves Interpretation

It is a commonplace today—as contrasted with a mere generation earlier—that our knowledge of the world is interpretational. Knowledge invokes an active transaction between a mind and the external world. Although we might argue that the prior account is validated experimentally, the conditions of this or any experiment themselves draw on prior interpretations. They rest on a host of data and assumptions that are part of our common world. But our common world is different from that of prior generations, and the interpretations that govern the experiences we have are also different. We do not understand nature or human nature as our predecessors did. We could not do so, for many of the things that we "know" are fundamentally different from what they "knew."

We do not believe with Aristotle that there are slaves by nature. We reject the divine origins of government. We know that objects do not rise because they are light, and we acknowledge their capture by gravity. We know that names do not capture the essence of things and that we cannot control things by manipulating formulas verbally. We do not believe that the shape of the head determines character or intelligence. Hence, what we perceive when we see a head differs from what the believer in phrenology perceives. We believe we know that the stars are vastly distant suns and not tiny dots of light or angelic beings.

The things that we know constitute a framework that influences how we perceive, how we reason about, how we conceive hypotheses about, and when we look for evidence concerning the events both of everyday life and of the more highly disciplined world of science.

Our experiences, thus, are the evolving products of our transactions with a world external to us and not merely passive copies of "something out there."

It may help to understand the implications of these differences if we start with a simplified view of some alternative natural worlds as they were understood in their time and then move to an account of our contemporary world. Aristotle's world was a world of perfect forms and final causes. Thus, a tree already was contained in the seed as a final cause. A final cause produced the individual human from its fetus in a natural process unless some abnormal circumstance intervened that impeded one of the other Aristotelian causes. Everything in the Aristotelian scheme had a nature that fitted into a definite place in a world that was itself hierarchically ordered according to a unified scheme of final causes that produced a limited number of real kinds.

Theories were believed to be true not because of predictions that were validated experimentally but because their premises, which the mind had a natural capacity to know, were necessarily true. It was self-evidently true that space was Euclidean. Although politics and ethics were not theoretical subjects—and hence could not be reduced to axiomatic structure—still it was possible to know what the good was and to place men and their virtues in a natural order. One could then assess empirically how particular political orders contributed to a polity in which human nature could find its best expression.

Descartes and Hobbes helped to formulate the "modern" scientific worldview. Descartes undermined a view of language in which language resembled things and replaced it with the thesis that language permitted the ordering and representation of phenomena. However, once stipulated, the relationship between language and things was invariant. Hobbes accepted Aristotle's concept of theory but applied it to governance as well as to physics. Motion was the key term. Life and politics were variants of motion.

Descartes' concept of language played a key role in the development of modern physics. Instead of investigating the natural ordering of things, one would investigate the quantitative ordering of the qualities of things and of the relationships between these qualities, for instance, force, mass, and acceleration.

Some of the French philosophes, Laplace and Condorcet, for

instance, developed the concept of a hierarchically organized and fully determinate world in which God could predict every future state of the universe provided only that He knew the initial conditions of the atoms. Both humankind and the world were predictable machines. (*L'Homme Machine* was the title of one of La Mettrie's books.) This was the best of all possible worlds because it was the only possible one. However, many of its unhappy features were produced by an ignorance that had removed humans from their happy conditions in the state of nature.

Although closer analysis would have revealed a problem in their deduction of this conclusion from these premises, they believed that it was possible for science to determine how to make men free, even if they had to be forced to be free, by structuring a perfect society. This general philosophy gave rise to a conception of the rights of man and of nations that was believed to be derived from the nature of the world. Deism—a philosophy that ascribed the creation of the world to God and then removed him from the scene—was the chief theological concept.

The Scottish philosophers Hutcheson and Hume were sceptical of this much determinism. Kant, who was "wakened from [his] dogmatic slumber" by Hume, distinguished between pure and practical reason. Hegel's great knowledge of Eastern philosophy led him to make a frontal attack on this type of positivistic science with its completely knowable and completely deterministic existential world, although he maintained a deterministic view with respect to the Absolute (as Marx did with respect to the Totality). But nothing really shook the modern worldview deeply until the discovery of non-Euclidean geometry in the first half of the nineteenth century.

The Contemporary Worldview

The classical and early modern view of the world as a strongly ordered hierarchy that the mind had a natural capacity to understand began to break down with the discovery of non-Euclidean geometry, for what could be more self-evidently true than the Euclidean character of space? However, it was the fact that the special theory of relativity established non-Euclidean geometry as the geometry of actual space that shattered the earlier paradigm.

We inferred from the evidence that supported relativity theory that our local space seemed Euclidean because the local deviations from non-Euclidean space were too small to be noticed visually. This led many to reason that if the mind did not have a natural capacity to recognize fundamental truths, then truth could lie only in experimental validation. (This was the apparent basis on which the logical positivists rested their doctrine, even though it was inconsistent with an appropriate reading of relativity theory and especially of quantum theory.)

But matters became even more disruptive in terms of what had been natural understanding. If space was non-Euclidean, still it might be independently real. However, time, the fourth dimension was paradoxical from the viewpoint of natural understanding. If two independent inertial systems were in motion with respect to each other, an observer on each would assert correctly that time was going more slowly on the other. But how could time simultaneously be going more slowly on each system? (Einstein was later to state that the concept of simultaneity was an error.) Only if time is not an essence—a thing in itself—but relational would this be possible.

Worse shocks were in store for the then current worldviews. The statistical mechanics of Ludwig Boltzmann and Josiah Gibbs already had made the concept of a less than deterministic world somewhat familiar. But this perhaps was merely a measurement problem. Only with quantum mechanics did it appear possible that the laws of quanta were themselves probabilistic. Einstein thought that God would be playing dice with the universe if this were the case, and he refused to believe it. With Podolsky and Rosen, he devised a thought experiment designed to show how absurd such a world would be because local realism would not hold in it. (The most recent experiments indicate that what Einstein thought to be absurd is the case, and that photons of common and identical origin, for instance, "coordinate" their positions without communication.)

Niels Bohr attempted to provide a philosophical foundation for quantum mechanics with his Copenhagen thesis. Many things in the world are in a condition of complementarity, he said. For instance, the position and momentum of a quantum do not exist as such but only as transactional products in the context of incompatible experimental apparatuses that cannot be used at the same time.

Hence, to ask where the position was when momentum was being measured was to reify the concept of position. Similarly, he argued, it was a mistake to ask whether a quantum is a wave or a particle unless one asked in what respects and in what contexts.

Bohr's principle of complementarity solves what had been a perennial problem: How did mind evolve in a material universe? If information and matter/energy are in a relationship of complementarity, then information is present in the world even in the absence of minds. Given sufficient complexity in the organization of matter/energy—namely, the development of neurological networks—then information may complement neurological systems in the form of awareness. Eventually, as self-reflexive neurological networks evolved, self-awareness would emerge.

Hence, one need not ask what state of the neurological system produced a thought, for the two modes of analysis—of neurological and of mental states—are pursued by incompatible, but not contradictory, means. Brains and thoughts no more fit into a deterministic, hierarchically patterned universe than do the positions and momenta of quanta. But they are different and legitimate subjects of study that do not contradict each other, that complement each other, and that can be fitted into a worldview that accords with the contemporary state of knowledge.

It is possible that more finely grained determinations would reduce the weakness of prediction from particular individual frameworks of reference. However, if complementarity is a feature of the universe, it excludes the possibility of a strongly ordered world that fits together in a neat package. If one accepts the Copenhagen thesis of Bohr—that is, of the ultimately probabilistic character of the laws of quantum theory—then there is an irreducible element of weakness in accounts of the world that is only somewhat, but not completely, reduced by the large-scale character of macrophysical phenomena.

The Role of Language

The understanding of language also must be adjusted to the contemporary worldview. Words do not naturally indicate their objects as they would in an Aristotelian universe. Nor are they linked arbitrarily but univocally to different referents, as they would be in a Cartesian universe. Instead, words (that is, signs) link concepts to referents in ways that depend on the entire economy of concepts. "True" does not mean the same thing in a syllogism that it does in an empirical attribution, a fact that undermines the Kripke/Putnam theory of necessary truths. The analytical "true" is a stipulated concept that governs logical inferences. The empirical "true" is a judgment that in some circumstances can be treated as if identical with the analytical "true." Its meaning shifts with context.

"Green" means different things to a man and a tiger. The optic apparatus that produces colors is different, and so is the framework of interpretation. The same green object will be perceived differently even by a single individual, depending on the colors with which it is surrounded, the lighting system, and the state of the optic apparatus with which it is viewed. The corresponding concepts and the linguistic signs (or language elements) that are linked to these greens also vary contextually.

This view of language fits with chaos theory. A scientific theory is a set of signs linking a set of concepts with external reality from a frame of reference. It does not exhaust the referent because other possible frameworks of reference also apply to it, although they define and circumscribe it differently. For instance, the two-body laws governing the path of heavenly bodies do not account for effects that over time might destabilize planetary paths. Every regularity is likely to break down at some extreme limit when there is a major lack of fit, resulting from processes accounted for by other frames of reference, between the equilibrium model (theory, system, set of signs) and the underlying real system that is the referent of the model.

The prior discussion is designed to set the stage for a discussion of morality and liberal democracy. There is no better place to start the discussion than with contract theory, for, philosophically speaking, the origins of liberal democracy and contractarian theory (and its offshoot, natural rights) seem to be symbiotically interwoven.

Contract Theory

It is generally believed that the concept of liberal democracy rests on contract theory. When the belief in divine authority for government broke down, Hobbes and Locke could find no basis other than consent.

Contract theory, however, misrepresents the intellectual problem of obligation. It is misled by its state of nature assumptions. As a hypothetical device, Hobbes' state of nature is without support. Most animals, and all primates, are social animals. There have been controlled experiments in which monkeys have been raised with mothers, with broomsticks, and without even broomsticks. The monkeys raised with mothers became normal monkeys. The monkeys raised with broomsticks were able to learn to socialize, although with difficulty and without great success. The monkeys that did not have even broomsticks for support became not merely asocial but dysfunctional as well.

Hobbes, moreover, was misled, as more recently Nozick was, by the analogy between physics and society. Newton could rest his axioms on action in a vacuum because his equations could take into account gravitation or friction. Hobbes and, later, Nozick had no way to make adjustments within the frameworks of their theories for factors of altruism or human cohesion. Hence, their counterfactuals were vicious rather than fruitful.

Given a seventeenth-century worldview that included a deterministic nominalism that made of the individual an isolated atom, it is possible to understand Hobbes' assumptions. But a contemporary worldview would not produce such ideas, and specific ethnological and anthropological evidence is strongly inconsistent with them. Although a contemporary position is inconsistent with obligation based on contract and the concept of universalized natural rights, those concepts can be controverted without resort to it. Hobbes reached his conclusions only by sleight of hand.

No contract in a state of nature is binding in the absence of a moral duty or need. Because Hobbes provided no moral ground for the observance of the contract that established the state, he placed the requirement in the sovereign's power to punish. Still, he knew that the sovereign, unlike God, could be neither omnipresent nor omniscient. So he changed his definition of liberty. In the state, he said, we did not have liberty to oppose the sovereign because of the threat of punishment. In the state of nature, however, we were free unless physically constrained. That was the trick.

Leo Strauss believed that Hobbes' logic was sound. Because failure to keep the covenant would return men to the brutal war of all against all of the state of nature, it was a natural law that keeping the covenant was mandated. However, Hobbes' logic was flawed with respect to making and keeping the covenant. Because men were equal in the state of nature, no specific person was singled out by nature as ruler. Thus, only combat could decide this issue. But engaging in combat for this purpose would be more dangerous than remaining in the state of nature, for it would be fiercer. Hence, none would seek to lead unless they desired rulership even more than they feared death. Yet Hobbes disallowed this choice. And, if such combat began, one was more likely to survive if one remained neutral or joined only when the issue appeared settled.

On the other hand, if the state was in existence, breaking the covenant would not be dangerous if one was not caught. Even staging a coup would not return men to the state of nature, for historically many coups had been successful and had merely changed rulership. Thus, Hobbes' deduction of a law of nature that mandated keeping the covenant was flawed. His starting conditions were not sufficiently constrained to necessitate his conclusions. This perhaps was an excusable error on Hobbes' part, for he wrote before game theoretical analysis had been discovered. More likely, because Hobbes feared civil war, he made a deliberate error because he wanted men to believe it.

Contract theory will not sustain the legitimacy of government in any form, let alone liberal democracy. Two grounds need to be prepared for a defense of liberal democratic government. One would be in its efficacy in achieving or avoiding certain ends in the conditions for which it has been proposed. For instance, few would argue for a democratic vote among citizens on how to proceed with a heart transplant operation. The other defense would be in the values promoted by democracy. Few would want a successful heart transplant operation on an Adolf Hitler. And many would reject a democratic government if it produced a majoritarian tyranny.

The Good and Justice

To make a case for political obligation, we must first make the case for objective morals. Both relativity and quantum theory provide contextual reasons for believing that objectively true phenomena are true not as such but only relative to some framework of reference. This position was foreshadowed philosophically by Peircean pragmatics, which itself was responding to the problems bequeathed by the Hegelian legacy. This understanding is inconsistent with the concept of objectivity in all natural law theories and also with the concept of objectivity involved in Toulmin's *Reason in Ethics*, which led him to dismiss the notion of the objectivity of the good.

Toulmin argued that unlike the taste of sweetness, which might vary among individuals, green was green, unless one had defective vision, and hence objective. If one denied this, one was simply using words differently. What is good, however, cannot be distinguished in this fashion. Hence, according to Toulmin, it could not be objective.

Toulmin failed to note that dogs see colors differently than we do and that there are angstrom wavelengths we are incapable of perceiving. Color is a product of a transaction between us and an external world. Moreover, although he referred to the scientific basis of colors, there are no colors in physics, only angstrom wavelengths, which themselves are the products of transactions. The angstrom wavelength we see as green may not be green under different lighting, including that of some other star. Hence, it is variable also, although, from our normal frame of reference, it is less variable than sweetness. Toulmin's notion of the objectivity of color—that is, of a quality that is independent of transactions with others—was similar to that of the natural law theorist's concept of the objectivity of natural law. This casts additional doubt on most theories of natural law.

The discussion thus far also entails conclusions with respect to language. Language does not match an internal concept with an external object, either as a copy or as a universal correspondent. Green things, except as potentialities, are not out there independently of how we engage in transactions with them. Instead, language uses signs to mediate between a concept (and its environment) and a referent (and its environment) to produce meaning. The greenness of external objects is dependent on conceptual coding as part of a transactional process. Because this is so, concepts are not such as such but only from a frame of reference. Laws are sets of signs that link sets of concepts with external reality from a frame of reference and that do not exhaust that external reality. Hence, every regularity is likely to break down at some limit.

To understand the role of morality in political obligation, it is necessary to move away from universalistic worldviews that do not take context into account in reaching conclusions. Let us lead into a contextual account of morality by returning to the simpler problem of color perception.

We cannot perceive greens or solids in the absence of a framework of coding. So, too, we cannot perceive something as good in the absence of a relevant coding system. This does not mean that the infant has a sophisticated coding system that would be responsive to what adults recognize as moral qualities. The infant's coding system for good things may be something very simple. For instance, the sight of the mother's breast may be interpreted (nonlinguistically) as the availability of a particular kind of good: food.

Moral understanding develops through acculturation and with experience. Our moral universe has its origins in primitive codings for good things, things perhaps as simple as the "goodness" of the breast and its milk. Much as our knowledge of colors becomes sophisticated after much simpler beginnings, the criteria and reasoning applied to the conception of good things develop out of experience with relatively simple phenomena. Judgments related to such discriminations are shaped by their fit with other elements of experience. Thus, contrary to what Kant stated, we know that there are circumstances in which lying is moral. The greater our experience, the more likely we are to be able to make satisfactory, and more finely shaded, moral discriminations.

It is important to understand the difference between definitional and dispositional referents if one is to understand the differences between goods and some other types of things. Trees, for instance, are definitional objects. They are recognized for what they are, although they also have dispositional aspects. Goods are recognized by what they do. They are dispositional.

The reason this process is difficult to recognize as objective is that we have become used to the myth that we prove or disprove theories only by the results of tests. Thus, we assume a relatively simple test that many statements concerning the good cannot meet. In fact, many determinations in physics cannot meet this test either. We ignore many experimental results that do not accord with accepted theories because we assume that they are mistaken or that they will be accounted for by further knowledge. When conflicting theories contest with each other and the experimental data are insufficient, we prefer one theory over another if it better fits the current framework of knowledge. Indeed, the experimental evidence itself depends for its coding upon assessments that are employed within a wider realm of knowledge. It is this kind of assessment that is the paradigmatic case with respect to goods.

Because some philosophers misunderstand this process, they believe that objectivity has been undermined. They then retreat to different concepts, such as that of uncoerced discourse in the case of Jurgen Habermas. It may be the case that on the average it is easier to find truth if inquiry is uncoerced. But that is not always true. Try reasoning with a sadistic psychopath or someone who refuses to look at evidence unless forced to. And sometimes the evidence would be so misleading that ordinary people, who do not share a background that would place the evidence in proper context, would be able to accept the truth only if evidence that they would misinterpret is withheld from them.

The determination of when it is better for inquiry to be free cannot be made in the absence of other criteria. It may be true that political decisions, particularly in contemporary modern societies, are accorded greater legitimacy when all affected interests are consulted. But the criteria that determine application of this rule are not in turn determined by it.

Let us move from a discussion of the objectivity of the good to the objectivity of justice. Justice—in a simplified and preliminary sense—involves giving everyone his due. What this due is will differ from society to society. The same process of assessment that enables us to critique conceptions of the good also permits us to critique conceptions of justice. I discuss this elsewhere under the rubric of the "test in principle."

The Matrix of Knowledge

Languages, logics, beliefs concerning science and the philosophy of science, and our notions of good things and justice all develop out of a historically conditioned matrix. The idea of pure reason, which lay behind the French Revolution, is nonsense. Any attempt to jettison entirely the received store of knowledge can lead only to chaos.

Traditions are important buttresses for the assimilation of eufunctional change in society. And because the web of interrelationships is densely connected, the weight of tradition is not to be jettisoned easily or quickly. In the absence of catastrophic necessity, it is important to change slowly to provide time for assimilation and understanding.

Morality and ethics are not disembodied, abstract subjects. Their subject matter is concrete. They apply to particular kinds of beings in particular kinds of environments and with particular historical experiences and understandings. Marx's concrete universal "man" is an aberration that is detached from every quality that makes a person concretely human. Marxian man has no history, no ancestry, no individual human wishes, no particular physical characteristics or personality. He is a myth who can never have real existence, for he exists only as a denatured concept in the mind of Marx. The humans of Rawls, Nozick, and Gewirth are equally denatured.

Human Nature and Moral Inquiry

What does it mean to argue, as I do, that moral inquiry must be related to a conception of human nature? It does not mean that we can derive a prescription for a good society from knowledge of human nature. But then we cannot derive a prescription for a good bridge from the laws of physics, even though, unlike human nature, the nature of macrophysics is only peripherally dispositional. It does mean that the approaches of philosophers such as John Rawls and Robert Nozick, who devise schemes of ethics that are unrelated to either more general or more specific and dispositional accounts of human nature, are doomed to irrelevance except in highly special circumstances. But then we cannot build a theory of physics unless we have some conception of the character of the forces or elements of physics.

There is a thesis that nature is selfish and disposed to self-reproduction. That is an oversimplification that reifies particular boundary conditions. It treats gene pools in virtually the same noncontextual way that was criticized earlier in the discussion of colors and goods.

The gene pool will vary with the ecological niche and chance factors. Moreover, one could as easily argue that mutational evolution, which involves changes in the gene pool, is natural and, hence, that there are altruistic tendencies toward evolution inherent in every gene pool. All gene pools are in process. They are dispositional and shift under changing conditions. The task of analysis is to make sense of this complex natural process.

It is obvious on purely evolutionary grounds that early social systems could not have survived if the individual members never placed the survival of the group over that of the individual. Therefore, some degree of group bonding, particularly within the family, must have played a role in selection. The great advantage of decentralized decision making most likely would have inhibited the selection of individuals who always subordinated the individual to the group. In fact, this does not occur in so-called primitive systems but usually requires a large society in which centralized control over a monopolized energy source is possible.

Thus, although unusual circumstances could make either authoritarian control or virtually anarchic behavior temporarily advantageous, societies would be well advised in most cases to avoid either extreme. Even during the period of absolute monarchy in Great Britain, the commercial and industrial orders were left substantially free of regulation. That did not occur in France, and industrial development in France suffered greatly.

Our knowledge of sociobiology, as contrasted with that of physics, is so limited that speaking about the constraints that nature places on political, social, and moral systems has authority only in extremely limited ways. Most responsive behavior is over-determined by contextual historical factors. We know that we need the assurance of relatively unconditional support in some areas of life and yet require the freedom to explore and differ. Probably much of our myth and fantasy life—and our receptivity to it—responds to a generalized preconscious coding. But this puts very few constraints on evaluation until we are in a position to judge the "fit" between our needs, more narrowly expressed, and a variety of institutional modifications.

We know that there are different somatotypes and that these somatotypes tend to produce individuals of different dispositions. One of the advantages of modern society, along with concomitant disadvantages, is the complexity that provides opportunities for those of different psychological dispositions. I have watched a litter of cats from birth and observed traits in the exit from the womb that persisted through life.

Although humans may differ in the strength of their competitive behaviors because of genetic differences, there is no such thing as an inherent store of aggressive instinct. There instead are predispositions that are activated under a variety of circumstances and dampened under others. Life circumstances, experience, social arrangements including the roles particular individuals play, and culture have crucial roles in arousing various forms of active and passive behavior. Thus, no deductions can be made from relatively unstructured social behavior to activities invoked by complex social structures.

The difficulty of speaking with authority on the relationships between nature, human nature, and society does not rule out reasoned speculation about some serious contemporary controversies. We know that humans have great adaptability and that they may differ in their predispositions to respond to certain kinds of situations. Yet great plasticity does not mean infinite malleability. Humans have a great capacity for autonomy, and this is supportive of liberal democracy. Yet many contemporary individuals have made the mistake of divorcing the concept of autonomy from that of transstable character, which can maintain a firm sense of identity throughout external change, and of identifying it with the pursuit of transient pleasures, to the detriment of character and a sense of identity. Our minds, as in the case of the compulsive loser, may lead us into dangerous bypaths, particularly if we resort to abstract thinking, whether individualistic or collectivistic.

Democracy and Contemporary Society

If we wish to inquire into the appropriateness of democratic institutions in contemporary society, we need to inquire into those characteristics of individuals and society, both in general and in particular, that make democracy an appropriate solution to the problems that we face. If there were genuine and vast biological differences in the intelligence of individuals, democratic government would be questionable, although not necessarily ruled out. Even if the differences in intelligence were the consequence of differences in life chances, similar conclusions might follow.

I do not think differences in biological intelligence are a key factor in actuality. There are individuals with astronomical IQs whose practical judgment I would not trust for a moment. There are others with modest IQs whose judgmental ability is outstanding. On the other hand, the decline in practical intelligence, and even more in knowledge, that is resulting from contemporary schooling could become inconsistent with democracy particularly as we head into an age in which skills become much more important than they are even now in job holding and in political judgment. It is perhaps ironic, although not surprising, that the decline in educational standards has coincided with its most egalitarian, and thus democratic, extension. The highly skilled teachers who were available for the elite in a relatively primitive economy have not been reproduced in a mass educational system and an industrial economy.

Democracy depends upon the relative equality of skills and judgment in individuals, for, in its absence, democracy will not work; and, in its presence, nothing else will be accepted failing the myth of selection by God or control of a scientific theory of history. Democracy is supported by the potential for autonomy of individuals, by the great efficiency of decentralized decision making, and by the ability of people to "throw the rascals out" when they are judged to have failed. The historical development of empathy from tribe to ethnic group to nation supports the extension of democracy to previously excluded groups that reside within the state, and perhaps beyond it.

The Market and Liberal Democracy

In an age in which the superiority of the market over planned economics and the relationship of a decentralized economic system to political democracy are generally accepted, it still would be a mistake to regard market decisions as invariably desirable. Friedrich Hayek and Antony de Jasay have made a powerful but overstated case for market methods.

For instance, I disagree with the evolutionary case Hayek makes in *The Fatal Conceit: The Errors of Socialism* for what he calls the extended order, the market.[1] I do not agree that the distinction between "mine" and "thine" is entirely an externally imposed constraint that is foreign to animals. My dog may beg from my plate, but he will not take from it. However, if I take something from his plate, he jumps at me and takes it back. The well-known phenomenon of territoriality is one aspect of animal recognition of the difference between mine and thine.

The forms within which self-centered and other-centered activities occur are learned—and they do evolve over time—but the distinction has been built into our nature by evolution. Although the infant has no clear recognition of self and others, it is as predispositionally disposed to learn these distinctions during maturation as it is to learn how to walk. Furthermore, every successful culture must satisfy the need for both the *gemeinschaft* and *gesellschaft* aspects of human nature.

Hayek is so impressed by the productive power of the market that he believes conceptions of justice are destructive. But we would not want laws that increased the conviction of innocent people, tax evasion, or starvation among the poor. A society so radically unfair would lose its legitimacy.

Although an effort generally to pay people according to nonmarket evaluations of their worth would undermine productivity, it does not follow that no considerations of justice or aesthetics should ever be applied. Italy's subsidization of the opera is not indefensible. Private and public donations to universities may produce an amount of human capital that improves society as well as individual lives when other mechanisms to produce similar results at this early stage of life are absent.

The market does not really maximize, or even optimize, goods because it is constrained by the mechanisms of choice. An individual who would otherwise play his high-fidelity equipment loudly may still prefer an ordinance that forbids this. Perhaps Gresham's law applies to atomized tastes. The state of television might be used to support the conclusion that bad taste drives out good taste. If so, carefully considered support for countervailing tendencies would make good sense. The fact that legislatures and award committees often make us regret these choices does not mean that we should never make them.

I also differ with Hayek on the subject of planning. If by planning he means rationality of the type sponsored by the French philosophes—which attempts to plan an entire society on the basis of a few definitions and axioms—then, of course, it will fail. If, however, we think of rational planning as assessment, as I use that term, then it can work, although any particular plan may fail. Although the danger may have been exaggerated, society needs a plan to prevent ecological disaster. The recent report (April 10, 1991) of the National Academy of Sciences on global warming is germane. Furthermore, European planning of urban growth and mass transit has produced cleaner, more livable, and more accessible cities than in the United States.

De Jasay has shown brilliantly how vacuous the concept of freedom is when it is discussed in its generality rather than in terms of specific freedoms and the tradeoffs they involve.[2] However, his defense of unimpeded contract suffers from the fact that he treats the concepts of justice and social goods as abstractly as others treat the concept of freedom.

If the market continues to produce an underclass that is uneducable by current techniques, then I would not want to live in a society that did not raise tax money in an effort to correct this. If individual contract produces a plenitude of highly visible porno shops and movies in the heart of New York City and Washington, DC, then I want government to do something about it. If freedom of contract has produced a decadent atmosphere in our national capitals, it has deprived me of the freedom to walk with pride in the center of those cities.

I do not apologize for being prepared to limit the freedom of those who turn the national capital into a pigsty. Even if we knew how to add freedoms and to calculate them—and there is no way to do this—and even if counterfactually there were no tradeoffs among them, the qualitative determination of which freedoms to facilitate would take precedence over an abstract analysis of the problem of freedom.

New York recently passed a law outlawing the use of midgets as bowling balls. The columnist Mike Royko took the position that if midgets, who, like the rest of us, had to eat , liked earning $2,000 a week by impersonating bowling balls, they should have the right to do so. This is not an unreasonable argument. If we could know that this would occur only in a few cases in remote areas, I perhaps would agree. But widespread activity of this type would run the risk of desensitizing us to the rights of all humans, including deformed and crippled humans.

There is no doctrinaire solution to this problem. Some might try to outlaw ethnic jokes or irreverent remarks. Both the absence of limits and an abundance of limits can be dangerous to liberal democracy and human autonomy. There is no neutral framework and no substitute for good sense. My own preference would be to err on the side of liberality. But I would not raise this to high principle.

De Jasay suggests that we have to choose between the socialist principle that society distributes goods and the market or contractual mode of distribution. That is too general. We can choose between the areas in which we want the market to operate and the areas in which we want some other principle to predominate. Food stamps or the distribution of surplus goods to the poor may be quite defensible choices.

We do not have to choose between a level playing field for individuals and that which the market produces, as de Jasay states, because society can decide to restructure the field when imbalances produced by the market begin to offend our sense of what is just, of what is politically feasible, or of what is socially desirable. In any event, the actual playing field is highly imperfect and never entirely neutral. The belief that previous defects will repeat themselves is overstated, although new defects may be expected. It is not unreasonable to expect the political system to compensate periodically for the imperfections and biases of the playing field. On the other hand, it is important to exercise great care in deciding how to accomplish this. And de Jasay, of course, is correct when he warns against extending socialist principles to the process of the production of material goods.

Unlike Rawls, I do not object to the benefits that stem from luck, whether it is a matter of genes or land of birth. It is part of our human heritage, part of our concrete reality. And it is up to us whether we make use of it. On the other hand, I am collecting rent from those who came before me and from Dame Fortune. I do not have to choose between keeping all the benefits provided by good fortune or giving up all of them. Decency requires that I recognize a moral obligation to others, including those who follow. If I am unwilling voluntarily to respond to this obligation, and if too many others join me in this refusal, then others have the moral right, even the moral duty, legislatively to compel us.

Thus, although I am fearful of easy invocations of concepts of social redistribution and aware of many of their deadly results, I fail to see that all redistributions are undesirable. A purely contractual society, whatever its other defects, would so deprive us of the deep need for membership in collectivities that it would be as self-destructive as a socialist society. Moreover, the discontent the acute perception of injustice would foster would provide ambit for demagogy.

The Weaknesses of Democracy

Democracy has its weaknesses. It is slow to respond to crises. Often it requires violence before great injustices are responded to. The racial question in the United States is an example of this. Policies are often determined by veto groups at great expense for the polity. Fortunately for the defense of democracy, Leninist regimes are not good at this either. Not only did Gorbachev experience severe difficulty in imposing perestroika in the Soviet economy, but it took a severe crisis—the threat that the Soviet Union's economy would degenerate to a Third World level—belatedly to produce Gorbachev's early reforms. And his efforts hit a dead end even before the unsuccessful coup.

Democracy appears to be a cultural failure in the United States. It does not take extensive inquiry into television, the movies, newspapers, novels, or even contemporary social science to document this conclusion. On the other hand, we may be in a developmental trough. American food, for instance, became homogenized in the postwar era as a consequence of economic efficiencies. However, we are now seeing a recrudescence of specialty stores, as the efficiencies that made food and other products cheap produced the wealth that creates demand for better products. One may hope that a similar process will occur with respect to the other features of life where higher standards are required for democratic systems to work well.

Liberal Democracy

Liberal democracy, in the older and more legitimate sense of liberal, implies a form of majority rule constrained by the values of liberty or freedom. The older English and Scottish philosophers were inclined to think of freedom negatively, that is, as absence of external constraint. This had some justification, for Rousseauian concepts of forcing people to be free raised the specter of authoritarian government.

Yet the distinction between positive and negative freedoms depends entirely on frame of reference. We are not free to float as butterflies because we do not possess wings. If we are born without legs, or if they are bound, we are not free to walk. If we are abandoned at birth to the care of animals, we are not free to talk or even to think in ways that require certain kinds of concepts. And every facilitation that permits certain kinds of freedoms inhibits others. The marvelous structure that permits a bird to fly prevents it from moving the huge loads that a pachyderm can move.

Negative and positive concepts of freedom are bound together in an inextricable symbiosis. It is dangerous to apply either abstractly rather than in historical and comparative context. One is not free to make rational decisions if under the influence of drugs. One is not free to be a concert violinist except under conditions of strenuous study and practice. One is not free to behave morally unless there are internalized constraints on the pursuit of individual wants. One is not free to live at peace unless the police constrain criminals.

Both concepts of freedom are dangerous when treated abstractly. Freedom can be used to destroy freedom even when external constraints are not imposed on individuals. One of the possible dangers in the legalization of hard drugs is that the legitimation of drug taking may erode the cultural constraints that limit it. The concept of those things that injure others and those that do not is dangerously misleading when taken abstractly, for it fails to recognize the consequences of social legitimation and example.

The abstract rejoinder that we should be independent enough to make our own decisions—apart from its failure to understand that impressionable children are members of society—responds to a real problem with an ideal type that few, if any, individuals match. It ignores the process of socialization and of how the concept of the self is formed. And it substitutes for the complex self—a self that is not a simple or fixed process, let alone a thing—a doctrinaire and abstract concept.

Every proper concept of freedom develops in a historical matrix that limits its application through cultural standards that constrain what is meant by freedom and also what is meant by "human." Surely a future in which we would be linked voluntarily to pleasure machines that constantly entertained us, stimulated our pleasure centers, and fed us would not now be regarded as human. The freedom I want is the freedom to be human.

It is the rapid extension of the concept of freedom that threatens freedom by threatening the matrix within which it has appropriate meaning. And it could be the "slippery slope" extension of the concept that could take us to the point of cultural "no return."

The Ends of Society and Polity

Every political system, and every society, ought to be evaluated according to the types of human beings who are sustained by it. Slaves and members of a permanent underclass are turned into inferior human beings. The types of polities and societies that increase their incidence are unjustifiable if alternatives exist. Greek and Roman society at least encouraged the education and manumission of slaves, whereas the American underclass seems to be self-reinforcing. Perhaps smallness of human spirit, the pursuit of transient pleasures to the neglect of enduring character, bureaucratic self-protectiveness, dishonesty, and neglect of wider human interests are inevitable by-products of any social organization, but their incidence in contemporary American society and politics is deplorable.

The degrees of intelligence, moral understanding, and human sensitivity fostered are among the most important factors in judging a society. Economic productivity, although essential, is only a means to these ends. The degrees of selfishness, dishonesty, and addiction to drugs and transient pleasures in American society today stand strongly against the United States as a long-term exemplar, despite its clear advantages over contemporary alternative types of government and society. It cannot be true that with the resources available to us we are unable to do better than this. The belief that history has ended, that the superiority of our present system is self-evident, is dangerously wrong. Even apart from the problems that technology will present to us—and that I shall discuss shortly—satisfaction with American society and politics is uncalled for, however much we may applaud the demonstrated inferiority of totalitarian, authoritarian, and centrally planned alternatives.

Legitimacy and Democracy

Legitimacy is a key concept for political systems, and it has not been well served by the definitions of Max Weber and David Easton. To say that the political system possesses a monopoly of legitimate force or that it authoritatively allocates values at best is truistic because the key terms *legitimate* and *authoritatively* contain the essential material.

The political system (that is, the political subsystem in society) is the government. The scope of its authority depends upon its legitimacy in various circumstances. It has authority to the extent that its prescriptions will be obeyed. It has legitimacy, either in general or in particular, to the extent that such obedience is regarded as rightful.

The key to understanding the political is to understand legitimation. There are three levels at which this subject can be understood. The first is that of the mythical observer from Mars. If he looks at the actual behavior of people and if they obey established authorities, he might assert a concordance between the actual behavior of people and the legitimacy of government that, at least at this level, makes clear what is meant by a monopoly of legitimate force or an authoritative allocation of values.

But this would miss important elements of legitimacy. It is also necessary to investigate the mental states of people, for this gives a clue to what they might do under different conditions. If they see the authority structure as effective in maintaining control, as governing in accordance with reasonable rules of justice, as coping reasonably well with disturbing influences in the environment, and as not grossly inconsistent with their interests, they will tend to view it as legitimate. What will be regarded as such, however, depends on the backgrounds of those making the judgments. For instance, few doubted the divine right of kings at the time of Louis XIV, but many Frenchmen doubted it at the time of Louis XVI.

If we left the discussion there, it would lack an important dimension. One would be left in a relativist or historicist position in which all judgments are made in light of a parochial setting. There is, however, a reflexive process of thought—the "test in principle"—that can be applied to the subject of legitimacy and that takes into account comparative knowledge of both the system under analysis and the broad sweep of human history. This range of knowledge can include human nature, social science, judgments about environmental possibilities, procedures, justice, and so on. If the political system is adequately responsive within the framework of such an examination, it retains its legitimacy, and citizens have an obligation to support it because of their interest in good ends. Even when it fails this test to some extent, it may call upon obligatory, if limited, support if it can be replaced only at great cost.

The thesis that history has ended with the current forms of polity and society fails at this third level of analysis. Although contemporary American society and polity warrant unselfish support against external threats under contemporary forms of organization, this support should not exclude an active search for superior conditions. Although the society and polity toward which we move may retain important elements of pluralism and market, their context likely will be substantially different.

This third level of legitimacy invokes one of the key concepts of liberal democracy: individual autonomy. One of the most important functions of liberal democracy is to assure the autonomy of the individual in making political and moral choices. It is the possibility of autonomy that makes freedom valuable.

However, one of the crucial and sad defects of contemporary democracy lies in the identification of autonomy with the pursuit of transient desires rather than with the type of transstable character that makes moral and political judgments reflexively and with appropriate consideration of responsibility toward others. It is this type of responsible behavior to which Aristotle referred when he spoke of the pursuit of happiness, not transient pleasures.

Please note that nothing has been said about the political system's embodying the will of the people. Its legitimacy stems from its achieving reasonably good ends by reasonably good means and from its accountability in democracies if it fails to do so. The intellectual puzzle posed by the Arrow paradox of the agenda order—in which no unique solution is available to maximize the joint preferences of individuals—is of interest only if one believes both that political decisions should express in some maximal way the will of the people and that preference orders are transitive both for groups and individuals.

The first proposition is uninteresting except to mathematical economists, who are more interested in intellectual puzzles than in realworld problems. No one could engage in the calculations required to determine what the maximal will of the people is with respect to a particular legislative proposition. Moreover, it could be formulated in so many different ways that no determination could be made with respect to maximal consequences, even apart from wills. The second proposition is incorrect.

Even for individuals, let alone for groups, preferences are too context dependent for transitivity to hold. Ross Ashby provided an amusing illustration of this. An Englishman went on vacation without his wife. He went to the post office to send her a cheap telegram. The clerk said there were two choices: "Having a wonderful time" and "Wish you were here." The man said, "Send 'Wish you were here.'" The clerk then remembered a third choice: "Please join me at once." The man said, "Send 'Having a wonderful time.'"

If one took seriously the assumptions underlying Arrow's analysis, it would follow that any law that maximized collective preferences should be obeyed. Why, however, should an American Indian who desires a tribal life take obligation to the American polity seriously, apart from the penalty that might be invoked? The right of the American Indian to vote and to take part in the political process in ways fully equal to all other members of society may be entirely beside the point if the Indian identifies with tribal society and not with American society. To use as a metaphor the clock paradox of relativity theory, these Indians and ordinary Americans may be on different inertial paths.

If this is so, it follows neither that the Indian has an obligation to recognize the legitimacy of the American government nor that the government has an obligation to recognize his right to rebellion. Although moral individuals will search for some acceptable compromise if different legitimate considerations are at stake, war is sometimes the only solution to otherwise insoluble problems.

There are multiple identifications in contemporary society. One identifies with oneself, one's family, one's ethnic or religious group, one's nation, humankind, the animal kingdom, and so forth. Which of these identifications takes primacy cannot be determined in the abstract. Such examinations can be agonizing and often, because of the looseness of the web of considerations, inconclusive.

There is a huge potential for tragedy in such conflicts. If justice were purely abstract—if justice were a system for ghostly humans without particular characteristics and histories—if the world were only strongly ordered, then there would be an identical answer for all questions and only bad, evil, ignorant, or stupid people would fail to accept it.

Humans working through history grind these tragedies out of existence or submerge them by superior force. Tribal society cannot be restored meaningfully for the Indians, for the tribe within the United States, and the life and culture within it, are poor and dysfunctional substitutes for what tribal life was before Europeans occupied the land. Few of us would be willing to agree to end the existence of the United States even while empathizing with the tragedy of the Indian and regretting the inability or unwillingness of many Indians to assimilate. But the democratic procedures of American society are neither a solvent nor, from the Indian frame of reference, a justification.

The Future and Democracy

The current democratic systems and their social, cultural, and technological environments are the matrix out of which future political systems will arise. Their unfolding surely will create tragedies for some individuals and groups--tragedies that cannot be justified from their frame of reference—and perhaps tragedies for all if we fail to apprehend and respond to some of the unfortunate, or perhaps even evil, potentialities that are present in the contemporary matrix.

It is not difficult to project a desperate future if some tendencies in contemporary society continue to grow. The functional illiteracy of vast numbers of Americans and their inability to perform at the simplest levels of skills is frightening. The declining number of Americans with skills in mathematics, the sciences, and engineering raises serious questions with respect to the continued health of the American economic system. The growth of crime and dishonesty at all levels of American society is extremely troubling. These problems could give rise to waves of discontent that could be exploited by demagogues. The low level of discourse in the last presidential campaign provides a hint of how far we can decline.

Let us examine a few of the technological developments likely to emerge in the first half of the next century and briefly examine how they can affect the prospects of our value system and also of democratic government. Manufacturing will be largely automated and robotic. There will be few workers in factories, and these will be highly skilled technicians, professional people, and managers. The molecular basis of materials will be understood, and materials will be produced to order. Power—solar or perhaps fusion—will provide cheap energy. The genome will be fully mapped, and microsurgery will permit the elimination of unwanted characteristics and the substitution of those wanted. Chemical enhancement of learning will be achieved. (It is important to understand that this will have only marginal value in the absence of sustaining cultural and social conditions.) The chemical and electronic control of behavior will become possible.

Universal surveillance will be easy. Both visual and auditory means will be light years more efficient than any devices now available. The major problem that has always impeded intelligence organizations—the massiveness of the data base—will be overcome by cheap supercomputers that utilize enormously efficient scanning programs that select key terms from the stream of information in which they are embodied and that interpret them.

It should be clear even from this brief selection of items that the means will be at hand to produce a relative utopia or a "Brave New World." It is fortunate, indeed, that the Soviet system entered its crisis in the contemporary world rather than in this world. But it does not follow that either we or they will escape the disastrous possibilities that are pregnant in the contemporary matrix.

How many in Washington, let alone in Beijing, could be trusted to solve these problems in a humane way if they had the opportunity to solve them in ways that perpetuated their rule and their perquisites? Are the values placed on the sanctity of human life, values beyond the state (God for many), respect, concern and empathy for others, honesty, and humility so strong in contemporary society that the survival of democratic institutions is assured?

I am an optimist, despite the weight of evidence to the contrary, but surely it is time to anticipate these developments. The institutions that should be in the forefront of these examinations, the universities, are particularly deficient in their attention to them. They are caught up in the race of specialization. The linkage between realms of knowledge that makes for civilized discourse and understanding is neglected and devalued.

Even apart from these problems, how will humans convince themselves of their value sufficiently to preserve decency, let alone democracy? As computers begin to mimic reason more successfully, the distinctions between humans and machines may seem smaller. Substitute parts for the body will be manufactured, again diminishing our sense of uniqueness. Some will argue for genetic adaptation to different environments—the sea for instance. Once we start, where will we stop? Will we begin to adapt humans to particular tasks?

What will individuals do with their lives to make them fulfilling? Most work, both blue and white collar, will be done by machines. How much service work will be left? How many can write novels, paint pictures, or compose music? (And perhaps the computers will do many of these things also.) What vocation will give life its value?

If computers begin to mimic intelligence, if individuals are adapted to different environments, if they are improved by prosthetic devices, if robots begin to perform more skilled tasks, how will this affect the self-conception and identification of humans? Will it undermine their sense of uniqueness and the humane qualities of life that are essential to liberal democracy? Or will it lead to greater sensitivity?

We have the myth that if only we can solve life's material problems—if only we can abolish hunger, sickness, and inadequate living conditions—we can create a utopia. But that may create only worse problems. Men used to get satisfaction from unskilled jobs because that provided for the family. Women received satisfaction from the important task of raising children. Both men and women seem less satisfied and more alienated in contemporary society.

Ambition will not vanish. It may get more intense primarily because the number of avenues through which it can be fulfilled are diminished. To what psychological dysfunctions will this give rise? To what political perversions?

Perhaps the reader may feel that I have vastly overstated the case. My optimistic side is inclined to agree with this evaluation. If there is an excuse for this exercise, it is to indicate that we should not be complacent in our defense of democracy.

Still, the future of liberal democracy is not secure. It is important to understand that liberal (in an older sense of the term) democratic institutions, which for the first time in human history make dignity a possibility for all humans, need intelligent defense if they are to survive and flourish through the next century.

There are many contemporary problems urgently in need of solution. The educational problem and that of moral values surely are among the most important. But other problems that could be even more serious may emerge before we become aware of them. It is good that contemporary society has set up committees of experts to discuss the ethical issues in such matters as gene splicing. We need to go beyond this, however. We need to examine how possible future developments may affect the solutions we institutionalize today. And we need to ask how these solutions today and in the future will affect the larger sets of values and institutions of society.

Many of these speculations will be incorrect. Surprises surely will be in store for us. Even so, I would argue that the comparative evaluations provided by speculation about the future, even if wrong, will open up ethical evaluation to a wider and more desirable range of considerations.

Notes

[1]Friedrich A. Hayek, The *Fatal Conceit: The Errors of Socialism,* ed. Robert Bartley (Chicago: University of Chicago Press, 1989).

[2]Antony de Jasay, "The Bitter Medicine of Freedom," *The Balance of Freedom,* ed. Roger Michener (New York: Paragon House, 1992).

PART FOUR

A SOCIOLOGICAL PERSPECTIVE

CHAPTER 10

THE RIGHT TO BE LEFT ALONE IS THE RIGHT TO BE NO ONE

Morton A. Kaplan

U nless sharply qualified, both Hobbesian and Millsian individualism are threats to a good society. Although it is surely more
benign than the Hobbesian alternative, the Millsian concept that the
individual should be free to do whatever does not directly harm others—the so-called right to be left alone—also is not without its dangers for liberal democracy. This "right," when expressed abstractly,
fails to take proper account of the nature of human personality and
social identity.

The "right to be left alone" with respect to social and moral matters is a very popular position, particularly with the intelligentsia.
Although the Supreme Court, in its decision on the use of contra-
ceptives *(Griswold v. Connecticut)*, defended privacy only in this particular matter, it moved to an acknowledged generalized defense of
privacy. The doctrine of privacy, however, is counterproductive as a
generalized doctrine, a fault that can be attributed to its abstract
treatment of freedom of choice. It fails to come to terms with the
complex interrelationships between self and society that make the
concept of individual choice meaningful. Hence, rather than sup-
porting, it undermines, and in extremis would dissolve, that individual autonomy and human freedom it attempts to serve. In effect,
it would serve no one, for the self—the subject of ethical discourse
that freedom serves—would be minimized.

The doctrine of the "right to be left alone" is dangerously seduc-
tive because we tend to restrict our attention to the many instances
of freedom of choice that enhance human life in our society. There
are clear and convincing reasons to support the "right to be left alone"

within some limits, and those limits are less restrictive in a pluralistic society such as ours than in a more culturally homogeneous society.

The rules that governed a more parochial America—for instance, the criminal law under which a Wisconsin married woman was recently convicted of adultery—cannot be imposed without social warfare on contemporary Americans. Because such rules remain important to such important institutions as the family, we must rely on social sanctions to preserve institutional strength. However, we threaten these and other vital institutions gravely if we transform the "right to be left alone" into a generalized constitutional doctrine.

The Millsian doctrine that we should be free to do those things that do not harm others fails to do justice to how identifications and conceptions of self develop within societies, and it misunderstands how the human mind works in solving problems. Because Mill misunderstood these processes, he also failed to understand that the generalization of the right of privacy—in his terms, the right to do anything that does not harm others—is destructive of the very values it is designed to implement.

In making my argument, I shall neglect some obvious cases of harm to others that arise under the doctrine. Excessive drinking or smoking and the taking of mind-altering drugs, for instance, impose large costs on society in terms of medical bills and lost productivity. But these costs are not the most important ones. They pale into insignificance when weighed against other costs imposed by the actual ways in which human minds work.

The Millsian doctrine is severely flawed with respect to its implicit account of the ways in which the human mind works. The utilitarian thesis—even apart from its question-begging concept of utility—assumed that the mind was some sort of calculating machine: Correctly adjusted, it could make the calculations required for a utilitarian determination. However, the mind is a complex and dynamic interpretive system that depends, for adequate functioning, upon its balancing of complementary but conflicting interpretive schemas, each of which becomes dysfunctional and pathological if used excessively. Rule following and adjustment to circumstances are the two interpretive orientations or perspectives that play a primary role in the operations of mind that are relevant to the following discussion.

The conflicts among considerations that affect human choices are inherent even in the simplest of systems that invoke more than one goal orientation. Air-raid warning systems, for instance, must meet only two simple requirements: they must give notice of raids, and they should not be subject to false alarms.

However, there is no simple or perfect way to balance between these considerations. A system that never was subject to false alarms would fail to report many air raids. An alarm system that would report all raids would give many false alarms. Thus, a system compromise that does not follow from a unique and clear criterion is necessary. It should provide some reasonable mix of the two considerations. This is even more true of more complex systems with more complex requirements, such as social and personality systems. No single principle can be generalized or absolutized without significant harm to society and the individuals who are members of it. And no unique criterion can determine the weight to be given to the considerations.

I have examined these matters elsewhere from both an ontological and a cybernetic point of view.[1] The categories of pathology most relevant to the discussion that follows are the compulsive/obsessive, which depends upon rigid adherence to strict rules, and the hysteric, which loses itself in the needs of the moment. Mental dysfunctions occur when minds tip too far in the direction either of rule following or adjustment to circumstances.

There is no such thing as a veridical path that is distinct from some balancing of rules and the desires that are related to specific circumstances. External social constraints and internal inhibitions are the complements to the enticements and opportunities that social structure, personality, and environment provide. They are required to diminish the likelihood of pathology and to preserve the integrity of the self that makes choices.

The Japanese culture is shame-oriented. It permits a strong sense of identification but submerges the individual within the group. The nineteenth-century American culture was guilt-oriented. As long as there was a hegemonic culture, it permitted a strong sense of identity that was consistent with considerable freedom for individual variance where key cultural values were not involved.

Difficult problems arose when the American culture became

pluralistic because of inconsistencies between the frames of reference of different social groupings. Transstable personalities are able to maintain a strong sense of identity in pluralistic cultures by adjusting expectations and behavior to different settings.[2] But there are few transstable personalities. And there is a tendency, which has become increasingly manifest in contemporary American culture, to invoke a doctrine of freedom of choice, regardless of the setting in which one finds oneself, that is responsive to the idiosyncratic needs of an isolated self. This can be inhibited only by an appropriate balance of internal and external constraints.

The deleterious transformations that are occurring in the American culture are supported by two concepts that are inherent in the Millsian doctrine and that are widely believed. The Millsian doctrine assumes that individuals can make choices that do not change the choices that others face; hence, that they are cost free to others if they do not directly harm them. It also assumes that the chooser is not changed by the choices that are made. Neither is the case.

It was no accident that Spartan nobles wanted to be warriors, that Dutch burghers developed bourgeois values, that contemporary children present their parents with what their peers do and get as justifiable grounds for their own demands, or that few would consider wearing a banner denouncing religion in a church. In the society in which we are acculturated, a fairly stable set of values and expectations plays a major role in the formation of our self and of its sense of identity. That self and its sense of identity provide the framework within which choices can be reasoned about, and this provides the foundation for our human freedom.

When change occurs, the meanings attached to choice also change and operate with uncertainty. Is bowing to a superior a sign of respect or one of self-denigration? If the former is the case, bowing does not decrease self-esteem. However, if a Japanese rejected this cultural value and did not bow, he preserved his self-esteem only at the cost of hurting his superior's self-esteem. When a culture is in flux, the meanings of transactions become uncertain and harm cannot be avoided.

When the cultural guideposts change rapidly, anarchy rather than reasoned choice is more likely. The conceptions of self that guide choice become increasingly uncertain. This is even more true of children, who are easily influenced by the practices that they observe or read about, than it is of adults. If rapid change is accompanied by the idea of the "right to be left alone," it would not be surprising if many adults, let alone children, believe there are no unacceptable social limits.

Some meanings are in flux in any complex society, but there is some limit beyond which changes in meanings call into question the social arrangements that make a body of consistent meanings possible. However, reasonably consistent meanings are integral to the sense and identification of the self and, hence, of its autonomy and freedom. Identity weakens and choice begins to relate to a less definite individual when the structure of meanings that provides context for individual meanings weakens.

Every society, even the simplest, requires sets of understood rules that underlie expectations. When a wolf loses in combat to another wolf, it saves its life by lying supine and permitting the other wolf to urinate on it. If not hard-wired, this agonistic behavior is close to such. Humans have much greater flexibility, but even modern man has taboos.

For instance, we could use the flesh from nondiseased recently dead humans to feed starving people, but an effective taboo operates to prevent this. Is that taboo irrational? Perhaps. But then again, perhaps it sustains, or at least helps to sustain, other important inhibitions in the treatment of fellow humans. It would be a serious mistake to test this possibility except, perhaps, under the hardest circumstances. We cannot reason about it abstractly and in isolation from the web of understandings that underpins the culture without gravely distorting or rendering senseless the conclusions we reach.

From birth to death the individual develops a sense of self as it interacts with others who provide support and constraint. Both constraint and support are required if the self is to have coherence through time and, hence, to be a focus for decisions that respond to more than transient pressures.

These supports and constraints transform potentially dangerous and antisocial impulses by constructing a web of sentiments and understandings that focus behavior. The supports provide assurance that one is not alone and that mutual expectations characterize one's society. They permit the postponement of pleasure in favor of longer term goals and provide incentives to take into account the needs of others. The constraints promise sanctions of various kinds if one does not respond positively to the socially appropriate expectations of others. It is this complex of supports; and constraints that sets the cultural terms for what freedom means for individuals in a particular kind of society.

Later Roman society was decadent. Its elites gorged themselves with food and vomited to eat still more. One of the purposes of the training at West Point is to develop in cadets a sense of self that excludes the sybaritic life. The function of an army is to be ready to defend the nation. It is not desirable to have generals who, by indulging themselves, display a lack of that self-discipline that is essential in combat. Even if a particular general is an exception to this generalization, acceptance of such conduct might legitimate this and other behaviors that would erode the fighting quality of the armed forces.

Civil society is not an army, and the narrow standards that apply in armies are inappropriate for civil society, particularly if it is pluralistic. But it does not follow from this that no limits apply, even if behavior does not directly and immediately harm others. There is a limit beyond which the absence of agreed standards would defeat attempts to develop coherent selves that are capable of making meaningful choices.

Foucault captures much support for his proposition that every culture exercises power over its members, and, hence, that their similarities in undermining freedom outweigh their differences. However, Foucault fails to understand that every freedom is supported by a corollary constraint. This is true even at the simplest level of mechanics. An object is not free to roll unless it is roundish in shape. An individual is not free to think rationally if under the influence of mind-altering substances. A concert artist is not free to perform at concert level except under the constraint of long hours of tedious practice.

The freedom of human beings depends upon cultural constraints. The meaning and worth of human freedom in a society are intimately related to the types of human beings nurtured by that society's internal and external constraints. Stating that American democracy nurtures better individuals and more freedom than a Nazi concentration camp would not seem worthwhile were it not for the confusion spread by Foucault. Few former Soviet intellectuals would have been taken in by his formulations.

On the other hand, the thesis that one should be "free to be left alone" arises from examining the possible consequences of a particular novel freedom from within the framework of a relatively stable world of expectations. It may be possible to accommodate a small number of new freedoms without harm or even with benefit, depending on their impact on the web of cultural meanings. Yet it is surely not possible to analyze or to accommodate the program "to be left alone" in whole or in large part, for that would be sufficient to invalidate the analysis or to disrupt the stable expectations that characterize any possible stable society.

The desire to be free of any constraint is not merely the desire to be free of any dominating society. It is, in effect, the desire to be free of any set of individual characteristics that might constitute being a human being. It is pure fancy to suggest, as Derrida did, that one would be well rid of the constraints of language or logic. These are minimal conditions for communication with oneself, let alone with others. That way lies madness, as Derrida himself suggested.

If the system of constraints and supports is evanescent very early in life, a sociopathic personality may result that is innocent of concern for others, or even of understanding of their reality. Such individuals probably lack the neuronic interconnections that are required for bonding to other individuals and moral behavior. The nonrational inhibitions that restrain most of us would not be present.

In addition to supports, even the most "normal" individuals require constraints in the form of social sanctions, in the absence of which they are most likely to lose their sense of appropriate limits. Dictators begin to lose their sense of reality at least in part because they are insulated from opposition and the need to test their views against those of others. Those who are less than the best, or who are faced with desperate circumstances, may be containable, if at all, only by the force of law. An open season for actions that do not directly harm others would contribute to personality dysfunctions with respect to behavior and morals by insulating individuals from the constraints that sustain our "normality."

The process by which one develops an identity and sense of self is one in which limits are tested. This is typical of, but not limited to, adolescent behavior. It serves two immediate functions: to learn what the limits are and to test the veracity of the declaratory beliefs of authority figures. It produces the dynamic and evolving framework of expectations that makes possible complex society and the identifications that fit particular societies. And the more complex and pluralistic the society, the more this process is lifelong.

A social system and a personality system that did not exclude some patterns of behavior—even if they did not injure others—would undermine the system of rules that are required for a good sense of identity. The literally infinite complexity of deciding each issue on its merits would founder when standards were absent. The infinity of considerations would overwhelm our ability to make reasoned decisions. Our choices would be unrelated to our individual sense of self, in the absence of which freedom of choice loses its importance.

If, for instance, every social rule—whether to bow to superiors, to dress for dinner, and so forth—was subject to personal calculation, society would be in danger of collapse. But that is the direction in which the Millsian doctrine pushes us. Not all the norms of a society can or should be sustained by law. But a system will optimize its functionality and the autonomy of its members only when law is supplemented by effective social sanctions. When important institutions seek to render reasonable limits ineffective, and they are supported rather than challenged by social elites, a time of trouble lies ahead for a society.

The rules that guide decisions constitute the data that define us, because we then are the kinds of individuals who behave in certain given ways in certain kinds of situations. For instance, we are not the kind of person who copies someone else's paper when a teacher turns his back. Such rules provide a matrix within which change can be assimilated and concepts of the self adjusted without loss of identity.

It is highly likely that many of the asocial and antisocial activities of the current period—including drugs and widespread dishonesty—are caused in part by the philosophy that underlies the concept of a generalized right of privacy. When standards erode to this point, the very conception of harm to others—or even the capability to conceive of it—will be seriously diminished.

For instance, at what point does consensual sadism weaken the barriers against nonconsensual sadism? Are pictures of bullwhips in anuses or adults urinating into each other's mouths, as in the Mapplethorpe exhibit, really harmless? Even if these activities occur behind private walls, the effects might become significant if it becomes widely known that they occur and are permissible. This is even more true if they win awards and are regarded highly. If one wanted to break down the minds of other individuals, would not a barrage of material of this type, or knowledge about it, be effective? What does it say of a society that so many of the elite defend or even stage such exhibits?

Moreover, continued experimentation of this kind is likely to break down the personalities of those who engage in these actions. The Marquis de Sade, apart from the harm he did to others, did harm to his own personality. He transformed it in dysfunctional ways by exercising his "freedom" of choice.

The Manson group was not a totally illegitimate offspring of this philosophy. The motto of the sixties was "the greening of America." "Doing one's own thing" was the new golden rule. Timothy Leary was telling us in Playboy magazine how taking drugs would raise us to a new level of consciousness at which we could perceive the flow of the individual atoms in our bodies. It is the generation of the sixties that is the greatest force behind the dysfunctional changes that are occurring in American society today. When the sense of identity is gone, people either pursue immediate wants or, to escape confusion and indecision, they turn themselves over to a leader who can reinforce his sense of power only by formulating more and more bizarre demands. If the Manson group was an extreme result of this philosophy, it was such only because other internalized and external constraints had not broken down as completely in other elements of society.

On the other hand, the conception that we can return to the stringent standards of the Anglo-Saxon culture of the nineteenth century ignores the pluralism and complexity of modern American society. The strains that such an austere standard would impose would rival, and possibly surpass, those of Prohibition. For reasons already stated, no perfect solution is possible because the requirements are incompatible. Therefore, some compromise solution is required.

As a person who likes to do things my own way, I am sympathetic to the concept of being "left alone." In the best society, internal inhibition would be the chief means for regulating individual conduct. I surely do not wish to see individuals reduced to creatures of either a state or society in which conformity to generalized mediocrity becomes the rule.

But we also need to recognize that voluntary inhibitions often are insufficient. The concept of the individual is meaningless in the absence of society. The self and its identifications are the product of transactions with others. Hence, it is not possible or desirable entirely to eliminate external sanctioning.

Individual and society are symbiotic. I am a professor, but not a nineteenth-century German professor. I do not expect my students to stand when I enter the room, and I want them to challenge my opinions. Introduce in rich context my other roles as husband, editor, and so forth, and you have begun to understand who and what I am. In my understanding of my self—which is always subject to reevaluation as I discover it in new situations and when faced by new types of choices—I find my own grounds for autonomous choice.

Were I to be forced out of my roles into a strange society, I would have to remake and refind myself. Force me out of a system of meaningful constraints, and I would begin to lose the sense of identity without which the freedom to choose is meaningless. I would become a rudderless ship, adjusting to momentary pressures without a sense of the pattern of life I wish to lead. It is this most terrible condition, even worse than death, that the concentration camp imposed on its victims. Will we impose it on ourselves in willful surrender to one-sided doctrine?

No society can prevent harm to its members that results from individual or collective action. Most tax laws, for instance, will do immense harm to some, because general statements, no matter how carefully written, cannot take into account all possible contingencies. No matter how great the care we take to avoid such consequences, almost invariably a tax law will drive some individuals out of a business or job that represents a lifetime of accomplishment and that is essential to their sense of identification. Life is filled with tragic dilemmas that we can attempt to ameliorate but cannot entirely avoid.

Because this is so, what we owe each other is an orderly regimen manifesting care for the equities and the values that are involved. This kind of care reinforces values and identifications and protects our freedoms. This is what would be threatened by extreme application of "the right to be left alone."

Notes

[1]See chapter 11, "Ontological Dysfunctions of Mind," pp. 209-218.
[2]Ibid., pp.224ff.

CHAPTER 11

ALIENATION AND IDENTIFICATION

Morton A. Kaplan

I. Alienation

I have no interest in exploring the history of the use of the concept of alienation. The way I shall use "alienation" is more neutral with respect to the conclusions I shall draw than is usually the case. The set of terms— "alienation," "identity," "creativity," "authenticity," "productivity"—employed in this chapter will enable us to deal with the subject of alienation within a reasonably comprehensive and adequate framework.

The dictionary tells us that the alien is the foreign. If this is the meaning that is chosen, a man who is alienated would be in some sense foreign or separated from himself. In this case, do we refer to his feeling different from what he was previously or different from what he thinks he ought to be? Is he a stranger in his own society— one who does not belong? Is an alienated person abnormal? Would this imply that he differs from other people in this respect? Can an entire society be alienated? Would that imply that the society differs from others in this respect? Or from what it ought to or could be? How would we recognize a person who was not alienated or a society that did not produce alienation?

Ordinary usage leaves us with many problems. In one sense we might seem to be dealing with a verbal paradox. How could one be alien from oneself? Is it not true that one is identical with oneself and, therefore, not alienated? One could be alienated from one's work or from one's country but not from oneself. But perhaps this gives us a key to understanding the term. Alienation occurs when an individual perceives an absence of meaningful relationships between his status, his identifications, his social relationships, his style of life, and his work. As such situations often arise, alienation is a recurrent phenomenon.

All complex systems that are subjected to significant environmental disturbance, or that have important needs whose joint satisfaction cannot be managed within inappreciable time spans, become dysfunctional in some respects as capacity is drained to deal with disturbances or specific needs. In self-conscious systems with a sense of identification and life style, such draining of capacity produces alienation, that is, dissociation in the meaningfulness of the life of the individual. Part of one's life appears to be both "objectified" and "detached" from the rest of it: it appears to respond to external constraints rather than to personal desires or needs.

Yet the process is more general than this suggests, for living necessarily "objectifies" the various aspects of existence—that is, it gives them a form or content that often escapes control as circumstances change. This loss of control is experienced as a disjunction between the self and important aspects of the world. Thus, alienation is always potential in the human condition.

Differentiation

The first time that a man considered what he would do in the future, he treated himself as an object of his own thought. The first time that a man named himself, he differentiated himself from other people and from the fullness of his being. The first time that a man classified himself as human, he differentiated himself from other animals, from nature, and from inanimate reality. Life involves a continual process of differentiation.

When we think about a problem, we interfere with, or cut off, that part of reality that would be conveyed by a direct emotional response. On the other hand, if we allow ourselves to respond with emotional intuition, we have cut ourselves off, to that extent, from the information that thinking could present about the matter. When we think about ourselves or others, the categories of thought we use, the language we employ, the theoretical concepts we develop open up certain insights and cut off others.

To think of ourselves as human is to overlook our continuity with the animal kingdom. To think of ourselves as animal is to diminish the moral and intellectual capabilities that our biological organization provides. To think of ourselves as Americans diminishes our kinship with the rest of humankind. To think of ourselves as part of humankind diminishes our contribution to the institutions that maintain important human values in the United States.

Differentiation and Alienation

Some differentiations are so great that even the absence of a meaningful relationship is not perceived as an alienation. A female pig that is perceived by a male pig as an object of sexual attraction, for instance, is perceived by a plantation owner either as a source of income or as a potential plateful of ham. The average person does not think of himself as sexually alienated from pigs, even if they are of the opposite sex, for he does not perceive a potential identification.

Clearly, "alienation" and "differentiation" are related terms, for the former cannot occur in the absence of the latter. Clearly, "difference" and "distance," if only as metaphors, are required for alienation. The extent of "distance" or "difference" that is necessary to produce alienation is the core of the problem.

Therefore, if the extent of "distance" is the key variable, the potential for alienation is omnipresent. Yet not every distinction or separation produces an actual alienation. There is an obvious sense in which the farmer is "alienated" from an aspect of the pig that is central to the pig's nature. However, it is unlikely that this "alienation" alienates the farmer from an important aspect of his nature.

The primary source of alienation lies in the discrepancy between the identifications of people in actual societies and the satisfaction of their needs or desires in social activities. When the identifications of the individual appear to be subject to social or natural forces over which he has no control, he perceives himself as alienated from important aspects of his personality. Such alienations occur often if the society fails to produce what humans perceive as satisfactions of legitimate human goals. It occurs as social change disturbs identifications in ways threatening to the personality of some members of the society: for example, women's liberation in contemporary society becomes a threat to some male identifications. Equally, however, the failure to achieve it becomes a threat to new female identifications. Alienation occurs inevitably in complex societies because of conflicts between at least partly independent part-system needs. These can never be entirely reconciled. Thus, disorder and lack of symmetry are inherent in the human condition.

Marx's Solution

Marx was aware that alienation was related to differentiation. He was aware that social processes produced alienation by thrusting men into activities that divorced essential aspects of their humanity and that separated them from nature, although the sociological or class analysis on the basis of which Marx arrived at his conclusion is unsound. But perhaps a few words should be said about the philosophical presuppositions that led Marx to expect his conclusions to be valid. The concepts of internal relations and totality that Marx adapted from Hegel constitute the key. Marx's putative solution is substantially, if not completely, harmonistic, for it assumes that no antagonistic conflicts will exist between part systems of the larger social system under socialism. However, in all systems in which scarce resources must be used to increase more than one independent variable or social outcome, simultaneous maximization is impossible in principle. The greater the complexity of the system, the more likely it is, depending on scarcities, that conflict between independent goals will increase strain in the system.

Alienation and Existential Being

Alienation is an inevitable, although not an omnipresent, component of existential being. If one worker is alienated because his wages are set by the market and because his livelihood may disappear during an economic storm, another worker may be alienated because his diligently worked and beautiful product gets no special recognition. There is a constant tension between rewarding a man for being who he is and rewarding him for what he does. Either choice devalues some aspect of him, denies its relevance, and separates him from it. Such choices are so costly to some men that these men are alienated.

In the real world scarce resources often require choices concerning the fulfillment of desires in cases in which the attainment of one desideratum is not directly linked to the attainment of the others. Yet it would be intolerable if the strength of the desire behind a motive continued unabated in consciousness until satisfaction occurred. Usually without thinking about it, the conscious aspect of desire is suppressed until it can be satisfied. Nagging signals may rise to the level of consciousness, but the strength of the motive is usually rerouted to an area "below" consciousness. It is in another (alien) place, ready to be resurrected upon an appropriate signal. If circumstances forbid its satisfaction, it is denied, suppressed, transformed, or mitigated by some form of secondary gain; in these latter cases, alienation is present. Sometimes the suppression becomes relatively permanent. An aspect of being, rather than being temporarily delayed until an appropriate time, is "outlawed," and secondary gratifications are substituted for it. Such individuals lack authenticity—a subject to which we will return.

There is a routing system within the biological system. Certain types of signals are suppressed, delayed, transformed, diminished, intensified, and so on. Information is compartmentalized, transmitted, suppressed, and used. There is a complicated "economic" balance in the system. The maintenance needs of the subsystems of biological man are not identical with each other. There are barriers and thresholds within the system. It is not instantly permeable from an internal perspective any more than from an external perspective. And, as we know, the internal subsystems even play tricks on one another, as when an undesired thought or feeling rises to consciousness or an unanticipated word is spoken.

The very singleness of being we present to others, and to ourselves as well, is in part the product of control by that cortical subsystem that dominates consciousness and that, in some of us, tries to outlaw or alienate other aspects of our being. In some sick individuals, it gets its "comeuppance" in the form of hallucinations or of other disturbances produced by other subsystems that have broken through the suppressing mechanisms of the cortical subsystem. Are these antagonistic or nonantagonistic contradictions? Or should we eschew such obscure terms and recognize that opposition is as ineluctable an aspect of life as symmetry and cooperation and that, if this is the case, some expressions of it will produce alienation?

Some antagonisms arise from the fact that the environment is limited. The individual who has a heart attack while running away from danger could have avoided that attack if the danger had been eliminated. Two individuals on a boat with enough food for one would not have been faced with this problem if sufficient food were available. On the other hand, two individuals who wish to head a particular organization are in inevitable conflict. Although this particular conflict could be removed by providing an organization for each, honor, esteem, and other similar values are inherently comparative. These conflicts can be avoided only by changing motivation. But then esteem will be extended to those who efface themselves or who avoid competition. And esteem always has a comparative element. Nature can never be sufficiently bountiful to accommodate all ambitions, for comparative evaluations defeat such a condition. And those ambitions or values that are sufficiently denied will produce alienation.

The Illusion of Eliminating Alienation

The cases dealing with the limitations of nature give rise to the illusion that all could be harmonious if only nature were sufficiently bountiful. The cases dealing with the esteem awarded men give rise to the illusion that all could be harmonious if only there were a new man who was not motivated by envy, greed, or the need for esteem or honor. Essentially, alienation is to be eliminated through productivity and changes in social organization that eliminate competitiveness, and changes in the motivation or consciousness of men that eliminate competitive or egoistic desires.

Unfortunately, this process of reasoning involves a sleight-of-hand trick. Each particular focal point of alienation or "contradiction" is removed by rearranging some other elements of the system. Because each type of alienation can be removed in imagination, it is imagined falsely that all of them can be removed simultaneously. This is impossible for biological man, let alone for man in society.

Internally, the sophisticated human biology requires adaptation of part system to part system. As in the case of every other type of circuitry, system compromises are required. Moreover, in this case, there are a number of system compromises that have not been designed by skilled engineers but that have resulted from the processes of biological evolution. The physical organization of the brain involves the layering of new functions over older and more primitive ones rather than a completely redesigned unit optimized for the requirements of biological humans.

The illusory character of a claim to eliminate all forms of alienation becomes even more understandable and explicit when we move to the level of social organization. Will the society of the future require surgeons or physicists? These skills require training. Training is costly in terms of time and requires sacrifice. Time spent studying skeletal structure cannot be spent at museums, listening to great music, or engaging in any number of delightful activities. During this time, the psychological mechanism of denial is required to reduce the import of these losses. Rationalization is required to enhance secondary gains. Secondary gains might well include such things as recognition, which has value primarily in terms of ambition.

Human society requires police forces, garbage squads, industrial organization, legislative activities, judicial functioning, and so forth. These functions can be performed only if the organizations that perform them survive and if they are serviced by individuals who perform the functions that maintain organizations. Yet the survival function of an organization can never be synonymous with the survival of the society of which it is part. This introduces a necessary conflict of interest between an organization and the system of which it is a part.

An organization requires people to carry out its functions, and this requires that the people who are supposed to do this be motivated actually to do it. Yet their needs are never synonymous with the needs of the organization, and therefore there is an inevitable conflict of interest between them and the organization. Thus, on the average, people tend to rise in organizations if they are skilled in survival techniques. What is good for the survival and rise of officials within an organization is not necessarily good for the organization, although partial conflicts of interest need not be total. When these conflicts are great enough—and in complex systems, some will always be that great—alienation occurs.

The Universal, the Particular, and Alienation

Justice requires rules. Yet every rule is a general statement that abstracts from the particulars of a situation. In principle, justice should take into account all the particularities of a situation. In the absence of rules, no one could be assured that the relevant particularities would be considered. Yet, in complex systems, some rule applications will be incompatible with substantive justice. This is one of the sources of some of the problems discussed in chapter 4 of *Justice, Human Nature, and Political Obligation*, and it produces alienation.

Freedom, Necessity, and Alienation

The freedom of a stone to roll is dependent upon a spherical shape. The freedom of a person to think is dependent upon certain types of biological organization. Action requires some particular kind of structure. Thought requires some particular form of symbolism.

Particularity is ineluctably a limitation. And limitation always involves some form of separation. The stone would not roll if it were not separate from the surface. The mind could not engage in thought unless it were at least partly independent of other aspects of the body. Thought could not occur unless words or symbols were differentiated from each other. If everything were infinitely transformable at will, we could not think, for we could not make reliable projections into the future. We could not act, for we would have no experience on the basis of which to calculate the consequences of our own actions.

The object upon which we work could not be used by us if it did not have predictable characteristics. Those very predictable characteristics make it at least partly independent of our will. The language we employ in the process of thought could not be used publicly by us unless the meanings of words were independent of our individual wills. Yet these necessary characteristics become dysfunctional in some circumstances. Words cannot change their meanings fast or often enough for all uses. Language too, like all tools, can produce alienation.

It is the concept of alienation in the general sense that is a fetish, for it separates us from the nature of the problem. By positing the elimination of alienation, it holds out the dream of an alienation-free society. In effect, it promises a perfect disturbance-reducing control system that will eliminate all important conflicts. Yet, even in the narrower sense of economic alienation, its Marxian use is a fetish. Apart from his faulty method of defining social classes, Marx never offered a specific explanation of how socialism would remedy the particular defects he found in capitalism and, especially, the alienation of man as a consequence of commodity fetishism. It was not enough to establish how this alienation occurred under capitalism. It was required that he analyze how a socialist form of productivity would change this fact and not produce some other form of alienation. In fact, alienation is abundant in those socialist systems that have removed the market mechanism for determining value. The extent of absenteeism and sabotage in socialist economies provides striking evidence for this assertion.

II. Ontological Dysfunctions of Mind

If alienation is an ontological necessity in a complex world, the attempt to eliminate alienation will generate instabilities. Although particular alienations can be overcome, it is inherently impossible to eliminate alienation. These attempts to escape alienation will take a variety of forms.

The Compulsive Dysfunction

In the compulsive form of dysfunction the mind attempts to unite reality with subjective belief by making them identical. Thus the compulsive person fits external events into a constricted set of highly ordered categories. He has a strong, although impoverished, sense of who he is and a weak sense of his relationship to the world. The magic acts performed by the compulsive—stepping on cracks in the streets, making symbolic movements with the hands—have the meaning of restoring the ordered relationship between the perception of self and the perception of the world. The reality that does not conform is brought back into relationship by a magical gesture. In effect, alienation is overcome by psychic denial. This individual has a sense of identity that is continually buttressed by distorted perceptions of the world and by magical forms of control over it.

The compulsive is also an obsessive. Because the symbol is the instrument by means of which the external reality is reduced to the mental conception, the symbolic means of achieving this is a requirement—obsession—of the individual's state of psychic adjustment. As these obsessive means are the instruments of control, the sense of identity, although real, is fragile; it is constantly subject to assault because of the inadequacy of the magical means of control. The compulsive (obsessive) individual is alienated from his own emotions, because these are threatening to the psychic order he is attempting to impose upon the world.

Disorder continually threatens to break through the defenses of the obsessive-compulsive individual and must be guarded against rigidly. This requires strong magic. The magic pentagram, designed to contain the summoned devil, is a good example of this aspect of the compulsive's behavior. Its sharply angled lines, its rigid forms, and its perfect circles are particularly appropriate to the portended victory of form over spirit. Yet the pentagram is designed not to exclude spirit, but to control it, to contain it within the accepted forms. It thus seeks to overcome the alienation between the two by harmonizing them, by excluding the obnoxious, autonomous, intellectually uncontrollable aspects of emotional life. What it fears is the free play of spirit, the unbridled emotion that reveals its distinctness from form and from intellectual control.

I am not arguing that biological or libidinal drives and mind are inherently incompatible but only that they are different and not entirely adaptable. Whatever the reason for the origin of the fear of the independence of impulse, the meaning of compulsive magic lies in the assertion of the complete harmonization of mind and emotion. That such an extreme effort to overcome it emphasizes alienation is not paradoxical. The patient who refuses to recognize the sickness of his condition often worsens it. It is precisely the attempt to escape all alienation, as in the case of revolutionary Communist movements, that intensifies it.

The compulsive person is not anomic. He has a set of rules, but they do not provide him with directions that are sufficiently responsive to the richness of the external world. His actions are stereotyped; they are not productive.

The Sociopathic Dysfunction

The second form of dysfunction—essentially the sociopathic—is represented by the attempt to overcome all alienation by a plasticity of individual adaptation. Some sociopathic people present those faces to the external world that meet the requirements of particular situations regardless of their continuity with past behavior or their conformity with reasonable sets of rules for social intercourse.

This dysfunction may take a variety of forms including that of the true sociopath, who simply uses other people, and the essentially rudderless individual who is merely searching for approval. In the extreme case, this leads to loss of identity. The individual does not know who he is because he bends his behavior to the inconsistent requirements of a constantly shifting set of external pressures. The only constant in his behavior is inconstancy. He is incapable even of perceiving his character as changed, for there is no consistent pattern from which it changes. This person merely seeks to survive, or perhaps to prosper. He is an embodiment of the Hobbesian axioms which—rather than expressing true premises about the nature of man—rationalize the aberrations of dysfunctional character. Again, as in the case of compulsive behavior, this aberrational pattern is defended for the secondary gains it provides. However, the quest is both hopeless and costly, for the adaptations of the anomic person who lacks a robust sense of identity are inherently incapable of satisfying the demands that are made upon him by his personality. Thus, the sense of alienation gathers strength.

Dysfunctions of Sensitivity

Some of the forms through which the attempt to escape all alienation is pursued produce madness. The attempt to reduce the barrier between the individual and the external world in some cases leads to a heightened sensitivity that escapes control. Pater's imagined sensorium—an organ emitting different odors—is representative of the effort made by the decadents during the *Yellow Book* period in England. Attempt after attempt is made to heighten sensation, to distinguish different forms of sensation, and to exhaust that mode of experience. In its extreme form, this process becomes autonomous, escaping conscious control and severing the relationships between the individual and the everyday world. As external experience is unable to produce the range of experience the individual now requires, he turns to a world of imagination. The elements of this imaginative, kaleidoscopic process lose their ordered relationships. The most rapid changes of form, meaning, and appearance assault perception. The individual becomes the passive spectator of his own inner experience, merging with it almost as the clay merges with the intentions of the sculptor.

This form of aberration requires the most rigorous defense mechanisms against the intrusion of conscious control or interference by the environment. Even when induced by drugs, it is possible that the dependency of the individual is not so much upon the biological effects of the drug as upon the subjective impression of oneness with the world. However, this oneness is achieved at a price. Beyond the giving up of relationships with, and control over, the external world, the individual submits to the autonomy of the elements of subjective experience. He buys this oneness by attempting to lose himself within it. Yet this can never be achieved; for, if it were achieved, the experiences would belong not to him but to the individual elements of his experience, in which he merely appears to lose himself.

It is this ultimate incompatibility that drives the sequence into an ever descending spiral. Once the individual is caught in its power, each stage requires a further stage, for the inherent dichotomy in the experience defeats the unity that is sought. Always one appears to be on the threshold of the ultimate experience that will break through the barriers of being to produce a marvelous oneness in which no alienation occurs. Yet ultimately each new sequence of experience disappoints.

The price is enormous. By submission, the individual has given up those means of control that would enable him to interpret and understand the experiences he is having. The words and concepts his thought employs, and the logic he uses, cease to have determinate meaning. His subjective lucidity is an illusion. Through shifts of meaning, through the equation of incompatibles, through the derivation of illogical conclusions from premises, through the perception of different forms of illusory samenesses, the critical faculties of mind have been killed. The lucidity that has been achieved is the lucidity of the idiot. "Yes" equals "no," and the elementary distinction that is required for one bit of information according to the axioms of information theory has been lost.

The dysfunction of sensitivity may take another form—an excessive sensitivity to the subjectivity of other beings. We are familiar in everyday life with simple differences in sensitivity. The difference between eufunctional and dysfunctional sensitivity is often a matter of degree and circumstance. Some extreme psychopaths are willing to do anything to anyone, provided it is costless to them. Some recognize the needs only of their own families. Others have sensitivities that extend to the needs of their countrymen. Some give some consideration to all of humankind. Some are kind to animals but not to insects. Some are kind to their dogs but will eat meat. Others are offended by the eating of animals. In extreme pathological cases, some may view the eating of plant life as a form of cannibalism. In this last case, a complete equation is made among all forms of life. In principle, perhaps, this pathological sensitivity may be extended to all of existence.

This extreme sensitivity constitutes another method for attempting to overcome alienation. It identifies the self with all the elements of the rest of the world. Ultimately this quest is impossible for obvious reasons. The refusal to eat anything would soon result in death. However, depending upon the conditions with which the world confronts us, even much milder forms of extended sensitivity produce dilemmas that can lead to madness. Sometimes we must kill or watch others being killed. Sometimes we must see our family in pain or produce pain in others. We are continually confronted with situations in which we must produce pain—a pain we may feel empathetically but never directly.

Under ordinary circumstances, we solve these problems by various psychological mechanisms that depress our sensitivity, or that divert information, or that produce rationalization. In the person of exquisite sensitivity, however, these particular forms of self-protection are no longer available. His life becomes anguished. His attempts to avoid conflicts of this type become ever more exquisitely extended.

Each extension of his sensitivity, although designed to reduce the alienation between him and the rest of the world, increases the alienation. As the sensitivity to injury increases, no matter how great the empathetic subjective distress, the sense of ultimate disjunction between self and other is heightened. The sensitive consciousness is acutely aware that the real sufferer is an "other." To escape this distress, the sensitivity is heightened still further, thus again heightening the self-punishment and the subjective sense of alienation. If the earlier type of sensitivity represents a retreat to internal subjectivity (the perceptual level), the latter type of sensitivity is relevant to the religious spirit. It is pain and the body that must be escaped.

Both these forms of escape mechanism have their obversion. The individual who intuits the dangers of excessive inner experience, but who is susceptible to the need for such experience, may attempt to avoid it through rigid mental control. The individual who is excessively sensitive to the pain of others may attempt to escape through one of a variety of mechanisms. He may attempt to isolate himself from the world, or he may do deliberate injury as a form of denial, or he may attempt to attach others to himself as a way of denying their separateness. Or, alternatively, in some individuals sensitivity, rather than being genuine, may serve as a denial mechanism. It is designed to inhibit fear of external punishment for these attempts to obliterate the distinctions between self and the external world. This extreme fear of loss of control is related to an infantile drive for omnipotence.

The Dysfunction of "True" Autonomy

There is a third mechanism by means of which the individual may attempt to overcome alienation. In its extreme form, it will produce madness. This is an attempt to overcome alienation by breaking through what is perceived as the rigid structure of social or moral rules. Individuals who attempt this escape perceive the rules of society as artificial barriers to their desires, and, hence, to their "true" or authentic autonomy. Rules about neatness and cleanliness are seen as restrictions on natural behavior. Rules about theft, particularly theft from large corporations, are seen as artificial restrictions on the needs of poor people or free spirits. Rules against incest are seen as artificial restrictions on the varieties of love. Such rules individually and collectively are seen as barriers to spontaneity of behavior.

The "free" mind perceives such rules as alienating the self from inner being. Such minds see themselves as superior, for they believe they have seen through the fakery and artificiality of society. Such views are tempting, for many rules can be violated in the individual case without any significant harm. A single theft from the supermarket is a petty matter. Moreover, some rules, even within the same society, could be supplanted by some different rule without significant harm in the long run of cases. By rising to the "superior" point of view that rules are, therefore, arbitrary, the individual appears to have penetrated to an ultimate truth. Other individuals are seen as merely creatures of habit who follow rules blindly and without understanding because of training and propaganda. This is the Nietzschian delusion.

However, this attitude increases rather than decreases alienation (and anomie), for it detaches the individual from his orientation to the world. Lacking guideposts and standards of comparison, the individual case becomes even more difficult to judge than ordinarily. There is an infinity of rules to choose from in determining what is best.

Because we are dependent upon consistencies and continuities in life—we do not wish to analyze each cup of coffee for poison, or fear that a kind word will elicit a blow, or that today's friend will arbitrarily become tomorrow's enemy—the "free" spirit comes into constant collision with the requirements of his own existence. To maintain his posture, he is continually driven to further extremes. The world he seeks to unite to him eludes him. The necessity to force fate increases as do the demands he must make upon life and his associates.

As the intimate associates and followers of this free mind require some guideposts for their own behavior, he must play god, and provide such rules; and they must submit. Yet, in the absence of external standards, the standards he provides must be arbitrary, and they are changeable. Therefore, they can be accepted only as a manifestation of his power. As there is no external standard by means of which this power can be satisfied and as submission by followers may merely cloak the seeds of eventual disobedience, the leader must keep testing his power. Nothing can suffice to suppress doubt entirely. Thus, the fear of alienation keeps rising and his personality becomes fragmented. If any pattern or logic remains to his behavior, it is necessarily an internal pattern or logic that is disconnected from the external world and therefore alienated from it.

There is no solution for this case, for each further activity only increases the sense of alienation from the real world. Each act makes the individual and his group ever more peculiar and likely ever more destructive, for recalcitrant reality somehow must be brought back into connection with the self. The disconnection between the world and the self becomes so great that only destruction momentarily provides meaning by temporarily bringing the individual back into connection with the external recalcitrant world. By stamping out the disorder (disagreement with him) in the external world, he has assimilated it to himself and "proved" that he is real.

Biology and Dysfunction

If the category of alienation is an ontological necessity, it does not follow that every case of alienation is an existential necessity. Mention has been made of the fact that the human biological structure is the culmination of a series of mutations. The evolution of man did not entail the evolution of a completely new neurological structure that was fully adapted to his new being. Instead, new structures were added to the old, or related in new ways, as in the case of the cortex and the medulla oblongata. As in the case of every other system involving complex feedback relationships, the potential for instability and overload is present in such a complex system. We know very little about the complex structure of the brain, but evolutionary advantage did not likely produce a brain that is as efficient and eufunctional as possible. Even if its operation is far more marvelous than anything we can now conceive of from a theoretical point of view— even if it is far beyond our power of comprehension and understanding—there is room for enormous mischief in its actual operation under particular conditions. Moreover, even the best-designed system can be overloaded, in which case instabilities occur. The human brain is not likely a "best-designed" system; and there are genetic variations in the system among individuals as well as differences in its care, nurturing, and education.

Thus, the brain can be put into dysfunctional operation by biological defects, chemical inputs, electrical discharges, libidinal inputs, and informational inputs. Moreover, there can be an extremely complex relationship among these elements. For instance, a chemical strain upon the system may lower the threshold for a libidinal or informational strain and vice versa. This might operate in terms of step functions, each new level of which might stabilize, even if not optimally, or it might produce a progressively unstable series of step changes. In the abstract little can be said about this. Few audio engineers would be willing to make predictions about amplifier circuits unless they could study these in detail; and, of course, amplifier circuits, complex as they may seem to the layman, are idiotically simple in comparison with the human neurological circuitry.

There are many competing explanations of mental breakdown: psychological, biological, chemical, organizational, and ontological, for instance. Sigmund Freud speculated that every neurotic or psychotic disturbance had some biological foundation. Freudian and chemical explanations of psychoses may be inconsistent only from an extremely narrow point of view. Exclusive attributions of cause and effect may do more to obscure than to clarify the nature of the problem. Chemical and psychological phenomena are threshold phenomena. In principle, either type of phenomenon could trigger the other; and, in particular cases, they could do so to a greater or lesser extent.

Transcending Dysfunction

The real problems facing men are particular problems. These are the problems that provide meaning in men's lives and within the context of which they find their identity as particular human beings. Lives that are productive and creative do not eliminate alienation, but they cope with and transcend it.

The existence of alien aspects of life is necessary in the problem-solving process. It is the very existence of things beyond our control that enables us to employ control, that is, to change some other things. Thus, the human problem is not the abstract problem of eliminating alienation—for alienation is universally potential in life—but the more particular problem of changing the world in productive and useful ways. Under benign circumstances, particular problems can be solved. Universal aspects of life can never be eliminated and that is why the attempt to overcome them necessarily leads to dysfunction or even to madness.

It is perhaps no accident that the world before creation is thought of as chaos or that in some religions gods are thought of as polymorphous. Alfred North Whitehead may have understood a deep truth when he made his God primordial and unconscious. Consciousness entails thought; thought entails separation; separation entails limitation. Only entities that are limited can be related to other entities. Thus, without the potential for alienation, there cannot be particular lives, human relationships, or solved problems.

III. Aspects of Being

The problems of alienation, of authenticity, and of identity are intimately related to the nature of human being. Thus, their elucidation requires at least a minimal inquiry into existential human nature.

The Sensual

One element of being involves a glandular impact on behavior and mind. This operates in two forms: as an impulsion to act upon the world and as a receptivity toward emanations from the world. Anger, fear, love, but also receptivity to sights, sounds, and smells come under this rubric.

Although the particular and the concrete dominate the sensual mode of behavior, they do not exclusively represent it. Smells, sights, and feelings involve perception and not merely sensation. Perception always entails some element of form. However, this element of form can be expressed at the lowest level of abstraction; curve, for instance, rather than space. Even if these low levels of form involve some aspect of mind, it need not be conscious and the levels of form may be biologically embedded. It is a mistake to think of such concepts as the Jungian archetypes as purely unscientific. We know very little about the forms that invest our impulsive behavior, our libidinal motivation, and those aspects of our preconscious thought that are related to them.

This aspect of our being relates us to the most palpable aspects of the external world. This is the anchor that moors us to reality. A supreme designer might have designed the system more sensitively;

to detach ourselves from it entirely, however, is equivalent to eliminating our existential basis. We sometimes speak of individuals whose behavior is impulsive as superficial. This is correct from the standpoint of intellect; however, it is intellect that is superficial when divorced from immediate existence. The texture of life—of experience and of action—is intimately related to the richness of the concrete elements of life, even if it is not exclusively determined by them. A personality that does not tap the varieties of concrete, sensuous experience is "thin." In Thomas Mann's *Magic Mountain* both Settembrini and Naphta share these thin qualities. Neither resonates to other people or appears as much more than a walking theory. Their lives have been attenuated.

Rich lives are directly linked to the sensual (as well as to the scientific and to the sacred). The sensual is the realm of the immediate, and gives life its flavor.

Analytical and Theoretical Science

A second aspect of being involves the capacity to employ abstraction and reason analytically and theoretically. This is a large realm extending from simple problem solving to the formal sciences. However, its paradigmatic form is that of theoretical science. Science searches for laws, even if law must be related to boundary conditions.

Science does not deal with the concrete existent. It deals with classes of animals and not with any particular animal. It deals with classes of electrons and not with any particular electron. The existential correlates of the products of this aspect of mind may be palpable in some instances; but abstract generalization is invariably impalpable.

The activities of this aspect of mind may be triggered by an impulse, but the system is operating imperfectly if they are determined by an impulse. Functional separation is required. If these aspects of mind are useful to a society, then the value placed upon them may encourage certain individuals to emphasize them to the exclusion of other aspects of mind. If the generalizations, propositions, or laws formulated by this aspect of mind are treated carelessly, as often happens, the boundary conditions under which they apply may be forgot.

This aspect of mind tends to believe only what can be demonstrated and to respond only to what is not impulsive. If a plane in flight between two cities were suddenly to become self-conscious, it might believe that its function in life was to be continually in flight. If a fuel-regulation system were to become self-conscious, it might believe that the most important objective in life was to control the rate of flow of fuel rather than for the larger system to operate. Yet it is within the self-conscious cortical system of mind that further orders for the operation of the human biological system are formulated; and it may seize control of the entire system.

It has often been asserted that science is the engine of change *par excellence*. The history of the modern world since the origins of theoretical science is cited as support for this proposition. It is surely true that technology is the product of science and that in the modern age technology has produced almost ceaseless social and political change. Yet in a very profound sense the proposition is mistaken. Science introduces a fundamental conservatism.

As Aristotle pointed out, the first technique of science is classification. Classification produces hierarchy and order. Classification excludes. Traditional social systems with closed orders involve early applications of science. Science imposes boundaries and resists change. Science is essentially a scheme for death; for, by increasing the level of abstraction, it continually increases the distance between mind and existence. By insisting upon universals, it attempts to exclude novelty and accident.

What is demonstrated is timeless, for it can never be changed. Yet life is always changing, always overflowing boundaries, always exceeding schemes of classification. It is in this sense that a scheme for controlling nature is a scheme for destroying it, at least if not moderated by other aspects of mind. It is the very fecundity of nature and its resistance to schemes of classification that becomes the challenge.

If we were to construct a control computer to make governmental decisions for us and if this computer became self-conscious, it might begin to control the flow of information to protect its own functioning, thus divorcing itself from a more intimate relationship with the system it was designed to serve. We might have an analogy to the control computer in the activities of some intellectuals whose lives seem to be dominated by the cortical functions of their brains. Entire philosophies have been built around such abstract notions as that colors are not real but that angstrom waves are. The converse error lies in an excessive faith in the sensible, as in the notion that colors are real but that angstrom waves are not. Thus, those whose minds are oriented toward the "concrete" also tend to read all of nature into their particular interpretation of it.

Note carefully the actual character of the metaphor or analogy employed here. Cortical activity is instrumental, but so is perception of the palpable. Glandular and libidinal activity are also instrumental. All structure requires instrumentation. And all successful instrumentation responds to some actual aspect of existence. The error lies in reading the part for the whole. However, the error of the sensible is noted here only to contrast it with the error of the abstract.

I am not arguing for non- or anti-scientific premises. Explanation requires science and the use of generalizations. However, I am asserting that there is a tendency on the part of those using scientific method to act as if the entire world consisted only of rarefied abstractions. There is a tendency to forget that an explanation is always an explanation of some thing and that things include emotions, impulses, smells, sights, and other types of concrete phenomena. Science—at least in its confirmatory or explanatory phases—requires strict control. Life, and creative science as well, cannot stand that much order.

The Sacred

The third aspect of being is the sacred. If science requires the formulation of boundary conditions, the sacred requires the stripping away of all conditions. If science depends upon closure, the sacred depends upon holism or all-inclusiveness.

When man attempts to answer the question of who he is or where he belongs in the world, he enters the realm of the sacred. The concrete responds to things as they are existentially. Sciences in the theoretical sense tear things apart in the development of theories. The sacred attempts to restore unity but in a non-immediate sense.

If formal science attempts to differentiate among universals, the sacred attempts to find identities among them. If science stresses functional relationships, the sacred stresses syncretism, consistency, "fittingness," and partial relationships. Yet, as in the case of Mann's Naphta and Settembrini, who both represent death, theoretical science and the sacred have in common timeless being. They represent different modes of expressing truth.

Some religions that represent themselves as standing for revealed truth are nondevelopmental. Science in its dogmatic form also takes this guise. What are presently understood as the laws of nature are presented as final and ultimate truths. Most scientists are aware that they have no warrant for dogmatic assumptions of this kind. They know that at best they can assert warranted belief in the truth of their current notions of the laws of nature and of their conceptions of science. If the realm of the sacred is regarded as an aspect of being, the understanding of which is pursued by mind, then obviously the same considerations apply to it that apply to the ordinary concerns of science. Indeed, as part of the realm of nature, the sacred, as understood by mind, can be viewed as that aspect of science that is relevant to the search by human beings for the meaning of their existence as this is revealed by the way in which knowledge of man fits with knowledge of society and the physical universe.

Let us examine a few concepts from systems analysis that are relevant to an understanding of the problem. Although they will not give us a precise and complete understanding of the operations of the human mind, they do provide a more precise understanding than ordinary vocabulary permits of the way mind functions in certain respects. They at least point us in the right direction.

Different types of systems are distinguished by the equilibrating processes that occur within them. In the physical sciences, the equilibria primarily are of the mechanical variety. The concept of equality in mechanical equilibria is meaningful because there are independent measures for the variables that have general applicability. Therefore, genuine equalities between them are possible. When we turn to examples of homeostatic equilibria—and all social or political "equilibria" are variations of the homeostatic variety—we no longer have independent measures for genuine equalities. Therefore, the implication of equality in "equilibrium" is not related to covering laws. Hence, the concept of equilibrium is not in this case an explanatory device with respect to "why" questions but is merely a categorizing device that tells us something about "what" we are dealing with.

There are many different types of homeostatic equilibria. The physiological system is homeostatic. For instance, the temperature of the human blood is maintained by processes that compensate for environmental disturbances. In cold weather, constriction of the blood vessels occurs, whereas in hot weather, perspiration takes place. The thermostatic system that maintains room temperature is also homeostatic. When the mercury reaches the desired range, the furnace is turned off. When the mercury goes below the desired range, the furnace is turned on. In both examples, there are related mechanical systems to which the equalities of physics apply within the framework of covering laws. However, homeostatic systems are not systems of equality. The process of perspiration continues until the required temperature change occurs. If, for some reason, this process cannot occur, as would be the case if the human body were covered with paint, either sickness or death would occur. There is no independent measure that will establish the equality between the perspiration and the lowering of temperature.

Some systems are merely homeostatic whereas others are ultrastable or multistable. Consider an ordinary homeostatic system such as the automatic pilot in an airplane. If a plane deviates from level flight while on automatic pilot, the automatic pilot will sense this and, by the application of negative feedback, will adjust the flight pattern of the plane back to level. Consider, however, the case in which the automatic pilot has been incorrectly linked to the ailerons of the plane. If the plane now deviates from level flight, the automatic pilot mechanism will sense this. It will now make an adjustment, but the adjustment, instead of bringing the plane back to level flight, will throw it into a spin. To the extent that purpose implies a capability to pursue a given end by alternative means, this system lacks purpose.

In principle, it would be possible to build an ultrastable automatic pilot the behavior of which was not critically dependent upon the linkages to the ailerons. That is, the automatic pilot could be so built that it would reject its own behavior patterns if these increased the deviations from level flight. It could then "search" for a set of behaviors that would restore the level character of flight. When it found it, it would continue to use it as long as it maintained the critical variable within the established limits for variation. In a sense, this system is capable of adjusting the internal rules by means of which its behavior is governed. This type of ultrastable system would have distinct advantages for survival over a merely stable homeostatic system. Even ultrastability, however, is not sufficient for complex biological survival. W. Ross Ashby, who developed these concepts, therefore applied the term "multistability" to those cases where multiple part functions of the system are individually ultrastable and where they can therefore "search" relatively independently for critical behaviors consistent with the maintenance of the system.

If a visitor from Mars observed the behavior of a machine incorporating the ultrastable automatic pilot suggested by Ashby, its behavior in some respects might seem purposive to him. He would observe it making adjustments in its own internal control system to find an arrangement that would restore level flight to the plane. It would then overcome external obstacles such as large wind gusts in achieving this objective. However, he likely would recognize that this system could not shift from one "purpose" to another, substitute one "purpose" for another, or "choose" a goal that partly matched the perceived requirements. Although further inspection would reveal that the system was designed by an engineer, this would be inessential, for purpose resides in the character of the system rather than in its origin. A being produced by the union of a sperm cell and an ovum, both of which had been designed by a geneticist, would be as "purposeful" as a human produced by "natural" sexual conjugation.

If the visitor from Mars examined the ultrastable system in detail, he would note that it was relatively simple to specify exhaustively the environmental variations to which the machine could adjust. The variable that is to be maintained, namely level flight, would be simple, easily recognizable, and invariant in every environment. It would soon become clear that even if the system were self-conscious, it would never be in any doubt as to its own purpose. Conflict and tragedy would never be part of its internal life. Development or growth of character would be meaningless. It is the continual process of discovery—not of what one is but of what one can become—that gives rise to the concept of the sacred. The concepts of ultrastability and of multistability fall too far short of explicating this. Therefore, we must search for a new concept that expresses the meaning we are searching for.

The term "transfinite stability," or "transstability" for short, will be used for this purpose. It may not be fully adequate, but it at least comes closer than the concepts of ultrastability and multistability. The transfinitely stable system is one with a complex system of purposes. These purposes are not necessarily fully consistent and they may give rise to gross conflict under many environmental circumstances. Some, and perhaps most, of these purposes cannot be translated into an easily recognizable and univocal set of external behaviors. Implementation of purpose depends upon alternative and changeable environments. For individuals, this permits the development of values over time and the building of character. For humanity, it implies a process in history in which learning about human potential takes place. Although every manifestation of this process is finite, no manifestation ever completely satisfies the posited value structure. For every satisfactory state of the world, there is always some potentially superior state or at least some state that is better in new circumstances. It is in this sense that the process is transfinite.

The incompletion that is an inherent characteristic of any finite state of being gives rise to the quest for completion in a transfinite system. This is primarily the source of the sense of the sacred. This quest becomes perverse when it posits the completion of the search in historical time. In this perverse form, all potential conflicts among goals, all failures of understanding, all alternative tolerable variations of satisfaction, and all human particularities are stripped away. All of life is reduced to particular System. This misconceives and corrupts the character of transfinite process.

The transfinite process is one of discovery—fundamentally of discovery of what is to be human as this is illuminated by the test in principle. If being human involves being moral—as I believe it does— then transstability is the process by means of which men, in their learning of their humanity, become human and learn how to build a society fit for humans. In this sense, being human involves subjection as well as freedom: subjection to moral rules and consideration for others, and freedom to express one's humanity. Because this transstable process takes place in the realm of praxis, these conceptions develop through comparative understanding of how human behavior, social institutions, culture, and science are linked in alternative possible or real worlds, each of which is characterized by a worldview. Thus, a developed conception of humanity is not derived from, or reducible to, any specific theoretical or propositional foundation.

It is textured and enriched by the entire web of social existence and deepened by comparative understanding of alternative possibilities. Unlike classical philosophy, however, the standards for this process are objective in Dewey's sense of public communicability and in Peirce's sense of the pragmaticist test. In this sense, the quest for the sacred primarily employs the methods of praxical science (assessment) rather than those of theoretical science.

Differences between Science and the Sacred: Transfinite Stability

We may now further explore the differences between the realm of science and that of the sacred. Although our knowledge of science may develop over time, we normally assume that the laws of science, as distinguished from our knowledge of them, are invariant. Most laws are not developmental. A few cosmological theories appear to be developmental; and our knowledge concerning their invariance is only of low confidence. Human beings live for too short a time to observe the cycle of growth and decay that would occur if one of the competing developmental cosmological theories is correct. However, in principle only one cycle of observation would be required to confirm any specific developmental cosmological theory.

Knowledge of human nature is not in principle penetrable through the intensive study of a single cycle of development. Human nature develops (either progressively or retrogressively) as we learn about ourselves under different external and informational conditions. This dependence upon comparative information does not make the subject of human nature totally recalcitrant to study. However, this dependence upon a comparative historical record implies a development of that which is under study such that knowledge cannot in principle be complete within historical time, let alone within a single human cycle. This does not mean that reasonable inferences are impossible but only that the level of confidence we achieve will be low. Man is not a book to be read at one sitting, and the reading that finally occurs will be to some extent at least dependent upon historical accidents.

From this perspective, we perpetually make discoveries about human nature and society. As we learn about ourselves, sometimes erroneously, the sense arises within us of a moral imperative. In this way our nature speaks to us of the things that we must do. Recognition of this need, of this aspect of being, is an inherent element in its utilization. If and when such recognition occurs, men who are constrained from acting according to moral necessity will recognize themselves as unfree.

Transfinitely stable systems always involve compromises, for there must always be sacrifice with respect to some value in order to achieve some gain with respect to another value. For instance, love is sacrificed for honor or vice versa. This is necessarily true in an environment with sufficient variety to provide genuine choice. If the environment is sufficiently benign, then the price paid with respect to any particular value may be small. In this case, strong characters would be capable of fully facing the facts. However, during history, few environments have been benign. To achieve some goals, severe prices have had to be paid with respect to others.

Even people not ostensibly reduced to such conflicts of choice in severe environments have been forced to restrict their human sympathy for those in less fortunate circumstances. If, as some have hypothesized, human sympathy and the recognition of the sacred in each of us are basic elements of our character, then the psychological mechanism of denial is required. Whatever one may think of this particular example, if he can construct some other example to the same point, it will become evident that techniques for the exclusion of information are required by such systems if they are to maintain internal psychic equilibrium. Their attention then becomes diverted to other gains—the kinds of gains Freud termed secondary—which are then perceived as if they were primary. In addition, human beings go through a long period of learning. If they learn inefficiently, they may fear striking out on more productive paths. In this case also, they learn to value secondary gains.

I do not wish to push this discussion too far, as the investigation of the mechanisms of information regulation are not directly pertinent to this inquiry. However, it is important to recognize that transstable systems do employ information-processing mechanisms and that they can become dysfunctional. Thus, many problems can arise from the misprocessing of information. Among these problems some of the most severe are those we have already discussed: those dealing with the elimination of alienation. Because of faulty inferences, because examples are often employed without consideration of differences in boundary or environmental conditions, because inherent limitations are sometimes imaginatively stripped away, inherently infeasible and destructive quests are initiated. It requires only the adding of a suffix such as "less" to a word such as "time" to believe that one imagines a timeless entity having an existence similar to that of concrete being or the adding of the word "overcoming" to "separation" to convince oneself that all limitations of existential being can be overcome.

Transstable systems never overcome limitation. However, they are capable of a development that better fulfills the necessity of their own being. They are capable in most environments of finding ways to a productive existence and of making changes in the environment such that their prospects are improved.

Transstability and Search Procedures

The transstable system requires much more sophisticated search procedures than the ultrastable system. In the first place, it must seek to interact with a much more variable relevant environment. In the second place, the set of requirements it must satisfy is far more complex. In the third place, it does not possess a set series of responses that can be tried in serial or random fashion. The internal system and the external environment are simultaneously complexly variable. The combinatorial potential is astronomical. Any systematic search procedure at the conscious level, even a relatively random one, would likely overwhelm the organism and incapacitate it for its daily tasks.

Even if we speak metaphorically and speculatively, there is probably a very complicated division of labor in transstable systems in which most of the search procedures occur at a preconscious level. The kind of signaling or recognition device that is required for determining the admission to the level of consciousness of possible solutions that are worthy of consideration is not even hinted at in the current literature on brain functioning. We do not even begin to suspect how this combinatorial search is triggered off either by conscious activity or by some other form of bodily impulse. We do not know how the conscious mind decides which of the hypothetical solutions that rise from the preconscious level are worth systematic scientific investigation. Some process of recognition and identification, and perhaps of reasoning, is involved, but we do not know that the primitive methods we are now employing in the coding of computers bears any significant relationship to it.

IV. Identification

Identification and Alienation

Perhaps the reader wishes a concrete discussion of identification. I cannot oblige him in a work of this kind. What we identify with depends on the realm of knowledge and our location in it. As the former differs with time and place and the latter with the individual, the problem of identification can be discussed in detail only if the scope of reference is strictly bounded. Yet such a bounded discussion would be irrelevant to this chapter.

Although the ethologists may overgeneralize this point, imprinting may lead a duckling to identify with the human who takes it as the egg hatches. The process by which bonds of relationship become internalized by humans and the reasons that are acceptable in justifying these relationships will differ with time and place. The consistency and "fit" of the realm of praxis provide the constraints within which the process operates. Anything beyond a general discussion of the concept would take us beyond the confines of this chapter.

Identification involves a sense of membership: in a species, a nation, or a family, for instance. Membership implies differentiation from other membership groupings. Identity involves an individual history and, in particular, a history in which problems are overcome by a particular being. Particular histories are always differentiated from other particular histories. And alienation is always induced by a disjunction between an identification and the relationship it makes relevant to the self.

To understand the importance of a sense of identity in coping with alienation, it may be useful to contrast Adam Smith's use of "alienation" with Karl Marx's. When Adam Smith asserted that the worker in industry was pursuing a meaningless task, he meant that the worker was unable to perceive a meaningful relationship between his portion of the task and the finished product, whereas the artisan carried the task of production through from beginning to end. When Marx spoke of commodity fetishism and the alienation of the worker, he was indulging in a romantic confusion. The subjective concern of the worker with the problem of his alienation, to the extent that it exists at all, does not arise from the fact that he is paid a salary directly related to his economic input into the productive process. Most workers are concerned primarily with their economic well-being and not with the problem Marx discusses. To the extent that some workers are alienated, this stems primarily from the fact that under many forms of market economy they are subject to cycles of business over which they lack individual control. It may also arise from the fact that workers have no competence to deal with major accidents: great depressions, terrible illnesses, floods or hurricanes, or other social or natural catastrophes. Under these circumstances, some workers may perceive themselves as prisoners of fate who are treated as objects of life and who therefore lack dignity.

As man is linked to other men in institutional structures—and to the rules, moral or otherwise, that characterize them—life acquires meaning and specific goals are legitimized (in the absence of which the definition of rationality as optimization of preferences has no realworld referent). As these existential identity factors change, the criteria by means of which goals (and individuals) are evaluated change also. We change both the problems that people face and the potential solutions that attend them. But we can never eliminate problems and the potential alienation that new identifications will make relevant to the human condition.

The attempt to overcome alienation in general represents an attempt to achieve perfection in life. However, existence is always necessarily flawed. When we ignore this, we indulge in a flight of fancy that removes words from their mooring in particularity. Utopias of this type are not peopled with real individuals with real conflicting interests. They are peopled by phantoms of the imagination: and necessarily of the conscious imagination, for the phantoms of dreams often act contrary to the wishes of the dreamer. Marx, alas, suffered (at least in one common interpretation of his position) from the disordered dream that conflict could be removed from life and that then true history would begin, whereas the real problem in life is that of arranging conflicts in the most productive and least harmful fashion. We rearrange them, not to eliminate alienation, but to reestablish identity. In that way we reduce anxiety and, perhaps, if we are lucky, eliminate anguish and despair.

Identity and Anxiety

Emphasis on a sense of identity has been stressed so often that it has become banal. Psychologists note that those with a poor sense of identity suffer from anxiety in situations that "normal" people accept calmly. This should surprise no one. Systems with a self-conscious internal governor require the interposition of cognitive decision processes between motivation and behavior. In short, they must find some rule for action. A rule is not helpful if there is no way to choose between it and a conflicting rule. Thus, a human actor needs knowledge of the environment and of the objective that a rule is designed to serve. The formal rule, for instance, that citizens should serve their country could not be applied unless the person employing the rule knew of which country he is a citizen. If this is obscure to him, or if he must choose from among conflicting rules, he may not know how to behave. His anxiety is a manifestation of this indecision. He is impelled alternatively to various courses of action, none of which seems satisfactory and each of which, at least for a period of time, rises to the level of consideration, only ultimately to be rejected. Perhaps toward the end of this process he is driven toward an impulsive action which is again a source of anxiety as he reflects upon it. Anxiety is an ontological necessity in a system that is self-reflexive; that employs goal-oriented actions; and that lacks awareness of rules, the criteria for choice from among conflicting rules, or a means of employing them that is relevant to its existential situation. Anomie thus tends to accompany a lack of identity; and the overcoming of anxiety requires the finding of meaning and of identity.

Meaning and Identity

Meaning always includes definite reference, even if the reference is to an abstraction. There is no such thing as meaning in general or meaning that is abstracted from all relationships. There are no rules that are valuable or valid in general. There are only rules that are valuable or valid in particular types of circumstances. Light has meaning only in relation to darkness. Words have meaning only in relation to the meanings of other words and to the syntactical structure of language. The meaning of an action requires knowledge of the context in which it occurs. Laughter at a comedy does not have the same meaning as laughter at the agony of another individual. Parallel lines do not mean the same thing in Euclidean and non-Euclidean geometry. A gesture does not mean the same thing when a friend makes it that it means when an enemy makes it. An offer to arbitrate a dispute does not mean the same thing after years of litigation that it means at the beginning of a dispute.

For life to have meaning and for an individual to have identity, there must be ordered sets of relationships within which particular actions have meaning. These ordered structures include the physical, the biological, the psychological, the social, the economic, and the political. Even within the narrower realm of the social, the political, and the economic, the most violent revolutionaries never dared change many of these elements at once.

This should not surprise us. The tool we use to build a piece of furniture would not be useful if its shape and form changed under our hands. We could not think if the significance of words changed as we used them. This does not mean that we cannot form different tools with different shapes or even pound our present tools into alternative shapes. It does not mean that we cannot change the significance of some words at one time and of many words over longer times. It does mean that the changes can be meaningful only if the general framework within which they occur is relatively unchanged, in the short term at least.

Our sense of identity and the meaning we achieve in life depend upon the persistence of form and structure. Yet it is form and structure that permit alienation, for it cannot exist in the formless. The purposeful individual lives a life filled with meaning because his subjective awareness is directed more to the identifications in his life than to the alienations.

Identity therefore depends upon the continuities in life, including primarily those that affect one's defined roles. (Of course, the understanding of identities is enriched by comparison with differences.) A person has expectations about the behavior of others and about the states of the world. As long as these beliefs about the world accord with experience, or are rationalized subjectively, the individual will maintain a sense of identity. If doubts arise about these expectations, anxiety will develop with respect to those roles and institutions to which the doubts apply; and there will be a tendency to anomie in these areas.

Because of the importance to an individual of his sense of identity, his belief in it is often protected by dysfunctional regulatory mechanisms that resist with greater or lesser effectiveness information to the contrary streaming either from the environment or from internal aspects of the personality system. Thus, a sense of identity may be consistent with inauthenticity and great impoverishment of character. In malign environments, a sense of identity may even depend upon inauthenticity of character or personality except in the most philosophically wise individuals.

Identity and Traditional Society

The sense of identity seems open to least doubt within traditional societies. Traditional societies tend to be hierarchical; and, if they have plural hierarchies, these tend to be consistent with each other. Changes of individual status within a hierarchical structure tend to follow prescribed paths. The rules of behavior change extremely slowly. They are usually highly specific—and thus easily applicable—rather than general. Traditional societies also employ ritual; and rituals symbolically relate man to a group and to the universe. Symbolism has meaning at the intellectual level, but it also has meaning at the sensual level. Rhythms, melodies, colors, artistic forms, dances, intonations, and gestures play roles in reinforcing the bonds among humans and with nature. Traditional societies often provide great dignity to the individual, at least with respect to those in the ranks to which honor accrues. Dignity includes a sense of worth and thus confers a sense of identity. However, the sense of identity in these societies will not be transstable, for the framework of comparison is extremely limited.

The Sense of Identity and Modernity

The workers of whom Adam Smith wrote or those whom Marx called alienated more accurately lacked a stable sense of identity, for the former could not identify with the task they performed and the latter could not identify with a world that treated them as flotsam on the waves of economic distress. The former performed by rote a mechanical operation that they could not relate to the larger system in which it occurred. The latter found their value as human beings changing rapidly with the vagaries of economic dislocations of which they had little understanding and over which they had little control. Within these aspects of their human experience, they had lost their sense of orientation. The former had no sense of the worth of what they were doing and the latter had no consistent sense of their worth. Their sense of identity was fractured.

To categorize such phenomena as instances of alienation is to grossly misunderstand them and to seek a solution to the wrong problem. The problem is not one of eliminating alienation; it is rather one of recreating a sense of identity. The former conceptualization of the process sends one in search of an apocalyptic solution—a solution that is ontologically impossible. The latter conceptualization of the process requires an examination of the specific processes of socialization and of production within a society in the search for those specific transformations most consistent with a sense of individual identity.

Identity and Transfinite Stability

So far I have dealt with the conception of identity at the simplest level. Expressed so simply, it would seem to suggest a restoration of a previous golden age, of a search for traditional forms. Although such a conclusion is not incorrect merely because it is impossible under current conditions—for tribalism can never mean in industrial society what it meant under pastoral conditions—that way of conceptualizing the process is excessively narrow. If one examines the concept of identity from the standpoint of human potentiality, the sense of identity under traditional conditions is seen to be extremely restricted. Identity, more fully understood, involves the relationship of an individual to the social systems or subsystems that are relevant to his membership roles, his place in a hierarchy of being, and his responsibilities and prerequisites as a social actor. The last involves the relationship of an action to a rule or of a rule to the set or sets of rules relevant to behavior, the conditions under which rules are applied, the conditions under which rules change, and the conditions under which changes in the sets of rules occur. With the last qualification, transstability is required. (The way in which taste adds to transfinitely stable identity is discussed on pp. 254ff.)

Transstable behavior requires a sophisticated intellect. The sense of identity in modern society breaks down if an individual either cannot or does not know how to make appropriate transstable distinctions. For example, it is often asked why the use of force within a nation is not justifiable if its use by a nation against other nations is justified. Without attempting to answer that question in any absolute way—or even to argue that under no circumstances should force be used within the nation—it is surely legitimate to respond that the characteristics of a centralized polity differ so much from those of a decentralized one that it is similar expectations with respect to the use of force that require justification. It is sometimes argued, for instance, that because war is cruel no one should be punished for extreme cruelty during war or that everyone should be punished for engaging in cruel actions. This argument fails to distinguish appropriate differences in the applicability of rules under different sets of conditions. If accepted, it would interfere with an effort to maintain any standards with respect to the use of force in war either directly, as in the first formulation of the argument, or indirectly, with respect to the second formulation, as a consequence of the impracticability of the standard.

Modern society creates problems that impair the sense of identity of many individuals who lack an effective transstable personality. Events may move so swiftly that they lack the intellectual or emotional capacity to relate to them in any meaningful way. Events beyond their control may fragment their lives and make meaningless to them their relationships to institutions of which they are defined members. If their tasks are taken over by animals or machines, even their sense of identity as human beings may become attenuated.

Modern society thus includes many types of individuals with many different types of identity problems. Individuals who follow rules only to gain the approval of other people lack a sense of identity. Individuals who pursue objectives exclusively for self-gain have a diminished sense of identity, for they have a diminished capability for identifying either with particular institutions or with society as a whole. Individuals who compulsively follow rules regardless of external circumstances have a diminished sense of identity, for that kind of rule-controlled behavior becomes a crutch without which the individual is unable to function.

Thus, modernity creates serious problems for individuals who lack transstable personalities—problems that diminish their identification with important elements of society and that tend to produce anomie with respect to these. If authentic behavior responds to all aspects of being—and that is the theme of the next section—a society that produces transstable personalities will also produce authentic individuals. However, transstable identity and authenticity are independent, if related, concepts. Conceivably a price must always be paid in terms of one for a gain in terms of the other. This price would likely be greater in some conditions than in others. Whereas, for instance, puritanical individuals may have a distinct sense of identity in puritanical culture, the penalties of law and custom that would be applied to authentic humans in such a culture might shatter their sense of identity unless they had the strongest of personalities and the most philosophic of minds. Similar shocks might await a moral person in an exclusively pleasure-seeking society. However, appropriate social and natural conditions may decrease the conflict between identity and authenticity and permit major improvements in the manifestations of both. Both are requirements of being.

Identity and Justice

The process of identification is an important key to the applicability of moral rules. The identifications of individuals and the resolution of conflicts among them depend upon understanding, socialization, and environmental conditions. It would have been silly to have asked a sixteenth-century Frenchman to behave as a world citizen, because, except in a very peripheral sense, that concept would have been irrelevant to the moral choices facing him. Moreover, there is not necessarily a univocal hierarchy among identifications, for a person appropriately may decide to identify as a world citizen with respect to ecological matters and as a national citizen with respect to more narrowly conceived national security interests.

To the extent that important moral choices involve conflicts among actual or potential identifications, they are at least partly relative. To the extent that these conflicts involve identifications the individual has internalized strongly, such moral conflicts will alienate him. The solutions he finds for this alienation—repression, sublimation, affective isolation, reconstruction of institutions—depend upon understanding and the means at hand; and some will worsen rather than improve the condition. These latter aspects—understanding and the means at hand—will determine the arrangement of values and normative rules best suited to these circumstances.

How identifications relate to alienation and justice, therefore, is kaleidoscopic. The realm is one of praxis. No theory can be developed that can be applied provided only that enough is known about initial conditions. And philosophical theories that pretend to answer problems concerned with values or alienation in this fashion are illusory.

V. Authenticity

The Particular and the General

Sometimes destructive actions that issue from hostile emotions are called genuine or authentic and they are contrasted with hypocritical good manners that respond to social custom from habit or fear. However authentically such destruction may represent a particular emotional feeling, it is not clear that it authentically represents man, for such a view reduces man to his momentary passions. Yet, these may stand between him and authentic action as surely as social hypocrisy on occasion does. Being is both particular and general. With evolutionary development, complexity of structure increasingly permitted an elaboration in the complexity of the interactive processes of society. With the elaboration of the cortical aspects of neurological structures, complexity became possible not merely in the particularities of interactions but in the intellectual understanding of them as well. Behavior is not authentic unless it genuinely represents this.

Cortical Complexity and Inauthentic Behavior

Cortical development introduced an extremely powerful control factor, or governor, for the human system: a governor that became capable of suppressing important aspects of human nature and of diminishing its richness. The power of anticipation introduces the possibility of foresightful fear. Because of the particularities of individual nurture or social experience, various aspects of human motivation, thought, and social behavior can be repressed or "outlawed." The life of feeling, of mind, and of interactive behavior can be impoverished. Men become blind to the play of light and color, deaf to the harmonies and cacophonies of sound, insensitive to the varieties of taste, immune to the feelings of love and hate, resistant to the joys of thought, incapable of arguing in a logical manner, insensitive to the distinction between their interests and those of others, incapable of recognizing the autonomy of others, and blind to the shortness of human life and the infinity of its worth.

In some, impoverishment may extend over almost the entire range of being. In others, impoverishment in some aspects may coexist with exaggerated development in others. The decadents of the *Yellow Book* period and the "crazies" who do their own thing regardless of the consequences for others are examples of the latter phenomenon: that of an impoverishment of one aspect of being and an exaggerated development of another. Those who are impoverished lack authenticity. Their behavior does not stem directly from the nature of their being, but is distorted or rerouted by an intellectual belief, or an emotional blockage, or a defense mechanism.

Some might argue that both defense mechanisms and mental concepts are part of being and, therefore, that even impoverished individuals respond authentically. Note, however, the crucial difference between the decision or the defense mechanism that permits the expression of being through mediation, or that delays a mode of action until it can be safely employed, on the one hand, and that which forecloses its use, on the other. If one fears a specific danger and runs to a safe place where he can engage in other activities, that is quite distinct from possession of a fear that becomes so generalized that behavior becomes one long flight. There is a difference between the type of thinking that solves a problem, whether that problem is concrete or intellectual, and thought processes that are as diversionary as the fear that leads to constant running. In each case the motivation has been torn from its particular nexus, has been generalized, and acquires a life of its own that is independent and that "locks up" the behavior of the individual.

Think of an electric organ with a toy organ on top of it. Divert the wiring of the apparatus so that when the keys of the electric organ are played, it is the toy organ that sounds. What one hears now may be the authentic sound of the toy organ; but it is not the authentic voice of the electric organ. It is not the fact of alteration that makes for inauthenticity but the type of alteration. The fact that these distinctions are easier to make with respect to simpler systems—and that in the case of the organ the system is designed—should not obscure the fact that the distinction is real. And, by the test in principle, it would not be chosen by the person.

Impoverished behavior, therefore, is inauthentic. In the case of the literary decadents of the *Yellow Book* period, who explored the senses in such great detail, their behavior responds to an aspect of being. However, the decadent individual was inauthentic, for he closed off an essential aspect of his humanity. Think of a thermostatic heating system that operates in the following manner: when the temperature is too low, the thermostat turns the heating equipment on and the temperature continues to increase until the thermostat turns off. The thermostat now turns on the equipment and the temperature starts going up. However, the linkage between the thermostat and the heater is now cut off. The heater consequently continues to increase the temperature, at least until an explosion or some other accident occurs. The heater could be said to be behaving authentically but the thermostatic heating system is no longer behaving authentically. The test in principle of *Justice, Human Nature, and Political Obligation* provides the key for making the appropriate distinctions.

Control systems, rather than being inconsistent with authenticity, are essential elements of authenticity in the case of transstable systems. It is the type of linkage among the elements of the system that determines whether it is behaving authentically or not.

Although control systems, including the application of moral rules, are essential elements in authentic human behavior, not every application of control is consistent with authenticity. In section II, we examined various dysfunctions of mind, including the obsessive-compulsive. Many of these aberrations involve control mechanisms that have not been integrated into the human personality. For instance, some people may follow moral rules only because they have calculated that they will gain from doing so. Although they may obey moral rules, and although this may be better for society than if they did not, the moral rules are not an integral part of their personality but are superimposed upon it. In this sense, their behavior lacks authenticity.

Although the human system is so complicated that confident generalizations about its nature are reckless, our ability to distinguish authentic from inauthentic human beings is, if far less than perfect, still better than random. At least with respect to the emotional areas of life, it is not too difficult to distinguish, for instance, between individuals in contact with their libidinal mainsprings and those who are not. The authentic individual taps all areas of his being; and they are integrated into his personality.

Authenticity and "Balance"

I recognize, as I have stated previously many times, that the aspects of being are not entirely harmonious and that under unfortunate environmental conditions tragic conflicts of choice may be presented. The authentic man is not one who maximizes each aspect of his being, for that is patently impossible. However, he is a man who is not cut off from contact—as metaphorical as these words may be— with all the aspects of his being: the sensual, the intellectual, the sacred, the moral, and the creative. Yet, authentic man does not simply resonate, for there is a necessary interposition—the intellectual and the moral—between the expression of his desire and his judgment of its value.

This conception of authenticity obviously has much in common with Aristotle's concept of "balance," or even with Plato's discussion of the three aspects of being, or with psychoanalytical conceptions of the adjusted man. This should not be entirely surprising. It is rather late in the intellectual history of man to come up with an entirely new conception of the nature of humankind. However, there are a number of differences as well.

The nature of man is not something that can become known within isolated social settings. Comparative knowledge is necessary, for only comparative knowledge can relate behavior to the environmental constraints under which it occurs. Only comparative analysis can factor out the relationships between choices made and the constraints determining the character of the alternatives. Only a wide enough range of comparisons with other choices within the same social system and with other choices within different social systems can permit one systematically to investigate the moral consequences of different kinds of choices as called for by the test in principle. Moreover, the framework of analysis employed in this book and in *Justice, Human Nature, and Political Obligation* clarifies the fact that justice is a developmental concept. This emphasizes the need for a continual reassessment of the justification of social, political, and economic arrangements.

Authenticity and Alienation

Rather than being antithetical to alienation as some writers believe, authenticity requires alienation, at least potentially and perhaps actually. It does so in an ontological sense, in a biological sense, and in a moral sense. The concept of "self" would be meaningless without the concept of "other." Unity requires distinction and distinction requires unity. Hunger requires food external to the body. Love requires an external lover. Intellect requires a subject matter. Games require opponents. And morality requires a moral other for its meaning.

Would a love subject to our control be worth winning? If the laws of nature were subject to our whim, would they be worth studying? If our opponent threw the match, would the game be worth winning? If our arbitrary will determined the rights of others, would our moral stature be worth possessing?

The work of art when complete is beyond the will of the artist. If our children are to be moral works of art, they must become autonomous and freed from our moral control, although not necessarily from meaningful relationships with us. If our students are to be educated, they must become scholars in their own right and freed from our opinions.

We can express our nature, that is, behave authentically, only as we free our works from ourselves. And this process makes alienation likely in a complex environment. When we fail to free our works, our children, and our students from ourselves, we initiate dysfunctional mechanisms of regulation that impoverish us and those we seek to help in community with us. And yet such dysfunctional attempts must fail, for they increase our alienation from our own being and destroy the community of interest we might have had with genuine, independent others. Alienation cannot be eliminated. The attempt to eliminate it impoverishes the expression of being.

Thus, perhaps it would be more precise to say that authenticity requires the acceptance of alienation.

VI. Creativity, Productivity, Style, and Justice

Creativity

Creativity can become manifest in almost every type of activity: the design of a new style of architecture, the proof of a new mathematical proposition, the invention of a new gadget, the discovery of a new concept, the invention of a new game, a new deployment in chess or war, or the coining of a new word or expression.

Creative Thought and the Preconscious

Creative thought occurs at the preconscious level. The techniques of mathematical, logical, and linguistic analysis that we apply to the confirmation of theories or of praxical consistency are necessarily conscious and orderly. These aspects permit the public communicability that is essential to science. However, those aspects of judgments that underlie the assessment and reassessment of any field of knowledge whether of science, morals, literature, or art are not fully amenable to this conscious process. They require a widespread search activity and a recognition of "fittingness" that is sometimes based on a reordering of the entire field. This reordering may occur because the preconscious recognizes possibilities for greater relatedness—or for eliminating inconsistencies—in the field that others have failed to detect or because new information reveals these possibilities. In the latter case, the creative person is the one who is preconsciously alert to these potentials. This reordering is then subject to the procedures of public (objective) communication. For instance, we may test specific propositions for theories and organize evidence assigned to argue for the "fit" of the new theory or proposition in a reordered field. But this is an *a posteriori* process.

In creative individuals the (metaphorical) barrier between the preconscious and the conscious is very permeable. A barrier between the preconscious and the conscious obviously is required, or the flow of ideas would interfere with the reasoning of conscious thought: a reasoning that is directed toward constructive action on the basis of communicable experience or confirmed hypothesis. There also would be social costs if no barrier existed. Too many suggestions for change would undermine the perceived certainties that provide social sanction for accepted norms, in the absence of which predictable behavior would not be possible. Some degree of creativity has evolutionary advantage, but only up to a point.

However, mechanisms of social control may punish the use of creative thought and may "raise" the "barrier" higher than evolutionary necessity demands. Moreover, there may be conflicts between the macro and microneeds of society. For instance, parents may repress a curiosity seemingly disadvantageous to the family so thoroughly that insufficient creative talent is available to society. This may diminish an aspect of being and produce an unnecessary degree of alienation. Although science and conscious thought seek precision in the meaning of words, the creative process thrives on ambiguity in meaning. The confusions produced by ambiguity are amply compensated for by the richness of the creative associations and identifications that are triggered by them. However, there must be some restriction on ambiguity: otherwise there would not be sufficient differentiation among concepts for associations to be meaningful. The preconscious requires some degree of differentiation for creativity. Consequently, the preconscious also is a potential source of alienation. Because, however, it focuses more on identities than on differences, the preconscious is not likely the major source of alienation that many writers believe it to be.

Creativity and Alienation

Those who are alienated from society in general or from a particular elite group may be more receptive to a lowering of the threshold between preconscious and conscious thought than those who are comfortably "adapted." They may be disposed to search for a new unity as a form of rejection of, or opposition to, the old perceived disunity. That the sense of alienation is not a sufficient condition for creative activity, however, is amply shown by the fact that many people who feel alienated are not creative.

Some people may develop creative traits from a negative predisposition. They may then discover a strong affirmative fulfillment in artistically or socially productive activities that becomes an autonomous motive for their continuation. Alienation, therefore, may not be a necessary condition for creativity any more than it is a sufficient condition.

Transfinitely stable people with a strong sense of identity also may be disposed to search for new modes of expression or of social organization. They may be creative from a strongly affirmative quest for novelty in expression, improvement in their conditions of life, or improvement of the human condition in general. Recognizing that life is inevitably imperfect, they may accept the present as a reasonable set of "solutions" and still be strongly disposed to seek productive solutions to the problems, either personal or social, that remain unsolved. They may respond to transformations of society under new conditions, and to the new problems that arise from present "solutions."

Creative Style and Its Cycle

In the arts and literature, creativity seems to go through cycles of style. Thus, a romantic movement may give rise to an intellectual one: representational art may be followed by abstract art, or impressionism by metaphysical painting, and metaphysical painting by actionism.

Although art is superficially a sensuous activity, the history of art makes manifest the great differences in the temperaments of artists: in some periods art reflects the warmth of passion; in others it manifests the cool of intellect; and, in still others, the pure spirit of religious or moral ideals becomes evident. In some periods sensibility and fineness of detail are emphasized; in others simplicity and comprehensibility take a leading role.

These trends appear to occur in cycles, and we do not begin to understand the reasons for them. However, there are a number of convenient hypotheses that initially seem promising. The newer a mode of activity, the more extensive it would seem are the innovations that can be pursued within it. Thus, for instance, in the realm of science the major inventions of Galileo, Newton, Planck, and Einstein opened up vast new areas of scientific activity. In the same way, artistic innovations open up possibilities for other artists. Regardless of how the preconscious creative process may operate, the more open the terrain it explores—provided it is not chaotic—the more likely that creative discovery will occur.

Whether a major innovation finds a social response may depend upon a number of factors. There must be a readiness for it somewhere within the system. The discoveries of Galileo permitted successful experimentation by others. The vast conceptions of Newton permitted a meaningful explanation of diverse phenomena that were of interest to scientists and philosophers. The public may have hooted at Beethoven's music, but the musical avant-garde was ready for it. Moreover, his musical romanticism coincided with strong romantic movements in literature and in popular feeling.

As these new movements continued, their very success diminished the scope for further creativity within the same framework. On the other hand, their success encouraged others to continue to mine these fields until they ran out, as in many of the western gold rushes in the United States. As these motivating factors moved toward their margins, the interplay of motivations likely again favored those searching for new breakthroughs, although only particular efforts would combine novelty with public readiness in a manner productive of success.

From the standpoint of the consumers of art, much of the same motivational pattern may apply. The newer the movement, the richer the rewards to be gained by those who consume its products. As the rewards begin to diminish, novelty declines and acceptance increases. Finally, an important section of the public is sated and waits for something new.

Cultural innovations may initiate a similar pattern in the style of social life. With the introduction of a new style, one has a feeling of breaking through the constraints of past styles and of being liberated by the new. As time goes on, the style is sanctified by public acceptance. Ultimately the once new is perceived as a set of rigidified forms within which changes can occur only in small ways and at the margin. It is now experienced as a constraint on conduct and its costs rather than its rewards are at the focus of attention.

Creative Style and Authenticity

This tentative explanation would be merely interesting except for one possible problem. If expression of the three major aspects of being—the sensual, the intellectual, and the sacred—is essential if humans are to achieve authenticity, the cyclic process we are describing may result in cyclic inauthenticity and impoverishment of character. Yet, if the hypotheses concerning them are correct, there may be a semi-independent process generating them that it would be most difficult to control, especially under modern conditions.

Is this problem ineluctable? Although that question is fundamental, I doubt that it can be answered on the basis of existing evidence. However, even before attempting a hypothetical and very speculative answer to that problem, the related problem of productivity will be discussed.

Productivity

We use metaphors such as "breakthrough" and recombinations of particulars to stress what we mean by creation. Productivity might then simply be regarded as repetitive activity. In this sense, we would call an artist's painting creative and the work of a punch press operator merely productive.

We have a clear distinction in these two examples, but it is not clear that we have chosen the right examples. The punch press is a non-ultrastable machine. Consider the simplest type of ultrastable machine: Ashby's postulated automatic pilot. Is it creative when it readjusts its own internal connections to achieve level flight? What happens when we move to transstable cases: for instance, human beings? Is the salesman merely productive or is he creative as he sells his packages of hairpins from door to door? Is a traditional art that follows stylized form creative or merely productive? Is the maker of kitsch for K-mart merely a producer? Is the policeman arresting a drunk merely a producer? Is the writer of a hack textbook who plagiarizes other sources merely a producer?

Our problem stems from the fact that although we can establish a distinction between creativity and productivity without too much trouble, no human activity is purely one or the other. Yet, if we wish to characterize human behavior, we need both terms, often for the same acts. There are great creative artists who are not productive: that is, they are original but they do not produce a large body of work. And there are very productive artists who are not very creative.

There is still another, and more important, sense in which activity may be said to be productive. Merely repetitive activity may produce a useless output. Some activity, however, copes more or less adequately with real problems. Thus, increasing sales by a salesman may "solve" his family's economic problems. Increasing production by industry may "solve" a consumption problem. Acquiring friends may "solve" a personality problem. Receptivity to a stylistic change in society is evidence that the new style responds productively to some real need even though we may be unable to articulate that need and even though the "solution" may create worse problems than it "solves."

Changes in Productive Style

There are stylistic differences in productive activities as well as in creative ones. However, these do not seem to be cyclical in the sense that we noted in the case of creativity (at least for the elite). We do not deny the recurrence of some features of social style. Through much of human history we can note an alternation between the heroic and the religious spirits. Overlapping that dyad, almost as in a counterpoint, was the cycle of mercy and justice, sometimes as represented in moon (goddess, Marian) cults and sun (god, Jesus) cults.

Werner Sombart thought he detected an alternation of warrior and bourgeois spirits in the modern world. Max Weber was concerned with the rise of the bourgeois mentality and much of modern social science follows him in this. Much of the social ferment in the first half of the twentieth century involved a romantic rejection of the bourgeois spirit; indeed, much of the new left movement of today reacts to bourgeois values as did the protofascist movements of the 1920s and 1930s.

However, as long as we avoid the unilinear fallacy, social style seems to be developmental. The managerial and the scientific productive mentalities arose within the bosom of the bourgeois mentality. As capitalism developed, the reward structure of society fostered those mentalities that could make it work. As capitalism became dependent upon management and science, the incentive structure changed, thus partly eliciting a change in the productive mentalities of the period.

Although Adam Smith saw the relatively unskilled factory worker's job as meaningless—a theme repeated much later with graphic effectiveness in Charlie Chaplin's *Modern Times*—this did not correctly express the perception of the average worker. He did not think of his work primarily from the standpoint of its relationship to the completed product. His perception of himself during an era of scarcity was of a man contributing to the prosperity of the country and to the welfare of his family. Thus, contrary to what Adam Smith thought, the worker could have a sense of identity and could take some pride in his work, although perhaps not as much as that of the artisan whose work was often satisfying in its own terms.

With the rise of an affluent society, a welfare system, an availability of jobs for married women, a multiplicity of jobs for men, and an expansion of service activities that are not productive in the material sense, the relatively unskilled factory worker found it much more difficult to perceive a meaningful relationship between his work and a worthy role in the social system. His family's dependence on his labor was reduced. His dependence on a particular job was attenuated. The expansion of the concept of productivity diminished his perception of the importance of factory work. This tended to increase his awareness of a lack of relationship between his repetitive job and the final product. As a consequence, his sense of identity was diminished and his alienation increased.

It is with respect to developmental changes of this kind that generational gaps probably are widest. The older worker tends to retain his sense of the importance of productive work and therefore is able to take pride in it. Many younger workers, who grew up in the new milieu—at least prior to the recent recession—do not understand such attitudes. Nor does the older worker understand the newer attitudes or the social or productive styles that respond to them.

Contemporary problems may be at least as difficult to cope with as those that arose from poverty. Crises of self-esteem arising from relative abundance and the availability of social welfare may cut deeply into definitions of identity. Increased use of machines in sophisticated processes may cause many individuals, although fewer among the highly skilled or the unimaginative, to regard themselves as supernumeraries or even to become confused with respect to the distinction between the human and nonhuman—a consequence that could have a profoundly evil influence upon politics and upon social and productive styles.

This issue raises the question of a possible inherent incompatibility between productive achievement and the sense of accomplishment. If the latter is important to the sense of identity, as I suspect it is, material security may erode satisfaction in life, thus producing pathologies of behavior: apathy and a deadening of sensibility in some and a disordered search for thrills or a mission in life in others.

Whether we can control the exigencies of nature and at the same time confront humankind with creative tasks essential to the sense of productivity is a poignant issue for politics. Perhaps we need not worry, for the pollution problem and the energy problem do not seem to indicate an absence of challenge. Yet their seeming inaccessibility to intervention by any agency other than mammoth and impersonal governments is not entirely reassuring. And they may foster style changes in productivity and in society that are pathological.

The Individual and Social Costs

With changed attitudes toward work, it should not be surprising that there is a receptivity toward new life styles better adapted to these new attitudes. On the other hand, it does not follow that the new attitudes are genuinely functional. Large and unnecessary social costs are involved in sloppy manufacture and repair work.

We all recognize these problems in general terms. We deplore them when we suffer from them. However, on the whole, we fail to see the relationships between our attitudes and our lifestyles and their consequences. The interrelationships are too remote, too indirect, and too ambiguous. In the same way, individual acts of industrial sabotage seem relatively costless. And, indeed, they would be relatively costless if the individual engaging in them were the only one who did so. However, the attitudes that motivate him motivate many others just like him, and the resulting social cost is very high.

This illustrative example does not prove that each relative success with respect to some of the problems facing society generates new problems, new discontents, and new identity crises, although each change in the environment does change the perception of social relationships and social meaning. Yet, it surely suggests one or more of these consequences. Only the most original and perceptive minds of each generation will be capable of forecasting the ways in which social, economic, and political change will affect the future and the perceptions human beings will have of the meaningful character of their roles. It is hardly likely that they will be sufficiently influential to alert the mass of the population to these remote consequences, particularly if the present costs of avoiding them are clear and substantial.

Imagine the response if during the Great Depression of the 1930s some misguided genius had attempted to alert the nation to the perils of pollution under conditions of a future prosperity the individuals of that time would not have thought possible, and if he had suggested a modest tax scheme—or, alternatively, an increase in the cost of production—to protect against those perils. If any notice would have been taken of him at all, it likely would have been as a source of laughter or as a butt of anger. Moreover, this response, although not entirely appropriate, would have been not entirely inappropriate either. It was more important to deal with the problem of prosperity first, which we did not then know how to solve, than it was to anticipate the problems of pollution if the problem of prosperity were solved.

In the best of all possible worlds, some resources will be made available to explore the parameters of problems that can be anticipated by intelligent men. In a world in which resources are scarce, the mechanisms that guard against a diversion of resources to the study of hypothetical future problems are eufunctional. Even in prosperous worlds, resources are not unlimited. Thus, in present-day society, in which the ecological problem has become severe, there are serious questions as to who shall bear the costs of control and how they shall be borne. Each suggested solution sacrifices some alternative gain. Each principle of spreading the costs conflicts with some alternative principle and thereby conflicts with someone's sense of justice. Each putative solution will have differential impact on some human beings' perceptions of their identity or on the authenticity of their expressions of their being.

Despite the prior comments, it may be possible to acquire better insight into how social change affects perception and style of behavior. We know that our anticipations of the future will sometimes fail, that problems will always exist, that solutions will always impact differentially, that perceptions will always be altered, and that some senses of identity and some expressions of authenticity will always be injured. The certainty of such changes, however, does not mean that we cannot attempt to minimize damage, to facilitate authenticity, and to preserve the sense of identity.

Style Exaggeration and Its Consequences

We do not know enough about the social process to know whether damage from style exaggeration can be minimized in all cases. For instance, consider the political role in contemporary society. Some have suggested that the demands of the highest political offices, for instance, the presidency, are so great that only very abnormal individuals seek them. Yet, clearly we need people to fill these offices.

In some cases, where society greatly needs a role to be filled, the rewards attached to it may facilitate the development in those individuals initially predisposed toward it of those very motivations that are dysfunctional in excess. Thus, at least under current conditions, society may require roles that—although highly rewarded and serving as a source of a sense of identity—impede authenticity.

Perhaps a slight clue to a possible solution to this problem can be discovered by examining the possibility that the rewards offered by society may emphasize in political personalities those dysfunctional tendencies that make them successful in the role. In the first place, it is not clear that the success of political leaders in performing societal and political functions stems from an excess of competitiveness, although in an imperfect world some of it may be necessary for role performance. It instead may be the case that it is success in achieving the role, rather than success in performing it, that may require an excess in competitiveness.

If the latter hypothesis is correct, then a society that manifests prominent particular styles of behavior may encourage these styles in politically prone persons so much that they become dysfunctional for the society. In a heroic age, political leaders may romantically risk more than prudence would dictate. In a bourgeois age, political leaders may engage in excesses of deceit and calculation. In a scientific age, political leaders may too easily accept the technologies produced by science without considering the political and moral consequences of their employment.

In those cases in which a society manifests a style as strongly as this, it may be said to lack moderation. It may also inhibit authenticity, for each style represents an exaggeration of some aspect of being. This does not occur in any simple fashion, however. Some expressions of heroism are responsive to passion; others are responsive to idealism or the sacred. In the first case, they may be viewed as an expression of manliness; in the latter case, as an expression of a quest for sanctity. The bourgeois calculating style appeals to certain aspects of mind and exaggerates those tendencies in it. Heroism exaggerates a sacrifice of the self to the community or to spirit. The bourgeois spirit exaggerates the self and atomizes it. Puritanism exaggerates compulsive dysfunctions. Estheticism exaggerates hysterical dysfunctions.

Society and Authenticity

Exaggerated tendencies in style stem from different aspects of being. These different aspects of being cannot be homogenized. However, a society of sufficient complexity probably can provide roles that permit the manifestation of each of the tendencies. And, if this complex society is sufficiently permeable, individuals then can be encouraged to engage in a diversity of activities that manifest these often conflicting tendencies. Conceivably, if such variety does not confuse the individual, it might serve to maintain a viable level of authenticity, in which each of the aspects of being will find some substantial manifestation in behavior and serve as a constraint on excess.

A society with this type of complexity would not eliminate the potential for alienation—or even its occurrence to some extent—and it would not eliminate problems. However, it might reduce those exaggerations that generate unnecessary problems. A political leader who has been exposed to and constrained by such a variety of activities might be protected against the tendency of the chase for the office and the exercise of the powers of the office to exaggerate in him those abnormal characteristics that may have predisposed him to seek it in the first place.

I do not suggest that such a complex society would eliminate the cyclical nature of esthetic expression or developmental changes in style in society at large. Esthetic cycles probably follow an at least partly semiautonomous pattern, and social style is related to the problems generated by the complexly interrelated natural, social, cultural, and economic environments. Perhaps, however, sharp alternations of the pattern can be moderated, or at least offset, by countervailing influences. Whatever may or may not be true of some specialized social roles, where perhaps unbalanced or even impoverished personalities are required, perhaps we can at least avoid that extreme situation in which the bulk of the elite, or even of the population at large, is desensitized to essential aspects of being, whether these be sensual, intellectual, or spiritual.

Society and Identity

In addition to protecting influences and lifestyles related to the various aspects of being, thus facilitating authenticity, we require social, economic, and political arrangements that maintain the identities of members. This may involve relative equality with respect to a number of things: the vote, the right to education, the meeting of at least minimal medical needs, the assurance of meaningful work and meaningful recreational opportunities, and the assurance of meaningful (and not demeaning) assistance in case of adversity or accident. A human society will also permit equal opportunity to individuals to pursue those inequalities that respond to existential differences in their being and that do not demean or subject other people: in creations of the mind, in exercises of bodily skill, in developing productive techniques, or in the capacity to earn those of the goods of life that are needed to satisfy tastes, special abilities, or ambitions.

Society and Taste

A human society is one in which individuals exercise taste and sensibility. In discussing creativity, one of the distinctions I made between the conscious and the preconscious mind involved the capacity of the preconscious mind to scan for and to recognize "fits" among phenomena. The same capacity is made manifest when we recognize a particular individual. If the individual has a prominent characteristic, we can explain that we recognized him by means of that characteristic. Usually, however, our ability to articulate how recognition occurs is inadequate for teaching others how to recognize what we recognize: consider in this respect, for instance, the art of the tea taster.

For similar reasons, we usually cannot articulate those fine distinctions in social or moral situations that are necessary to account for our behavior. Much important social and moral behavior cannot be compressed within the framework of explicit rules. Thus, the concept of taste adds to our conception of transfinitely stable identity.

Taste and sensitivity—the ability to resonate finely to situations and to people—are required for appropriate social behavior. Some lack this capability because their behavior is derived from, rather than merely constrained by, a set of rules. Others interpret the behavior of people in terms of stereotypes or of their own needs. This impoverishment of perception diminishes their humanity and threatens their sense of identity.

Sensitivity to the needs of others is a necessary, but not a sufficient, condition for taste or sensibility. The sociopath is sensitive to the requirements of others. He could not manipulate them so easily were this not true. However, he lacks taste or sensibility, for he would not manipulate them if he understood the inappropriateness of manipulation or if he had a firm sense of identity. Thus, sensitivity involves openness to information whereas taste involves the sense of appropriateness in responding.

In some ways the sociopath is a bad example, for he lacks a comprehension of the existence of a moral order. Lack of taste could be even more clearly recognized in the case of those individuals who recognize the existence of a moral order, who wish to observe it, but who are incapable of making appropriate distinctions that are not directly reducible to rules. Thus, for instance, at the Democratic

Convention in 1968 the demonstration after the showing of the Kennedy movie was contrary to the rules. The chairman was within his rights in attempting to stop the demonstration. However, his action lacked taste. In the first place, it would have been appropriate to show some respect for so widespread a sentiment even if one disagreed with it and even if it was technically contrary to the rules. In the second place, the showing of respect under these conditions would have had a beneficial influence upon the political process. The chairman's action was neither wrong nor ill-intentioned, but it did lack taste.

Although taste can be dangerous if it becomes overly refined, as in the sensibility of the decadents, a balanced capacity for taste is essential to a human society. Civility, which requires taste, is a requirement for human politics. If one were engaged on a mission to undermine the foundations upon which a human society might be built, he would have no stronger weapon in his arsenal than that of incivility.

Society and Alienation

A human society is one in which alienation is accepted as a natural potentiality. It is only when one understands the ineradicable and ineluctable character of otherness that one is willing to concede autonomy to others, even at the expense of one's own alienation. Only such a willingness will produce that recognition of sufficient identity of interest between the self and others to solve particular problems. Those who will not accept this necessary potential for alienation will be driven to compel others to conform to the dictates of their own reason and needs. Anyone who resists, anything that defies understanding, anything that manifests an unexpected development thereby reveals itself as alien and invites destruction.

Society can be restructured to improve the sense of identity, and to facilitate authenticity, to encourage productivity, and to generate creativity if alienation is recognized as ineluctably potential in life. If we recognize that problems will always occur, that conflict will always exist, that resources are always limited, that every improvement in something involves differential costs for some people, that harmony and mutuality of interest can apply only to selected aspects and not to the whole of existence, we can better perceive those acts of reconstruction that can move us toward a human society.

There is an ultimate particularity that defies all our generalizations. We must continually return to the open world of experience to refresh our concepts, our ideas, our generalizations, and our theories. It is the union of the particular with the general that generates meaning and governs understanding. Except by accident, a human society will be built only by those who recognize this. Man's feet are in the mud and his eyes look to the stars.

GLOSSARY*

Abstraction. A *concept;* a *sign* in its role as a sign.

Analytical. Formally related, related by inner criteria (see *truth, logical);* alternatively, related in an abstract *system.*

Analyze, to. To separate into components.

Assessment. An *abstract sign system* that *mediates concepts* and *referents* and that employs the methods of *praxis.*

As such. As things are in their *essence.*

Bracket, to. To suspend judgment concerning the status of the appearance under examination (Husserl).

Centrality of logic. The more a definition or theorem is crucial to the logic of a *theory* or mode of inquiry—that is, the more that variance in it would produce radical change in the theory or mode of inquiry—the more central it is to its logic.

Characterize, to. To make a *concept* embodied in a pair of *correlatives* relevant to a *particular* by means of a *sign.* Characterizing is hypothetical in two senses. First, whether a particular *entity, process, sign,* or *quality* thereof exists: the concept "ether" in physics, for example, has no *referent.* Second, whether the attribution is correct: green, for example, may be experienced as red by a colorblind person. These problems are solved by *praxical assessment.*

Coding. An explicit or implicit routine for *characterizing perceptions* or *signals.*

Coherence theory. A *theory* that the *elements* of the world are *internally related* and that they *fit* together in a *strongly ordered, univocal* fashion.

---

*Terms in italics are defined separately in this glossary.

Complementarity. Aspects of an object, *event*, or *process* that contribute to *knowledge* of it but that require incompatible techniques for their determination are in a state of complementarity. According to Niels Bohr, the positions and momenta of quanta are in a condition of complementarity The measurement of one requires rigid instruments; of the other, instruments with moving parts. *"Mind"* and "body" are also *concepts* whose *analysis* requires incompatible techniques.

Concept. A *universal* or cluster of universals in their relationships. For example, the concept is "lightness," the *sign* is "light," and the *referent* is light. Clusters of concepts are *theories* or *assessments* and refer to *events, processes, structures,* and *systems.* Signs that mediate them include "ape," "scholar," "relativity," "revolution," and "fusion." There are external standards for the correct use of a concept: there must be an actual referent; there is none for unicorn, for example, except in fiction. Internal standards also govern the use of a concept: these may be set by definitions or by *theories.*

Concrete. Pertaining to a manifest *entity, process,* or *event.*

Concrete particular. See *Particular, concrete.*

Consciousness. The state of *knowing,* of having *experiences.*

Conventional. Artificial, chosen, not constrained by nature.

Copy theory. A *theory* that there is a descriptive correspondence between *ideas* and *concrete entities* or *processes.*

Correlatives. Qualitative pairs of *concepts* that *characterize* aspects of *experience,* such as "warm" and "cool." Because the *referents* of correlatives are always *particulars,* their use is always constrained by context and a frame of reference that produces inner connectedness.

Correspondence theory. A theory that there is an invariant association between *signs,* the *concepts* they mediate, and *concrete particulars.*

Covering law. See *Law, covering.*

Danda. Products of interpretations that rest on *worldviews* or "worldwide structural hypotheses," for example, organicist philosophies that distinguish between appearances and realities, the natures of which depend on the philosophy, for example, the *meaning* of Idea in Plato's theory depends on other elements of his theory (Pepper).

Deconstruction. A critical method designed to show how culture, including writing, inevitably produces incoherence in the presentation of the real world. Every signifier invokes an infinite sequence of signifiers, no one of which has a firm presence. Each produces its own gap or absence, in an infinite sequence. An example of deconstruction is the tearing apart of a text in an effort to find the one book that all existing texts hide (Derrida).

De dicta. A non-*univocal* relationship between *sign, referent,* and *concept.* How things are spoken of (cf. *de re*).

De re. How things are in themselves. A *truth* that will not vary from world to world.

Describe, to. To *characterize.* Description is always hypothetical.

Designation, rigid. The univocal relationship of *concept, sign,* and *referent* in all possible worlds. How things are *de re.*

Dispositional. A *concept* that cannot be defined, recognition of which depends on its manifestations under different circumstances, for example, electric charge.

Ego. The *self,* or the *conscious* subsystem thereof, to which all *first-order transactions* have reference.

Element. Member of a set.

Entity. A *structure;* occasionally used as a synonym for *system.*

Epistemology. The *assessment* of the standards for and the possibility of *knowing.*

Equilibrium, homeostatic. A characteristic of a *system* in which changes in one or more *elements* keep another element at a constant *value:* for example, when the room cools, the heater is automatically turned on.

Equilibrium, mechanical. A state of equality to which independent measures and *covering laws* apply.

Equilibrium, transfinitely stable. Refers to the ability of a *system* to adjust a complex *structure* of rules, goals, and *values* to circumstances, to substitute new rules, goals, and values for old ones, to develop new rules, goals and values and to relate its behavior to its understanding of itself and its world.

Equilibrium, ultrastable. Refers to the ability of a *system* to correct its code of behavior to keep at least one of its *elements* at a constant *value:* for example, if the coded behavior does not turn on the heat, the system will search for a new response that will.

Essence. That which underlies appearance and determines its character; underlying or basic character.

Event. An occurrence to which the concept of "space-time" applies and the *elements* of which are externally connected: for example, *praxical assessment* is an event.

Existential. *Concrete,* manifest.

Existentialism. A *theory* that the world is meaningless or that *meaning* is introduced into a meaningless world by human will. Existentialists may find meaning in the fear of nonexistence or in anxiety and often share with philosophical *phenomenology* a belief in Being.

Experience. Awareness of *entities, processes, events, signs, concepts, thoughts,* and feelings.

Explanation. An account that can be derived from a *theory* or *covering law* and applied directly to the real world when the boundaries of the theory or law are explicit.

Extension. Reference by pointing.

External Relations. See *Relations, external.*

Fact. An empirical *truth.*

Feedback. Produced by a control *system* in which the behavior of a *system* is monitored, modified or compensated for, and then returned to the system: for example, as by an automatic passenger elevator.

Feedback, negative. *Feedback* that controls output by reducing excess: for example, the control of distortion in a sound amplifier.

Feedback, positive. A *signal* that is amplified by the system, for which it is an input and returned to it for additional amplification.

First-order reference. The locus of reference of an observer, actor, or *system*.

Fit, to. To be consistent with, to complement; a *metaphor;* therefore, the criteria for fit must be stated each time the *concept is* used.

Function. The role an *element* plays in controlling *equilibrium* or change in a *system.*

Game theory. A mathematical *theory* that prescribes *optimal* strategies to be used in games in which players take into account the strategies of the other players (von Neumann).

Hermeneutics. The principles by means of which a text is *analyzed;* a set of *concepts* and *signs* divorced from real *referents.*

Homeorhesis. Maintenance of a direction of flow or of development in a *system* (Waddington).

Idea. See *Concept.* The *meaning* of idea that sustains idealistic *theories* differs from my definition; for example, *danda.*

Idealism. A *theory* that the reality underlying matter is *Idea.*

Idealism, objective. A *theory* that the world is the appearance of *essences* and, therefore, of *Idea,* but also that essences are inferred from existence; compatible with contingency in the temporal world.

Idealism, subjective. A *theory* that the world is phenomenal only or that it is, or consists of, *ideas* in the *mind.*

Idiosyncratic. Personal; dependent on the history of individuals, persons, or groups and variability in their environment.

Information. A *signal* that conveys *knowledge* to a *transceiver:* for example, the *characteristics* of an *entity* or *process,* the *signs* stored in a computer.

Intensional. Having significance or *meaning.*

Internal Relations. See *Relations, internal.*

Invariant. Deterministic; constant under specified conditions;

the quantum equations are invariant although quantum *events* are probabilistic.

Justice, procedural. *A process* intended to produce *substantive justice.*

Justice, substantive. *A* condition in which each actor, role, or *organization* obtains that outcome or participates in that state of affairs that it ought to obtain or participate in *(cf. Society, just).*

Knowledge. *Concepts* and *reals mediated* at least implicitly by *signs,* a triadic relationship that involves two *correlative pairs: "concept"* and *"sign"* and "sign" and *"referent,"* as well as relationships between *perceptions* of referents and *systems* of *concepts;* awareness of features of the world or of relationships among them. See *Mind.*

Knowledge, transactional. The *characterization* of a *referent* by a *transceiver* or perceiver.

Law, covering. *A system of signs* that specifies an *invariance* among defined *entities* or *processes* and that *mediates concepts* and *reals.* Requires independent measures.

Literal. Use *of* a *concept* that *fits* its *referent* exactly. A one-to-one relationship among *concept, sign,* and *referent.*

Locator terms. Terms that designate a qualitative or quantitative ordering of one of a pair of *concepts* that are *correlatives.*

Macrophysics. The domain in which mass points interact with force fields. Mechanics, field physics, and phenomenological thermodynamics.

Materialism. A *theory* in which the *real* is equated with the material and in which *mind* is held to be either epiphenomenal or physical.

Meaning. Meaning is given by the scope of the use by a *transceiver* or perceiver of the *sign-mediated* application of a *concept* (in its *correlative* aspect) or of a *system* of *concepts* (in their correlative aspects) to *referents.* As *reflexive* referents, signs in their relations to other signs can have intra-systemic *meaning.* There are external (and also internal) criteria for these applications; and, thus, the concept of *empirical truth* is applicable.

Mediate, to. To occupy an intermediate position in a *transaction.*

Message. A *signal* or signal set; a communication that conveys *meaning*.

Metacorrelatives. *Correlative signs* whose *referents* are other correlatives.

Metalanguage. A language within which another language is *analyzed;* language used to discuss language.

Metaphor. A *sign* that is complexly related to *concepts* and *referents*, that is, that does not fit them in some respects: for example, his elephantine walk, which can resemble the concepts or referents of "elephant" and "walk" only in some respects. External criteria are used to determine that a fit is not literal.

Metaphysical system. A systematic hypothesis of the nature of the world. If it were genuinely worldwide, it would be circular.

Metaphysics. The fundamental principles that govern the world; the *danda* that shape the interpretation of data.

Metatheory. The principles that *characterize relationships* in the world; for example, part systems, first-order and second-order references. These principles are not *a priori* principles and, as part systems within a *worldview,* they are not circular.

Microphysics. Quantum physics. Quantum mechanics is the field in which we cannot assign location or velocity without reference to specific experimental contexts. In quantum field theory the quantification of fields yields particles. In quantum theory, the non-Aristotelian logic of complex probability amplitudes leads to *objective* probabilities.

Mind. A *system* that uses and transforms *concepts, signs,* and *perceptions* of *referents;* and the states and organization of which are affected by its processing of them.

Mysticism. The belief that there is a fundamental reality that is ineffable and inexpressible, certain aspects of which can be partly discerned through *metaphor* or intuition.

Name. An identifier of a *concrete particular* or a *system;* a noun.

Natural. Produced by the potentialities of the transactional process; the opposite of *conventional* or artificial.

Natural kind. Entities that fit within a scientific classification; according to Kripke and Putnam, a natural kind is determined by a *necessarily true* definition.

Necessary. Internally *related; deductive* or *correlative.*

Neutral. A *second-order invariance.*

Nominalistic. Existing only as *particulars.*

Normative. Pertaining to criteria that guide, or are intended to guide, judgment.

Objective. The state of being a referent; hence, in the object language. It connotes invariance, at least at a *second-order level* of reference, and includes thoughts and relationships insofar as they are the objects of *knowing* or *thinking.*

Ontology. The study of the nature and *relations* of being.

Optimal. Best under the circumstances of choice.

Order, strong. An order that is determinate and *univocal.*

Order, univocal. An order in which each state of the world, *entity,* and *process* is associated with a specific locus that belongs to it alone.

Order, weak. An order that is not *univocal.*

Organization. A *system* in which participants have goals or tasks.

Paradigmatic. *Fitting* a *concept literally:* for example, a paradigmatic example of a free market economy would be one in which *information* is free, assets can be transferred without loss, and products are indistinguishable.

Particular. Distinguishable from other *entities, processes, events,* or *signs* of the same kind or classification; a member of a class that can be denoted by "this" or "that": for example, this apple.

Particular, abstract. A *sign* or *sign set* that qualifies a *concrete particular:* for example, "green" is an abstract particular that qualifies a concrete particular. "Greenness" is the *concept,* that is, the *universal.*

Particular, concrete. An *entity, process, event,* or *quality:* for example, the White House, World War II, or that green baseball.

Part system. A *system* of sufficient stability and independence so that it can be studied while changes in related systems are ignored, at least tentatively; a subsystem.

Perception. A holistic, analog process of *minds* that *codes* neural *signals* and inputs from the environment. See *prehend.*

Personal. Not *subjective,* but related to the individual (cf. *idiosyncratic*).

Phenomenology. As a method, the *analysis* of *experience;* as a philosophy, the attempt to penetrate to the *essences* that underlie appearances by analyzing appearances. Its emphasis is on human psychology, and it is often *characterized* by the thesis that Being has a *meaning* beyond types of *particular* beings or types of being.

Positivism. The claim that science starts from sensory data and that *theories* are built from this ground up.

Potentiality. The capability of becoming manifest or of producing or contributing to the production of manifest *entities, processes, events,* or *properties.*

Practice. How things work or how they are done; for example, how pilots fly planes rather than what the regulations specify (cf. *praxis*).

Pragmaticism. Charles Sanders Peirce's *theory* that the *meaning* of a *concept* is inferred from the infinite totality of its *relations* and effects. Peirce rejected the notion of *essences,* but accepted the *idea* of a *telos.* He coined the term "pragmaticism" to distinguish it from William James's misuse of the term "pragmatism."

Praxical assessment. An account that is not entirely deductive and that employs *concepts* such as *fit, centrality* of *logic,* and *relevance.* My employment of praxical assessment includes *second-order* and *part-system* analysis and, therefore, takes observers into explicit account. I drop the concept of an infinity of tests in favor of sustained comparative testing.

Praxis. A reasoning *process* in which the explicit or implicit employment of *concepts* such as *fit, centrality of logic,* and relevance are used in the evaluation of *theories,* propositions, and data; thus, the *practice* of scientific method as distinguished from the construction and testing of formal theories provides an external standard for theories. Not, however, practice in the ordinary or the Marxian sense.

Preconscious. *Potentially conscious.*

Prehend, to. To grasp by means of the senses. See *perception.*

Process. The regular changes that *functions* produce in a *structure.*

Quality. The *referent* of a *concept* that *characterizes* an *element* of an *entity, process, event,* or *sign.*

Rational. In accordance with internal and external criteria.

Real. An *event, entity,* or *process;* the *potentiality* of a *particular* entity or process; the properties of particular entities, events, or processes. To Hegel, *essences* were real.

Referent. A *particular,* including *relations; signed.*

Reflexive. Self-referring.

Reify, to. To treat an *abstract concept* as *concrete;* to treat a *process* as an *entity;* to treat a function as the whole; to treat a relational concept as independent; for example, the concept of class in Marx and of wants in neo-classical economic *theory.*

Relations, external. Relations among *concepts* or their *referents* when they are *mediated* by *assessment* rather than a *theory;* relations between concepts that are not *correlatives.*

Relations, internal. The relations among *correlatives* or among the *concepts* or *referents* of concepts in a *theory* or in the theoretical subcomponent of an *assessment;* a *necessary* relationship. *"Mind"* and "body" are correlatives and thus are internally related. The *meaning* of mass depends on the theory in which it is imbedded and, to this extent, is internal.

Second-order reference. A reference standpoint that is independent of the locus of particular observers, actors, and *systems:* for example, relativity *theory* provides a *neutral* perspective for observers on independent inertial systems.

Self. The *reflexive* subject that experiences the world; the "housing" of the *ego*.

Self-consciousness. *Knowledge* of *consciousness; reflexive* consciousness.

Sign. A symbol or word that is associated with a *referent*.

Signal. The content of a transmission from a source to a *transceiver*.

Signal source. A *referent;* a *real*.

Signed. The *referent* of a *sign*.

Sign set. Related *signs;* the signs of the *real elements* associated with a *name*.

Society, just. A society in which a good way of life, good *values*, and individual and *organizational* virtues are manifest.

Structure. The static relationships between *elements* of a *system*.

Subjective. The *correlative* of *objective; consciousness*.

System. *Abstractly*, a set of *elements* and *functions;* in *real* terms, an *entity* and its *processes:* for example, this man, that telephone network.

System, definitional. A *system characterized* by an *invariant structure* and/or by invariant *processes* carried on within or by that structure.

Telos. A direction of development (Peirce).

Test in principle. A *thought* experiment to test *values*.

Theory. An *abstract sign system* that *mediates concepts* and *referents* and that employs undefined terms, definitions, axioms, and theorems in a deductive way within explicit boundaries. In addition to the two senses in which *characterization* is hypothetical, there is a third sense in which characterization of the real world by a theory is hypothetical: there are internal standards for judging whether its predictions are accurate and, therefore, whether the theory adequately *characterizes reals.*

Theory sketch. A reasoned account, the *elements* of which are only loosely or plausibly related, although there may be occasional instances of strict deduction. It differs from Hempel's "explanation sketch" insofar as Hempel assumes that a *potential theory* always underlies a sketch.

Thinking. A *process* in which *concepts* are *mediated* by *signs* in theorizing about or assessing interrelationships in the world.

Thought. An *element* in *thinking;* a single proposition, express or implied.

Transaction. A *process* the outcome of which is produced by relations between *entities.*

Transceiver. A *system* that characterizes *entities, events,* and *processes* by *coding signals. Minds,* that is, perceivers, are transceivers but not all transceivers are minds.

Transmission. A *process* involving a *transceiver,* a *signal* set, a medium, and a *signal* source.

True. Something is true if it follows from internal criteria, if it fits external criteria, or if it is axiomatic.

Truth, empirical. The fit between an *entity, event,* or *process* or a *theory, assessment,* or proposition and external criteria. As applied to theories and the theoretical aspects of *assessments,* it meets internal criteria as well.

Truth, logical. An axiom, deduction, or inference that satisfies internal criteria. (cf. *analytical).*

Universal, abstract. A *concept* that *characterizes* an *entity, event, process,* or *quality* thereof. *Mediated* by a *sign,* but one that does not name a *particular.* Greenness but not green.

Universal, concrete. *Concrete* and generic; that is, its concreteness actually or *potentially* invests more than one *particular* of the same kind. To Hegel and Marx, the *essence* of something: for example, humanity or the working class. Whitehead's "eternal objects" are universals, but they are *real* and not *essences.*

Univocal. See *Order, univocal.*

Values. Goals, rules, or criteria that guide judgment.

Verisimilitude. A first-order *univocal* mapping in which each prediction of a *theory* corresponds with a descriptive position or *relation.*

Worldview. Includes *metatheoretical principles, concepts,* and an *assessment* of how things and *processes* fit together. Although it includes *"internal* relations," it is *characterized* even more by their *correlative, "external relations."*

INDEX

ABOUT THE CONTRIBUTORS

JUDE DOUGHERTY is the longtime Dean of Philosophy at The Catholic University of America and editor of the *Review of Metaphysics.*

LLOYD EBY, who has a doctorate in the field of philosophy, has taught philosophy at the State University of New York at Albany and at the University of Maryland. He is now an editor in the Currents in Modern Thought section of *The World & I.*

MORTON A. KAPLAN is Distinguished Service Professor of Political Science Emeritus at The University of Chicago and editor of *The World & I.*

JOHN H. SIMPSON is Professor of Sociology at the University of Toronto.